AMERICAN LITERATURE

AMERICAN LITERATURE

An Interpretative Survey

BY

ERNEST ERWIN LEISY

THOMAS Y. CROWELL COMPANY

PUBLISHERS   -4/30-:-   NEW YORK

Printed in the United States of America

PREFACE

Interest in American literature since the World War has grown very markedly. With the shift of the world's financial capital from London to New York there has come also an intensifying of interest in our national culture, an interest elicited in part by an unusually rich period of creation in every field of endeavor. Foreign as well as native critics speak of "America's Coming of Age." It is a happy phrase. It implies that culturally we have "arrived." The ailments of childhood we have left behind us, along with our elder brother's cast-off clothes. We are growing a beard and are ready to take upon ourselves all the duties and prerogatives of manhood. The prospect allures, but the retrospect is sweet also.

If the War removed our feeling of "splendid isolation," obviously one of its sequels is a revaluation of our literature. In this, perhaps the first connected account of our literature to be written since the newer stock-taking, an endeavor has been made to recognize some of the changes. Accordingly, an author like Melville receives more attention than in the older histories, and one like Holmes, less. A discussion of recent and contemporary literature is included. Throughout the book there has been an attempt to include only those writers whose work has value as literature or real significance in the literary unfolding of the American mind. Many minor writers, usually of historical rather than of literary importance, have been left out altogether. If the reader misses any of these he may supply his needs from the books listed in the appendix. In such books, also, he may learn more of an author's life, if that be desired, for it has been the intention in this book to supply only those biographical facts which had direct bearing upon an author's work. Such a plan has allowed more space for the criticism of his writing, on the theory that an author's work is after all the only justification for any interest in his life.

Another departure from the older histories is the attempt to group authors by influences and movements. It is not possible always to put writers into categories that are mutually exclusive, and it is quite likely that others may not agree with the arrangement here given; yet the author is firmly convinced that some such assignment is the logical one in a literary history.

As writer after writer is discussed an attempt is made, first, to "place" the man with reference to the movements of his day; next, to give the essential biographical facts; and, finally, after a critical inspection of his work, to suggest what he has to say to posterity. In connection with the latter, pains have been taken not to offer purely personal judgments. Extracts have been introduced into the text from the earlier writers whose work is not readily accessible. The author of this book is under no undue delusion that American literature is great artistically, but he is convinced that it reflects the ideals of an increasingly important people whose social development cannot be understood without an endeavor at a just appraisal of their literature.

The author owes much to all who have preceded him. He has found Professor Norman Foerster's analysis of American literary history suggestive. He is under obligation to Professor R. D. O'Leary, of the University of Kansas, for his careful reading of the manuscript. To Professor J. B. Hubbell, of Duke University, and to his colleagues, Professors John O. Beaty and J. H. McGinnis, he is further indebted for helpful suggestions; to his classes in American literature at Illinois Wesleyan University and at Southern Methodist University, who have listened amiably to these discourses while they were in the making, he is under the greatest obligation of all.

E. E. L.

Dallas, March, 1929.

CONTENTS

AMERICAN LITERATURE

I

THE PURITAN TRADITION

34902

In its beginnings American literature was the work of transplanted Englishmen. It did not, like the literature of most countries, evolve from primitive conditions. No legendary hero or events stirred the popular imagination to compose ballads or romances which in time might develop a national tradition. Yet there were apparent compensations. The language which the new-comers spoke had behind it the rich literary heritage of the English race from Caedmon to Shakespeare. And in the wilderness to which they had come there was such an abundance of the strange and the exciting as to stimulate even the most sluggish imagination. The modern romantic attitude toward nature, however, had not as yet developed; poets did not seek the wilderness for alleviation of their woes or stand in awe of its picturesqueness. Nor could the literature which had grown up largely around the court or the town serve for models in a country remote from civilization. For that matter, the men who first came were little concerned about questions of art. Men of action they were, rather than of words. Their emotional needs were satisfied by their religion. Such writing as they produced does not rank high aesthetically, but it deserves consideration, if for no other reason than to show "the clay whence we were digged." When, through the eyes of the historical imagination, such writing is viewed in relation to its setting, much of what appears old-fashioned is seen to be manner and dress, not thought. Accordingly, the course in American literature takes account of much besides the work of Emerson and Hawthorne and Whitman and Poe; it includes the contribution of pioneer annalist and humble versifier, wherever that represented the trend of American thought. If, then, throughout the various periods of its history, the literature of the American people is considered a manifestation of social consciousness, the earliest writings reveal in common the Puritan tradition.

The colonists naturally held much the same views as their contemporaries in England, with only such slight modifications as pioneer circumstances might impose. What, then, were conditions in the mother country? During the second quarter of the seventeenth century, England was torn between two factions, the Puritans and the Cavaliers. Puritan democrats had since the reign of Elizabeth been rising in power over cavalier Royalists, and in 1649 had gained sufficient mastery to execute Charles I and establish the Commonwealth under Cromwell. By 1660 the pendulum had swung back far enough for Charles II, who had been in exile in France, to be called to the throne. The upheavals that had preceded his return were not without their effect upon the character of American immigration. Such times bred restless spirits, "nonconformists" and adventurers, many of whom sought their fortunes in the new world. The adventurers came first and settled mainly in the South; the Puritans came later, taking up their residence near Massachusetts Bay.

1. PIONEER ANNALISTS AND VERSIFIERS

The leader of the company who came to Virginia in 1607 was Captain John Smith. This robustious Cavalier, for all his escapades, real or fictitious, never ceased to be an Englishman. He and his motley crew were conformists. They believed in an established church and government. Nevertheless, they were here because they preferred the unconventional life of the frontier to the hazards of their compatriots at home.

Although only a sojourner, Smith is of interest because his narratives, *A True Relation* (London, 1608) and *A Map of Virginia* (1612), represent one of the early motives for writing—namely, the desire to make a report, to financial supporters in the home country, of whatever might conduce to colonization. Moreover, though Smith was more adept in the use of the sword than in the use of the pen, his style, despite the euphuism then conventional, has sufficient vigor still to command attention. In the following extract he gave currency to our oldest legend:

At last they brought him [Smith] to Meronocomoco, where was Powhatan, their Emperor. Here more than two hundred of those grim Courtiers stood wondering at him, as he had been a monster; till Powhatan and his trayne had put themselues in their greatest braveries. Before a fire vpon a seat like a bedsted, he sat covered with a great robe, made of Rarowcun skinnes, and all the tayles hanging by. On either hand did sit a young wench of 16 or 18 yeares, and along on each side of the house, two rowes of men, and behind them as many women, with all their heads and shoulders painted red; many of their heads bedecked with the white downe of Birds; but every one with something: and a great chayne of white beads about their necks.

At his entrance before the King, all the people gaue a great shout. The Queene of Appamatuck was appointed to bring him water to wash his hands, and another brought him a bunch of feathers in stead of a Towell to dry them: having feasted him after their best barbarous manner they could, a long consultation was held, but the conclusion was, two great stones were brought before Powhatan: then as many as could layd hands on him, dragged him to them, and thereon laid his head, and being ready with their clubs, to beate out his braines, Pocahontas the Kings dearest daughter, when no intreaty could prevaile, got his head in her armes, and laid her owne vpon his to saue him from death: whereat the Emperour was contented he should liue to make him hatchets, and her bells, beads, and copper.[1]

It is clear that Smith had a sense for the dramatic, though he did not make the most of his climax.

[1] From *The General History of Virginia*, Bk. III, Chap. 2.

Following the founding of Jamestown, there developed in the South a leisurely manorial life that slighted the production of literature. Slaves did the menial labor and the gentry dispensed social hospitality or indulged in fox-hunting and horse-racing. On account of the distance between plantations, there were few schools; sons aspiring to the professions were educated by tutors or were sent to school abroad. Governor Berkeley indicated the state of culture when so late as 1670 he declared: "I thank God we have no free schools, nor printing, and I hope we shall not have them these hundred years." If one wished books, it was easier to import them from England than to write them.

About sixty years later the most interesting of the Virginia writers of the colonial period, Colonel William Byrd, wrote for his friends an account of his adventures in traversing the Dismal Swamp while establishing the boundary line between Virginia and North Carolina. A landed aristocrat, with a large library and fine horses, Byrd wrote in a lively, sometimes vulgar manner, of domestic and public life in the Old Dominion. The keenness of his observation is apparent in this incident, from the posthumous *Westover Manuscripts* (1841), concerning one of his visits to the home of Colonel Spotswood, Governor of Virginia:

. . . Amongst other favorite animals that cheered this lady's solitude, a brace of tame deer ran familiarly about the house, and one of them came to stare at me as a stranger. But unluckily spying his own figure in the glass, he made a spring over the table that stood under it and shattered the glass to pieces and, falling back upon the tea table, made a terrible fracas among the china. This exploit was so sudden, and accompanied by such a noise, that it surprised me and perfectly frightened Mrs. Spotswood. But 'twas worth all the damage to show the moderation and good humor with which she bore this disaster.[2]

With Byrd literary activity in the South subsided, not to revive again before the period of the Revolution. The urbane manner of Byrd and the Cavalier spirit of Smith fall outside the Puritan tradition; yet so exceptional are they during the colonial era that, if anything, they serve to emphasize the dominance of the Puritan point of view.

In the colonies to the North the motive for settling was entirely different from that which prompted the settlement of Virginia. The Pilgrims who arrived at Plymouth thirteen years after the founding of Jamestown, from which original destination they had been diverted by untoward winds, came not for wealth or adventure but because conditions in England had appeared to them intolerable. Economic innovations and political infringements had caused them to separate from the Church of England and to migrate to Holland; but there they had undergone hardships, not the least of which was seeing their children take up Dutch ways. Accordingly, when

[2] From *A Progress to the Mines*, Sept. 27, 1732.

the first company of a hundred came over in the *Mayflower* it was on making a home that they were bent—a home in a land where they might worship as they pleased.

It is necessary at this point to distinguish between the Pilgrims and the Puritans who came slightly later and settled about Massachusetts Bay. The Pilgrims were petty farmers and artisans whereas the Puritans were yeomen and scholars. As has already been intimated, the Pilgrims were Separatists, while the Puritans preferred to reform, or purify, the Anglican Church from within. The Pilgrims were milder, less fanatical, than the Puritans who decades later absorbed them. Traditions and legends, of course, have idealized the Pilgrims. It appears now that they were not so badly persecuted as was supposed and that some of their hardships were self-imposed. Nevertheless, their virtue, simplicity, and democracy have come to represent a national ideal.

Up to 1640 when Charles I had tried to establish a despotic government Puritan migration to New England was heavy. During the brief period of the Commonwealth it subsided somewhat, only to become stronger than ever after the Restoration. A theocratic form of government was instituted, with collective control, the clergy serving in the double capacity of priest and magistrate. Because of adverse climate and soil, chattel bondage was unprofitable. Yet society was not un-

stratified: Massachusetts had her aristocrats as
well as Virginia her commoners. Citizenship was
based upon church membership, and the meeting-
house became the community center. Since the
citizen was to be learned in the Scriptures, every
child must be taught to read. Therefore, com-
pulsory education was established early, and by
1638 a printing-press was set up. In so compact
a community mind kindled mind; controversies
ensued, some of which were committed to publication.

Much of the early writing of New England
was composed on sermon paper. Following the
tradition of centuries in Europe, the intellectual
life of the new settlements was in the hands of
divines. The particular belief which the colonists
of Massachusetts Bay had in common was Calvinistic. They held (1) that through Adam's sin all
men had incurred the eternal wrath of God; but
(2) through the intervention of a mediator
(Christ) the justly deserved punishment had been
lessened; inasmuch as (3) God had decided to
make it possible for some who had had the right
sort of spiritual experience to be free from the
wrath to come. This doctrine of "pre-election"
produced great searchings of heart, unwarranted
persecution on the part of some, and, on the part
of others, smug self-satisfaction. Years after,
in his satire, "The Wonderful One Hoss Shay,"
Oliver Wendell Holmes, humorously but disap-

provingly, carried to its logical conclusion the theology of his ancestors.

It is fortunate that the earliest chronicles of the Massachusetts colonies were written by the chief actors in the drama of building the state. Later generations may have, as a consequence, an intimate picture of what went on as it appeared to those who were in a position to know. Governor Bradford, although not so romantically appealing to the imagination as Captain Smith, was a rugged person, who wrote *Of Plimouth Plantation* with straightforwardness as well as understanding. His chronicle related the voyage on the *Mayflower,* recorded the signing of the first compact, and included events in the colony to the year 1646. The simple dignity of his narrative had something of the prose melody of the King James version, from which its style was doubtless derived. Here is a sentence, describing the departure from Leyden:

So they left that goodly and pleasant city, which had been their resting place near twelve years; but they knew they were pilgrims, and looked not much on these things, but lifted up their eyes to the heavens, their dearest country, and quieted their spirits.

Though digressing from time to time to relate "special providences" or to indulge in a diatribe against the "heathen," the narrative is considerably more readable than the somewhat Job-like entries of Governor Winthrop's *Journal.* Because the manuscript was lost, however, from the period of the Revolution until 1855, when the Bishop of London graciously restored it to Massachusetts, writers like Hawthorne, Whittier, and Longfellow used as source material for their works relating to early New England life, not the work of Bradford, but the journal of the leader of Massachusetts Bay.

Winthrop's *Journal* records civic, domestic, and religious affairs in the northern colony from 1630 to 1649. It contains such interesting information as that about using bullets in exchange for farthings, punishing drunkenness by requiring the delinquent to wear the letter D for a year, and the placing of a cleft stick on the tongue of a woman for daring to reproach the elders. The laconic governor entered the circumstance of his son's drowning with the same brevity as the death of a cow and a goat from overeating. In this journal as in all Puritan writings there is apparent a consciousness of the hand of God in all mundane affairs. For example, the drowning of a little girl in 1648 is interpreted as punishment for the father's working after sundown the Saturday before.

It would be a mistake, however, to fancy that the life of these people had an entirely somber cast. There was a lighter side as well. Besides, many people came to New England who were not Puritans. We learn from Thomas Morton's *New English Canaan* (1637) of some lawless resolutes

who set up a maypole at Merry Mount and sold
rum and guns to the Indians. And, as to the
simple amenities, the love letters of John and
Margaret Winthrop furnish abundant evidence
of the pleasanter side of Puritan life. Their
mingling of love and kisses with matters of petty
business, sometimes to the relegation of the latter to a postscript, has the aroma of lavender and
old lace.

The Simple Cobler of Aggawam (London,
1647) was written by Nathaniel Ward to offset
some of the attacks already being directed at
Puritan rule. In his euphuistic sub-title this sharp
commentator assumed that England and America
were a pair of old shoes which he proposed to
help mend. His procedure was to censure women
for their following of fashions, religious leaders
for their toleration, the king for his militarism,
and in general, all changes. When Ward, in the
bitterness of his satire lacked for a word, he
coined one. Something of the vigor of his popular booklet may be gleaned from the following
extract:

I honour the woman that can honour herself with her
attire: a good Text alwayes deserves a fair Margent:
. . . but when I hear a nugiperous Gentledame inquire
what dress the Qvueen is in this week: what the nudius-
tertain fashion of the Court; . . . with egge to be in
it in all hast, what ever it be; I look upon her as the
very gizzard of a trifle, the product of a quarter of a
cypher, the epitome of nothing, fitter to be kickt, if shee
were of a kickable substance, than either honoured or
humoured. . . .

Such language as was used in *The Simple Cobler* was the expression of a temper that was being baffled in its endeavor to coerce the thought of others. It was at this time that Roger Williams made a strong plea in favor of toleration, and advocated independence in religious thinking. Though he was banished to Rhode Island for his pains and, it may be added, for his somewhat hasty manner, his controversy with John Cotton on "The Bloody Tenent" served to liberalize subsequent thought.

The writing of verse seemed on the whole too frivolous to be undertaken by men who were doing their best to subdue the wilderness. Moreover, the Puritans had almost no literary tradition. Aside from Milton and Bunyan they produced no writers of distinction, and even these were outside the main current of the English literature of that day. The Bible they knew well; they read it not for its literary value, however, but for its spiritual guidance. The uses of the imagination they mistrusted. Naturally, poetry found scant expression among them; such verse as did appear was largely elegiac in character.

The Bay Psalm Book (1640), the first book published in the colonies, was an attempt to adapt the Psalms to the meter of the few tunes with which the people were familiar. The compilers, Richard Mather, John Eliot, and Thomas Welde, made as literal a rendering as possible, stating in their preface that "God's altar needs not our polishings." The substitution of fidelity to the letter of the scripture for poetic inspiration resulted in such curious versions as this rendering of a part of the 137th Psalm:

> The rivers on of Babilon,
>   there where we did sit down,
> Yea even then we mourned when
>   we remembered Sion.
> Our harp we did hang it amid
>   upon the willow tree.

This far from felicitous psalmody is perhaps not quite representative of the work as a whole, yet throughout the book there were stresses on syllables that should not be stressed, and strained inversions appeared in many a line.

Somewhat more artistic was the verse of Anne Bradstreet, whose work an admiring brother-in-law published in London as the product of "The Tenth Muse lately Sprung up in America" (1650; 1678). This accomplished daughter of one governor of Massachusetts and wife of another did not live up to this bold declaration and would have been the first to acknowledge the fact. Yet she kept the lamp of poetry flickering in the wilderness. Curiously enough she made no mention of the features of the frontier or of its hardships. Her "quaternions," that is to say, poems of "The Four Elements," "The Four Humours in Man's Constitution," "The Four Ages of Man," "The Four Seasons of the Year," and "The Four

Monarchies," showed the influence of the ponderous English poet Quarles and the "fantastic" Sylvester, translator of her favorite French poet, Du Bartas. Her best work appeared in her more simple and natural poems of "occasions," or poems for relatives, and in some of the stanzas of "Contemplations." Her method of contemplating nature and moralizing upon it is illustrated at its best in such stanzas as these:

I heard the merry grasshopper then sing,
The black clad Cricket, bear a second part,
They kept one tune, and plaid on the same string,
Seeming to glory in their little Art.
Shall Creatures abject, thus their voices raise?
And in their kind resound their makers praise:
Whilst I as mute, can warble forth no higher layes.

* * * * * * * *

When I behold the heavens as in their prime,
And then the earth (though old) still clad in green,
The stones and trees, insensible to time,
Nor age nor wrinkle on their front are seen;
If winter come, and greenness then do fade,
A Spring returns, and they more youthful made;
But Man grows old, lies down, remains where once he's
    laid.

In "Contemplations" Mrs. Bradstreet displayed ability to write fluent and melodious verse in stanzas somewhat like Spenser's and not without thought and feeling. Had her work, instead of following the puns and quirks of the "concettists," exhibited more passion and imagination, it might not now be compared to "a ship that bears much sail and little or no ballast."

The most widely popular poem of the Puritans was "The Day of Doom" (1662). Its author was Michael Wigglesworth, well named "the doggerel Dante of the New England meeting-house." Kindly though he himself was, he pictured in vivid verse of ballad meter the prevailing conception of the Day of Judgment: the marshaling of the dead before the throne of God; the separation of the "sheep" and the "goats"; and the pronouncement of the final judgment. The author's unflinching sense of the awfulness of sin revealed a straightforward imagination bearing directly on the problems of life. It was an evil day, however, when he undertook to handle in a jigging meter, however easily remembered it might be, a theme as solemn as that of the Last Judgment. The harshness of his manner as well as the form of his verse may well be illustrated in the stanzas in which the "reprobate infants" make their plea and are assigned "the easiest room in hell":

> O great Creator why was our Nature
> depravëd and forlorn?
> Why so defil'd, and made so vil'd,
> whilst we were yet unborn?
> If it be just, and needs we must
> transgressors reckon'd be,
> Thy Mercy, Lord, to us afford,
> which sinners hath set free.
>
> *   *   *   *   *   *
>
> 'You sinners are, and such a share
> as sinners, may expect;
> Such you shall have, for I do save
> none, but mine own Elect.

Yet to compare your sin with their
    who liv'd a longer time,
I do confess yours is much less,
    though every sin's a crime.'

'A crime it is, therefore in bliss
    you may not hope to dwell;
But unto you I shall allow
    the easiest room in Hell.'
The glorious King, thus answering,
    they cease, and plead no longer;
Their Consciences must needs confess
    his Reasons are the stronger.

This baldly realistic poem of more than two hundred stanzas was "the solace," says Lowell, "of every fireside, the flicker of the pine-knots by which it was conned perhaps adding a livelier relish to its premonitions of eternal combustion." For a century it enjoyed a popularity in New England second only to that of the Bible and the Catechism.

With Wigglesworth the discussion of the verse of the Puritans comes to an end. Taken as a whole, it reflects mainly the sterner side of their life. There are traces in it now and then of the affection for home, but there is no love poetry. Rather is it the product of a people goaded by circumstances and environment into the belief that life is a continuous battle with the forces of evil. The pleasures of art, they felt, might "seduce the soul from God." Naturally no sustained piece of good work was produced, though here and there are passages of chastened loveliness.

2. THE AGE OF THE MATHERS

Toward the close of the seventeenth century New England was under the sway of the "Mather Dynasty." This illustrious family, founded by Richard Mather, an Oxford graduate and one of the compilers of the *Bay Psalm Book*, continued its rôle as minister-magistrate to the colony under his son Increase, who for sixty years delighted his adherents and terrorized his foes at North Church, Boston; it culminated in power under the grandson, Cotton Mather, the most eminent of the Puritan divines. Of these leaders only Cotton Mather has much historical importance, though the *Illustrious Providences* (1684) of his father, Increase Mather, preserves a quaint interest in apparitions and in remarkable escapes from lightning and the sea. Perhaps the chief importance which attaches to the Mather *régime* now is that it is approximately the era depicted in *The Scarlet Letter*.

Cotton Mather (1663–1728) was a precocious youth who was graduated from Harvard College at the age of fifteen and then became his father's associate at North Church. He was even more industrious than his father, producing nearly four hundred books and pamphlets. There was undeniably something of spiritual pride in the way he sought to outdo his fathers in piety; he prayed and fasted much, and fell into mystical trances. He was skillful in clothing with spiritual vesture his thinking about mundane things; he believed that God spoke directly to him and that divine communion gave him a right to exhort others. Like many another in that age of general belief in demonology, he was taken in by the witchcraft hysteria of 1692 but never admitted that his prosecutions had been in error.

Yet it should be remembered that in other respects Mather was in advance of his time. He was one of the few Americans with sufficient scientific curiosity to be elected to the Royal Society prior to 1750, and he was a pioneer in advocating inoculation against smallpox. In his scientific works appeared his best prose, relatively free from pedantic allusions. His "Essays to Do Good," however, have had a wider reading public, including among others the youthful Franklin. His greatest work was the *Magnalia Christi Americana; or the Ecclesiastical History of New England* (1702). This compendium of more than a thousand pages contained seven divisions: a history of the settlement of New England, an account of the lives of governors, biographies of famous divines, a history of Harvard College, a section on "acts and monuments of faith," a record of many "wonderful providences," and a division on controversies about heresies. The work, largely an attempt to justify the theocratic order then passing, appears to have been planned somewhat after Fuller's *Worthies* and his *Church History,* and in style resembles Burton's *Anatomy of Melancholy.* It is

often pompous rather than accurate, but it gave
Hawthorne the basis for his sketch of Sir William
Phips, and Whittier his material for the "Garrison of Cape Anne," and despite its puns and
frequent quotations from the classics, may interest the reader as the "prose epic of New England
Puritanism."

Toward the close of the career of Cotton
Mather the Puritans lost their hold upon New
England. Society, having prospered, became
gradually more secularized and more liberal. A
contemporary who reflected the transition from
the old order to the new was Judge Samuel Sewall
(1652–1730). Sewall possessed a more pleasing
personality than Cotton Mather and though he,
too, carried out the letter of the law in prosecut-
ing witches, he afterwards frankly admitted his
error, did public penance for his guilt, and spent
one day each year in fasting and prayer. Sewall
prepared himself for the ministry, but as his wife
brought him a handsome dowry he was diverted
to business, then to politics, and finally to the
bench, where for ten years he was Chief Justice
of Massachusetts. Though by nature a conservative, he voiced in his three-page tract, "The Selling of Joseph" (1700), the first anti-slavery pronouncement in America. It began a protest which
may be traced thereafter through the writings of
Woolman, Freneau, Dwight, Barlow, and others
who gave it increasing prominence.

Sewall's chief claim to literary recognition lies

in his voluminous and entertaining *Diary*. So
shrewd and veracious are his entries that this
work lays claim to consideration among the better
diaries of literature. Its entries extend from
1673 to 1729, and range in topic from trivial
household facts and personal concerns to the
most important events in colonial affairs. Its
frankness it owes to the fact that the author wrote
with no thought of its publication; consequently
it is a most authoritative picture of colonial manners and customs.

Most frequently quoted are the portions in
which this thrice widowed man at the age of sixty-
eight, when he was father of fourteen children,
laid siege to the heart of Madam Winthrop, a
widow of fifty-six, with twelve children. To further his suit, he brought her a piece of cake and
gingerbread, wrapped in a clean sheet of paper,
and she entertained him with wine and marma-
lade. How they got on is related in the following entries:

I got my Chair in place, had some Converse, but very
Cold and indifferent to what 'twas before. Ask'd her
to acquit me of Rudeness if I drew off her Glove . . .
Got it off . . . I gave her Dr. Preston, The Church's
Marriage and the Church's Carriage, which cost me
6 shillings . . . 8/19 . . . Visited Madam Winthrop.
. . . Was Courteous to me; but took occasion to speak
pretty earnestly about my keeping a Coach: I said
'twould cost 100 pounds per annum: she said 'twould
cost but 40 pounds . . . Came away somewhat late. . . .
8/21 . . . About 6 a-clock I go to Madam Winthrop's;
Sarah told me her Mistress was gone out. . . . She pres-

ently order'd me a Fire; so I went in, having **Dr.** Sibb's
Bowels to read. . . . After a good while and Claping
the Garden door twice or thrice, she [Mrs. Winthrop]
came in . . . I ask'd when our proceedings should be
made publick: She said They were like to be no more
publick than they were already. Offer'd me no Wine
that I remember . . . Nov. 7th . . . I went to Mad.
Winthrop; found her rocking her little Katee in the
Cradle . . . She set me an arm'd Chair and Cushion;
and so the Cradle was between her arm'd Chair and
mine. Gave her the remnant of my Almonds; She did
not eat of them as before . . . I told her I loved her:
. . . She said had a great respect for me . . . I did
not draw off her Glove as sometime I had done. Her
dress was not so clean as sometime it had been.
Jehovah jireh!

The reader who will browse over the pages of this
"Puritan Pepys" in an abridged edition now
available [3] will find many bits of humor, conscious
or unconscious, and will get at the same time an
excellent picture of the life of the period.

Another interesting journal, which for some
reason was not published until 1825, is Sarah
Kemble Knight's *Journal of a Journey from Boston to New York in 1704*. This sprightly narrative gives insight into the wayfaring life of the
time. The good nature with which Madam
Knight took whatever the fates sent makes her
account unique and thoroughly readable. As she
came to a stream across which her horse could
not take her, she was obliged to get into a canoe.
But let her describe the crossing:

[3] *Samuel Sewall's Diary.* Ed. by Mark Van Doren. New York,
1927.

The Cannoo was very small and shallow, so that when we were in she seem'd ready to take in water, which greatly terrified me, and caused me to be very circumspect, sitting with my hands fast on each side, my eyes steady, not daring so much as lodg my tongue a hair's breadth more on one side of my mouth then tother, nor so much as think on Lot's wife, for a wry thought would have oversett our wherey. . . .

Such a delightful sense of humor was none too common and is in pleasing contrast to the soberer note in our earlier annals.

3. Edwards and Woolman: Puritan and Quaker

Following the decline in the authority of the Mathers, Calvinistic theology was obliged to undergo considerable modification in the eighteenth century. On the one hand, the Arminians attacked the doctrine of predestination as allowing no personal choice between right and wrong, and, on the other, the rationalists, or deists, belittled the large place that had been allotted to evil in the plan of the world. John Wise in two able books on liberal church government defended the laity against the theocrats. With the Great Awakening of 1740 enthusiasts like Whitefield encroached upon the powers of the regular clergy, thereby leading to a schism within the church. At length, when Jonathan Edwards (1703–1758), the consummate logician of the eighteenth century, wrote his famous treatise in opposition to the freedom of the will, Calvinistic theology uttered its valedictory.

This lonely seeker after spiritual perfection
was born in the Connecticut valley, in the very
year of Wesley's birth. At ten the precocious lad
tried to disprove that the soul is material; at
twelve, with the keen observation of a true naturalist, he studied the ways of a spider. In college
he read Locke, performed many experiments, and
a few years after his graduation from Yale, took
up a pastorate at Northampton.

At heart Edwards was a poet. He communed
with God and nature enraptured like a saint. His
betrothed, Sarah Pierrepont, he described in a
prose rhapsody of unmatched beauty:

They say there is a young lady in New Haven who
is beloved of that Great Being, who made and rules the
world, and that there are certain seasons in which this
Great Being, in some way or other invisible, comes to
her and fills her mind with exceeding sweet delight,
and that she hardly cares for anything, except to meditate on him—that she expects after a while to be received up where he is, to be raised up out of the world
and caught up into heaven; being assured that he loves
her too well to let her remain at a distance from him
always. There she is to dwell with him, and to be
ravished with his love and delight forever. Therefore,
if you present all the world before her, with the richest
of its treasures, she disregards and cares not for it, and
is unmindful of any pain or affliction. She has a
strange sweetness in her mind and singular purity of
affection; is most just and conscientious in all her conduct; and you would not persuade her to do anything
wrong or sinful, if you would give her all the world,
lest she should offend this Great Being. She is of a
wonderful sweetness, calmness, and universal benevolence of mind; especially after this Great God has man-

ifested himself to her mind. She will sometimes go about from place to place, singing sweetly; and seems to be always full of joy and pleasure; and no one knows for what. She loves to be alone, walking in the fields and groves, and seems to have some one invisible always conversing with her.

Edwards at the time of the Great Awakening had become the foremost preacher in New England. But the doctrine of total depravity which he preached did not square with the relatively harmless village life. When the reaction to the revival set in, he was dismissed because of disagreement with his parishioners over church discipline and the sacrament. His "Farewell Sermon" (1750) was a masterpiece for its calm power. He now removed to Stockbridge, where he preached among the Indians, and wrote his famous treatise on metaphysics, "The Freedom of the Will" (1754). At the close of his life he became President of the College of New Jersey, but died from inoculation for smallpox shortly after his arrival at Princeton.

By his contemporaries Edwards was known chiefly as a preacher. In his pulpit manner he was not demonstrative; but his logic, couched in simple diction and uttered with terrible calm, produced among his hearers the utmost spiritual intensity. Such a sermon as "Sinners in the Hands of an Angry God," which threw his congregation into horrified repentance, was not so characteristic of this saintly and poetic spirit, however, as his "God Glorified in Man's Dependence," or the noble utterances of his "Farewell Sermon." Few of the writers, thus far considered, had his mastery of English.

It was not, however, until he wrote his polemic, "The Freedom of the Will," that Edwards gained a reputation in Europe, a reputation not incomparable with that of Franklin and Jefferson. In this treatise Edwards sought to refute liberal Arminianism by demonstrating the sovereignty of God. The will, he argued, is not free; otherwise there could not be an all-ruling God. But so central did he make the Deity in the scheme of things that He perforce became the author of evil as well as of good and man a mere puppet of circumstance. The only relief I had," said Boswell on reading the book, "was to forget it"; to which Dr. Johnson replied, "All theory is against the freedom of the will, all experience for it." Whatever disposition may be made of Edwards's theological determinism, there is no gainsaying the intellectual power with which he expressed it. Students of literature will prefer, however, his mystical prose rhapsodies.

John Woolman (1720–1772) was "a sort of provincial Piers Plowman whose visions of reform were far ahead of his day." [4] A gentle-hearted Quaker, a mystic rather than a materialist, he differed from the Puritans in placing duties before doctrines, in considering not the depravity of the mind but its possibilities for good.

[4] *Cambridge History of American Literature,* I, p. 86.

Woolman was born in New Jersey in an atmosphere of plain living and high thinking. He was self-educated, was for a time a store-keeper, and tailor, then traveled on horseback along the Atlantic Coast, visiting Quaker settlements and ministering to them. As a notary he demurred to drawing up wills perpetuating the keeping of slaves. He objected to the exploitation of the poor; he protested against the misuse of wealth; and he inveighed against the waste of war; but in all that he did he was sweet tempered.

At thirty-six Woolman began keeping his *Journal* (1775), a work which has received high praise from divers critics. Coleridge and Stevenson liked it for its beauty and tenderness. Lamb advised his friends to "get the writings of John Woolman by heart, and love the early Quakers." Whittier, himself a Quaker and the first editor of Woolman's *Journal,* called it "a classic of the inner life."

The exquisite simplicity and limpid purity of style in this *Journal* stand revealed in such a passage as this relating to an incident in the author's early life:

A thing remarkable in my childhood was, that once, going to a neighbor's house, I saw, on the way, a robin sitting on her nest; and as I came near she went off, but, having young ones, flew about, and with many cries expressed her concern for them. I stood and threw stones at her, till one striking her, she fell down dead. At first I was pleased with the exploit; but after a few minutes was seized with horror as having, in a sportive way, killed an innocent creature while she was careful for her young. I beheld her lying dead, and thought those young ones, for which she was so careful, must now perish for want of their dam to nourish them; and after some painful considerations on the subject, I climbed up the tree, took all the young birds, and killed them, supposing that better than to leave them pine away and die miserably; and believed in this case, that Scripture proverb was fulfilled, ''The tender mercies of the wicked are cruel.'' I then went on my errand, but for some hours could think of little else but the cruelties I had committed, and was much troubled.[5]

Such a carefully moderated utterance is in pleasing contrast to the heightening of the romanticist. The simple-hearted piety and benevolence which Woolman taught stand in refreshing contrast, also, to the more sophisticated expression of present-day practical idealism. According to him social solidarity is to be achieved not by legislatures or committees but by clearing one's own life of evil; by following the guidance of the ''inner light'' rather than by degrading another for profit. The chief value of Woolman's work lies in his serene application of his mystical intuitions to the affairs of this world. The gentleness of the Quaker, because it did not require the intellectual cultivation that Puritanism demanded, did not readily transmit its spirit to public affairs. Nevertheless, its indirect influence upon American idealism may perhaps have been more pervasive even than that of Puritanism in the strict sense.

[5] John Woolman: *Journal*, Chapt. I.

II

THE PIONEER SPIRIT

1. THE AMERICAN REVOLUTION

BY 1765 a considerable leavening had taken place in the temper of the Puritans residing in colonial America. Less and less did the traditions which the founders of New England brought with them govern the lives of their descendants and more and more did the physical conditions which from the first had imposed themselves upon the colonists determine their mode of thought. The distance from the governing country, the misunderstanding that naturally developed, and the spirit of self-reliance that was engendered by these circumstances, caused the colonists to seek a new way of expressing themselves politically. The seeds of the American Revolution may be traced to John Locke; but the establishment of the nation as a new departure in the government of men was in a very real sense the flowering of the pioneer spirit.

The leavening process, just referred to, was induced in part by variety in the stock of immigrants that were coming to America. Massachusetts, for example, had many more people who did not share the Puritan faith of her leaders than she had of those who did, and in other colonies the admixture of races was even more pronounced. These various settlers, because of the oppressions to which they had been subjected in the old world, appreciated thoroughly their opportunities in the new, and by virtue of their industry and thrift subdued untoward conditions on the frontier. When the policy of imperial rule and commercial exploitation became economically intolerable, it was these backcountry agrarians who helped turn the tide of the Revolution for the mercantile East and the tidewater planters.

a. CRÈVECOEUR, THE "AMERICAN FARMER"

One immigrant who was impressed with the privileges in America because he had known some of the sorrows of civilization in the old world was J. Hector St. John de Crèvecoeur (1735–1813). He had what Woolman lacked, cultural background and a keen appreciation of nature. He had been born and bred in Normandy, had continued his schooling in England, and, at nineteen had set out for Canada, joining the forces of Montcalm, and remaining with the French army to the time of the attack on Fort William Henry. After that he made his way down to Pennsylvania, where he married, and became for sixteen years an "American Farmer."

In *The Letters of an American Farmer* (1782, London; 1793), Crèvecoeur enthusiastically contrasts his lot with the bitter estate of the peasant in France. He describes such things as life on the frontier farm in the Middle Colonies; the ways of Nantucket fishermen and their intrepid wives; the refinements and atrocities of Charleston; and the habits of snakes and humming birds. When the author writes of birds and bees he does so with a touch of eighteenth century sensibility; yet his idyllic pastoral, despite its somewhat artificial style, smacks of the woods.

In the chapter, "What is an American?" Crèvecoeur defines clearly the working of the melting pot. "Here individuals of all nations," says he, "are melted into a new race of men, whose labours and posterity will one day cause great changes in the world. Americans are the western pilgrims, who are carrying along with them that great mass of arts, sciences, vigour, and industry which began long since in the east; they will finish the great circle." Unfortunately for Crèvecoeur himself, the idyllic American adventure shortly came to a tragic end in civil war. He seems to have had Loyalist leanings, but was mistakenly imprisoned as a spy by the British. Shortly thereafter he returned to France where he frequented the literary salons. His later papers have been collected and published as *Eighteenth Century Sketches of America* (1926). These realistic sketches, together with the *Letters,* constitute most vivid thumb-nail sketches of the pre-Revolutionary frontier.

"Crèvecoeur's idealized treatment of rural life in America," says Tyler,[1] "wrought quite traceable effects upon the imaginations of Campbell, Byron, Southey, Coleridge, and furnished not a few materials for such captivating and airy schemes of literary colonization in America as that of 'Pantisocracy.' " Hazlitt and Lamb praised it, and it was pirated by German and Dutch "penny-a-liners." The social historian and the lover of imaginative prose alike will rejoice over the pages of Crèvecoeur.

b. BENJAMIN FRANKLIN (1706–1790)

Beginning with Franklin, the progressive, curious type of man, developed by the frontier, became the leader in America. In him was exemplified the tendency toward secularization which was taking place in the colonies contemporaneously with the transition to nationalism. Franklin had in common with Crèvecoeur a material philosophy of life, a view to which the Frenchman gave a poetic turn but which Franklin expressed in the lucid prose of an Age of Reason. The first half of his life paralleled that of Jonathan Edwards, yet he was much more truly representative of his age. He had, in a way, the

---

[1] Tyler, M. C.: *The Literary History of the American Revolution,* II, p. 358.

same basis of ethics as Edwards, but the emphasis was different; his shrewd common sense instructed him that the Calvinistic experiment in New England would not work. When this utilitarian became the apostle of America, it was not in the sense of its being a place for a theocratic experiment, but rather as a place in which to live, apart from the ideas of Europeans and with its own problems of adaptation.

The *Autobiography* contains the outstanding facts of Franklin's life up to the time of his major public services. He was born in Boston in 1706 into a tallow-chandler's large family. His education was left largely to books that came to him by chance, he having been early apprenticed to his brother, printer of *The New England Courant*, the fourth newspaper published in the colonies. At the age of seventeen, rebelling against his arbitrary brother, he left home for the freer atmosphere of Philadelphia. The *Autobiography* indicates, further, Franklin's appetite for reading, travel, and politics; his experimentation with newspapers and with electricity; his invention of a stove; his interest in street paving, sweeping, and lighting; and his leadership in a multitude of public enterprises. But of the thirty-one years which are not recorded in the *Autobiography*, years during which he was one of the most cultivated and imposing men of the world, there are outstanding facts which the student should also know: his negotiation of the French alliance, his securing the terms of peace, and finally, his work as a framer of the Constitution.

Although it is apparent that Franklin found more satisfaction in the capacity of a doer of good than as a maker of books, and though he wrote only to promote immediate ends, he has to his credit ten volumes. These embody his exposition of political and economic theories, his explanation of scientific phenomena, and his essays on religious and moral subjects. The student of literature is concerned with the essays. They readily fall into such groups as the "Dogood" and "Busybody Papers," in which the author, after the manner of the *Spectator,* attacks social abuses; the plebeian "Poor Richard's Almanac," later re-published in part as "The Way to Wealth," with its interlarded lessons of thrift and frugality; such bagatelles as "The Story of the Whistle," and the "Dialogue between Franklin and the Gout"; his delightful familiar letters, the best in their day in America; and the *Autobiography.*

In many of his writings Franklin simply took over an idea and greatly improved upon it. The Almanac had been the "general intelligencer" in every home even before Nathaniel Ames first published his in 1726, but it remained for Franklin to see in it the possibility for diffusing wisdom among the rank and file of people. The bagatelles were in the form of the light essay then current in France, but Franklin gave it a moral turn, such as best comported with the taste of his readers.

The *Autobiography* was not a novel literary form in an age of memoirs, yet in its way it is unique. No other nation possesses quite so intimate a document, at once

> sinewy, naive and shrewd, direct from the hand of the most versatile of the founders of that people's greatness. . . . Entertaining, sober, wise, sedately vivid, with here and there a whimsical turn and now touched with caustic penetration, full of example and instruction for free men, written with such simplicity that a boy can enjoy it and with such acumen that old men love to reread it, it is our most valuable literary inheritance from fathers of the republic (not forgetting Hamilton's tracts and Paine's propaganda) and one of the finest specimens extant of a simple, lucid style.[2]

It does not school its readers in the heroic virtues but in the everyday virtues, leading them to fall in love with order, application, laudable curiosity and the independent thinking which proceeds from that kind of curiosity. To set free such processes of growth in a democracy is a service of the highest order.

Though literature was not Franklin's primary interest, he has become a classic because in his work his unusual personality stands self-revealed. His independence and fearlessness, his shrewd common sense, his wide curiosity, his tolerance and self-criticism are here intermingled and blended in a racy and concise style. As a thinker his ideas are firmly rooted in his experience, ever animated by the search for truth.

[2] James O'Donnell Bennett: *Much Loved Books* (1927), p. 361.

Throughout his long career Franklin happily combined frugal self-interest and enlightened public service. After overcoming countless obstacles along his pathway he attained to "the graces," an experience that has been repeated in varying degree by successive generations of his countrymen. America's long-standing pride in self-made men should not blind the reader, however, to the fact that Franklin's mind was limited to things, the things of here and now. For spiritual and aesthetic values he had little taste. But his twin virtues, prudence and industry, as extolled in "Poor Richard's Almanac" and elsewhere, have become a gospel for many. His shrewd homespun philosophy promises long to continue an integral part of everyday American thought.

C. THOMAS PAINE AND THE CONTROVERSIALISTS

It has already been suggested that the events following the passage of the Stamp Act up to the adoption of the Constitution of the United States evolved a new political philosophy. The Revolution was a war of ideas in which the self-sufficiency developed by American energy through its experience with the frontier was pitted against the conservative paternalism of British Tories. It did not constitute a cultural split—it left little animosity against the English behind it—yet it lessened, for one thing, the stream of European influence, and it caused the strongest minds, like Jefferson and the Adamses, to turn to the field of politics. The literature of this period was largely controversial; and most of the documents belong to the field of history. Yet to the extent that some of them, like the *Letters* of Dickinson, the pamphlets of Paine, and the satires of Freneau and Trumbull were consciously embellished with a view to securing the favor of the reading public, they deserve discussion here.

As a large part of the population was agricultural, special appeals were directed to this class. It was given the choice of following the presentation of outraged rights given by John Dickinson in his widely discussed *Letters from a Pennsylvania Farmer* (1767), or of seeing the wisdom of remaining loyal as argued in the racy diatribes of the "Westchester Farmer" by the Rev. Samuel Seabury. Dickinson's twelve *Letters* in the Philadelphia newspapers accustomed the people to the idea of resisting Great Britain, as Paine's broadsides later accustomed them to the idea of independence. If the style, though rather homely and forceful, was at times a little too fine for his public, the deficiency was made up by the more popular appeal of the speeches of Samuel Adams and Patrick Henry.

A more potent factor in the Revolutionary cause than the foregoing was Thomas Paine (1737–1809). This remarkable compound of sheer genius and philistinism came to the colonies from

England in 1774 to repair his somewhat dilapidated fortunes. In London he had met Franklin, who had given him a letter of introduction to prominent men in the colonies. Before long he was editor of the *Pennsylvania Magazine.* As a disciple of Godwin, he early espoused the cause of the oppressed, writing slashing articles in behalf of the emancipation of slaves and the rights of women, and evincing unusual ability as a pamphleteer. Not long after the Battle of Lexington he came out strongly for the independence of the colonies in an anonymous pamphlet, *Common Sense* (1776). In only three months 120,000 copies had been sold, and within six the *Declaration of Independence* was signed. Very skillfully Paine identified the American cause with the Rousseauistic theory of the natural rights of man, as opposed to man-made law, and by doing so arrayed England against common humanity. Reconciliation with an incapable mother, he argued, was undesirable. To prove his word by his deed he joined the ranks of Greene's army. Much farther reaching than his military service, however, were the winged words of *The Crisis,* beginning with "These are the times that try men's souls." *The Crisis* appeared at intervals in pamphlet form from December, 1776 to the end of the war. Paine was not a political philosopher, but as a plain partisan journalist of genius his pen served his adopted country well. His later association with English and French radicals does not concern this narrative; but he should be freed from the ridiculous charge once made against him that he was an atheist.

Of the state papers the *Declaration of Independence,* drafted by the great commoner, Jefferson, is yet alive with the human instinct for freedom. The Constitution, based largely upon British precedents, has been an unusually serviceable document. In defense of its ratification Hamilton, together with Madison and Jay published in two New York papers eighty-five articles, which in 1788 were collected under the caption, *The Federalist.* This work was not the equal of Paine's either in literary style or popular appeal, but it expounded statecraft sagaciously, and as an expression of the civic spirit it probably has no superior.

d. THE CONNECTICUT WITS

Not a small part in winning the Revolution was played by popular songs and ballads and by verse satire. Most of these, as is usually the case, were crude and extravagant. It is hard to tell who fathered some of the most popular, like "Yankee Doodle," or the best, like "Nathan Hale," but there can be no question about their native spirit. Most notable of the Tory verse was that by Joseph Stansbury and Jonathan Odell; for the Colonials the best satire was written by John Trumbull and Philip Freneau. In temper this work varied all the way from the good-natured fun of Hopkinson's "Battle of the Kegs" to the sharp acrimony of Freneau's "British Prison Ship."

The most important group of Revolutionary poets were the "Connecticut Wits," later known as the "Hartford Wits." The leaders, John Trumbull, Timothy Dwight, and Joel Barlow, were Yale men, who, as the country developed politically, sought with youthful ardor to sing her "rising glory." Though Minerva smiled unwillingly at their attempt to create by epic and ode a national poetry, they were something more than a mutual admiration society. They had a bias. During the period of constitution-mongering that followed the war, they satirized in "The Anarchiad" the anti-Federalism of the Jeffersonians. Dogmatic and stilted as their verse was, and incongruous as their union of the English classical manner and biblical themes now appears, they imparted at the time, as Parrington says,[3] "a certain sprightliness to a dour temper."

John Trumbull (1750–1831) was the most talented of the group. His rapid advance at school illustrates the forcing process then current in education. While he was practicing law he began to contribute to the newspapers Addisonian essays and verse satires in imitation of Prior and Pope. A notable application of the eighteenth century manner to local conditions was his clever satire on college education and on fops and

[3] V. L. Parrington: *The Colonial Mind* (1927), p. 358.

coquettes in "The Progress of Dulness" (1772–
1773). The adventures of Tom Brainless, Dick
Hairbrain, and Harriet Simper represented in
rollicking octosyllabics the social whims and
academic customs of their day. The work on
which Trumbull's contemporary fame rested was
a satire on the Tories, *M'Fingal* (1775–1782).
This mock-epic pictured a turbulent town-meet-
ing, with its long speeches, its liberty poles and
bonfires, the tarring and feathering of a Tory,
the robbing of cellars, and the like. The poem
lacked the wit and venom of Butler's *Hudibras,*
but its banter struck the popular chord and helped
to hasten the day of independence.

Timothy Dwight (1752–1817) was a more mellow Cotton Mather, carrying a conservative political and theological view into a new century and
adapting it to a more practical age. His duties
as a teacher, preacher, legislator, and, at length,
as President of Yale College did not interfere
with his devoting a couple of decades to writing.
"Columbia" was one of his best lyrics, full of
spirit and elevated enthusiasm. "The Triumph
of Infidelity" failed as a satire because its author
had no native sense of humor. His epic in eleven
books, "The Conquest of Canaan," with its in-
termingling of biblical and American heroes,
could have been produced only by a grandiose
imagination. In the tenth book, for example, an
angel reveals to Joshua the future greatness of
America. In the course of the epic so many

thunderstorms are described that the author's friend, Trumbull, suggested that he ought to furnish a lightning-rod with the poem. The best of Dwight's longer poems was the historico-didactic pastoral, "Greenfield Hill." In this poem, as in Denham's "Cooper's Hill" and in Pope's "Windsor Forest," the author proposed to go to some hill from which to describe the view. In each of the seven parts he sought to parody some contemporary British writer, but he relinquished that design before he completed the poem. The pictures were essentially local, and furnished an admirable record of New England life and thought. The fullest account of the author's observations appeared in his prose work, *Travels in New England and New York* (1823). Its four volumes constitute a mine of information on social customs, education, geography, and government.

More warm-hearted and versatile than Dwight was Joel Barlow (1754–1812). After serving as an army chaplain, he entered the newspaper field. Upon the failure of his journal he went to France where he became a Jacobin. On his return, after an absence of eighteen years, he was regarded by his former Federalist friends as a radical. Jefferson and Madison alone seem to have valued his counsel. His "Advice to the Privileged Orders," like Paine's "Rights of Man," has become more comprehensible in this day than when it was written.

In earlier years Barlow had been regarded by his group as the epic aspirant *par excellence.* His "Vision of Columbus" (1787), later expanded into *The Columbiad,* best illustrated in its sumptuously embellished pages and grandiose style the golden dream of the future which these Wits cherished for America. Beginning with a representation of Columbus in prison, the work continues with a vision given him of the future of America, followed by a rhymed geography of the continent, a song of Mexico and Peru, an account of the settlement of North America, a sketch of the French and Indian wars and of the Revolution, and, as usual, a retrospect and prospect. The epic note was not Barlow's forte, however; posterity has preferred his mock-heroic, "Hasty Pudding," especially such graphic lines as those on the husking-bee.

From a reading of the poets of the American Revolution the reader gains the impression that their experiences were too real and objective to encourage imaginative flights. Besides, the period was essentially prosaic, matter of fact. Its literature was cheapened by serving politics with excessive passion and vituperative expression. It followed paths that had been well worn by the poets of the Restoration and Queen Anne. Yet beyond this imitation one may occasionally find a forceful phrase or a stinging epithet that was new. The dominant element, of course, was satire, and satire is unfortunately doomed to early death.

2. THE FRONTIER IN LETTERS

When the Hartford Wits collaborated on "The Anarchiad" their defense of Federalism was the last echo of the *status quo*. A romantic ideal was directing the minds of men to the pioneering that was taking place in the newly acquired territory beyond the Alleghenies. The "literature of travel" lured attention to this region, and Brackenridge's widely popular *Modern Chivalry* (1792–1805) illustrated its democracy and back-country humor. Even in the more cultivated areas the new point of view served to emphasize distinctions between what was native and what had been European. In literature, imitations of Pope still appeared, to be sure, on both sides of the Atlantic. With the advent of romanticism, the new world looked upon itself as a needle-work world, "a world in which there was always moonlight on the lake and twilight in the vale; where drooped the willow and the eglantine, and jessamine embowered the cot of the village maid; where the lark warbled in the heavens, and the nightingale chanted in the grove 'neath the mouldering ivy-mantled tower."[4] But in Freneau the wild

---

[4] Henry A. Beers: *Nathaniel Parker Willis* (1885), p. 78–79. The statement applies even to the years before those referred to by Beers.

honeysuckle replaced the eglantine, and with Bryant and Cooper the primeval American forest, ever present and obtrusive, came at length into its own.

a. NATURE IN FRENEAU AND IN BRYANT

It was the distinction of Philip Freneau (1752–1832) to throw off the shackles of Pope, and, turning to Milton for inspiration, to become a forerunner of Wordsworth and Coleridge in the romantic treatment of nature. This native of New York, graduate of Princeton, and successively teacher, navigator, farmer, poet, and journalist, has already been referred to as a satirist during the Revolution. But the forward-looking aspect of his work is yet to be considered.

Freneau was an important transition figure. "The House of Night," in its gruesome romanticism, looked back to the vogue of Gothicism, or forward, in its power of imagination, to Poe. Such poems as "The Power of Fancy" and "On Retirement" appear to echo the "Il Penseroso School," and "Eutaw Springs" has the elegiac cadences of Collins and Gray; yet there is in each a genuine native strain as well. The author's conception of nature, like his political activity, grew out of his deism; faith in natural goodness made him an extreme democrat and turned his interest to native environment. Freneau romanticized the red man, in such poems as "The Dying Indian" and "The Indian Burying Ground," but he exercised restraint where others writing of the natives of the forests heaped sentiment. With the lightness of Cavalier verse he wrote "On a Honey Bee" and "To a Caty-did." In his best poem, "The Wild Honey-Suckle," he displayed a new strain of delicate feeling. The rare sympathy with nature expressed there so felicitously brought the eighteenth century in the poetic annals of America to a close, with such things as "The Fringed Gentian" not far away.

With the advent of William Cullen Bryant (1794–1878), nature was no longer used for mere setting but it became a profoundly moving symbol of God, speaking "a various language." Having dwelt as a youth in the Pontusac forest in western Massachusetts, and having been taught by the "Lyrical Ballads" to enjoy a region so analogous to the English Lakes, Bryant early rejected the unemotional measures of the eighteenth century for the freedom and glory of romantic expression. Already in "Thanatopsis" he was master of stately blank verse, with internal sentence structure, long rhythmic periods, and full pauses. It should be remembered, however, that the seventeen year old's imitation of Kirk White's "Time" has not the beautiful opening and close that he added later.

To Bryant belongs the credit of first presenting in memorable art the American scene. He said little of the mountains or sea, but he made his countrymen aware of the grand and spacious beauties of their landscape, and stimulated poets like Halleck and Drake to write on native themes. He made known not only the summer splendor, the autumn russet, and the winter lights and glooms of the New England countryside, but he manifested amid all the change he noted a consciousness of the eternal. Like Wordsworth, who had helped him to self-discovery, he found in nature a "healing power" and in the wind "the breath of God"; but he did not meekly repeat the naturalistic mysticism of Wordsworth. Nor did he, as may be observed in "A Forest Hymn," conceive of nature deistically. His Puritan ancestry which had felt awed by the "horrible Wilderness" was responsible to quite as large an extent as the elegiac school of poets for the somber note in much of his verse. His attitude was that of a Puritan, but of one who was to free Puritanism from its excessive Hebraizing, and find in nature not merely a reminder of the transiency of things but an incentive to aesthetic expression. The ethical note he sounded gave poetry in New England at last its currency.

Bryant's best poems are not many. It seems now that "Thanatopsis," "The Yellow Violet," "Inscription for the Entrance to a Wood," "To a Waterfowl," "Green River," "A Winter Piece," "A Walk at Sunset," "Hymn to Death," "November," "A Forest Hymn," "The Death of the Flowers," "I Cannot Forget with What Fervid Devotion," "To the Fringed Gentian,"

"The Prairies," and perhaps "Robert of Lincoln" and "The Journey of Life" comprise the list.

In these he forgets his eighteenth century manner and cries from a soul deeply stirred. They fall into two categories: poems of nature and poems of reflection. In "Thanatopsis" there is direct reflection upon the eternal process of change; the "Entrance to a Wood" depicts with rare delicacy the woods and creatures of God's out-of-doors; "To a Waterfowl" is as truly inspired a poem as he ever wrote; "Green River" is sweetly idyllic; in "A Winter Piece" there is spaciousness. In "A Forest Hymn" there are the larger and sterner phases of the primal feeling for nature, and in "The Prairies" there is the elemental simplicity of earth and sky; while in the "Yellow Violet," "Fringed Gentian," and "Robert of Lincoln" the lighter aspects of nature are handled with joyous grace. In his reflections on life and death, and on the purifying influence of nature on man, Bryant enlarges his treatment of the cosmic process.

Much of Bryant's energy in later years went into his work on the New York *Evening Post,* where for fifty years he did what he could to foster good government and good manners in a new land. Late poems like "Mother of a Mighty Race," "Song of the Sower," and "Sella" prove that his poetic muse still had strength and charm. His translation of Homer is faithful, and along with Longfellow's *Dante* and Taylor's *Faust*, contributed to the dissemination in America of old-world culture. As a critic he belongs to the best tradition.

There can be no question that Bryant was an artist. His chaste diction, his ear for cadence and rhyme, his organic style testify to that. His use of blank verse has hardly been surpassed by later writers. But to be a great poet one must have also intellectual intensity and imaginative concentration. Bryant's poetry is calm rather than great; austere rather than passionate. He has few ideas or modes and these have limited philosophic reach. They have, however, to do with primary feeling, with adjustment to the brute facts of life and death. Compared with those who had preceded him, his raciness, concreteness, and reticent simplicity mark a great advance in the expression of beauty. In his own field—as a poet of nature—America has none to put beside him. Truth, purity, and reverence animate his work and still exalt the reader. If there is little warmth in his lines, it will be remarked, on the other hand, that they are tonic. Bryant's position in his country's annals is secure. "He is," in the words of Professor Pattee, "a lone, cold peak on the horizon of our poetry, grand and solemn in the morning twilight of American song." [5]

[5] F. L. Pattee: *Sidelights on American Literature* (1922), p. 326,

b. THE PIONEER SPIRIT IN FICTION

At the close of the Revolution, America possessed no native fiction. The thought of its best intellects was directed to problems of statecraft. Throughout the early period the Puritan tradition had militated against any interest in fiction; novels were regarded as lies and corrupters of morals. This opposition to fiction was shared also by the utilitarians, to whom the reading of novels was a waste of time. There was a taste for fiction, however, chiefly among the Tories. Inasmuch as these were in close touch with the mother country, it was but natural that their taste should be based on the English novels then in vogue. If native fiction should arise it was fair to presume that it would follow the models current in England. There, Richardson and Fielding having done their work, a school of sentimental and didactic writers, who had followed them, were vying with the terrorizers of Gothic romance for the favor of the reading public.

The first signs of literary self-consciousness in the new republic appeared in the form of a recognition of the obstacles that stood in the way of dealing with native themes. The Revolution was too familiar to be a satisfactory subject. The story of Plymouth Rock might have served, yet it was a reminder of colonialism. Writers complained also that there were no class distinctions and that consequently they could depict no contrast in manners. Worst of all, local publishers preferred pirating English novels to fostering native authorship.

Despite these obstacles, tales began to appear soon after the Revolution, tales pertaining to the war, and tales about the Indians. *The History of Maria Kittle* (1793), for example, was a thrilling account of Indian warfare written in a sentimental vein; *The Female Review* (1797) was a "glorified" memoir of a female soldier who served in the Revolution. A picturesque novel of equal popularity was Hugh H. Brackenridge's *Modern Chivalry* (1792–1805), still a readable satire on contemporary manners. There appeared, moreover, a host of seduction stories, the best known of which were Mrs. Rowson's *Charlotte Temple* (1794) and Mrs. Foster's *The Coquette* (1797). These indicate the influence of Richardson even as the Gothic romances that followed closely upon them attest the popularity of Mrs. Radcliffe.

The outstanding novelist in the Gothic tradition was Charles Brockden Brown (1771–1810), a resident not of New England but of Philadelphia and New York. Under the influence of "The Friendly Club" of New York, he matured as a journalist, novelist, and critic. His earlier work had been inspired mainly by Godwin; but with *Wieland* (1798), *Arthur Mervyn* (1798–1800), and *Edgar Huntly* (1799), his headlong pen entered upon a series of romances that dealt with native material. The terror *motif* which underlay all his romances appeared in *Wieland* as spontaneous combustion, ventriloquism, and religious mania. The sensibility of the heroine Brown owed to Richardson, and his intense style and obvious moralizing, to Godwin. In the keen analysis of action as well as in the lack of humor, he alone deserved credit and blame. In his next romance, *Arthur Mervyn,* there appeared as a means for inspiring pity and fear an unusually vivid picture of the yellow fever epidemic in Philadelphia in 1793.

It was in *Edgar Huntly* that Brown made his most significant contribution, adding a new *motif* and a new background to American fiction. Instead of appealing to readers with "Gothic castles and puerile chimeras," he chose to wring their sensibilities, as he said, with "incidents of Indian hostility and the perils of the Western wilderness." In the discovery of these agencies for the use of fiction he antedated Cooper by a score of years. His Indians were not sentimentalized, but were fiend-like instruments of death.

The last years of Brown's brief career were devoted to advancing native literature by means of reviews and historical surveys. For this purpose he established *The American Register.* As a well-informed and penetrating critic Brown deserves more credit than has been accorded him.

He was one of the forces that developed a reading public and helped to crystallize a definite feeling for native productions.

What America lacked in order to have a literature of her own, according to the plaint of her early writers, was a storied landscape. Yet as the French and Indian wars had drawn men together, and as this exploit or that successful skirmish of the Revolution came to be retold, the imagination was occupied in creating folk-legends. Myths grew up around such figures as Washington and other heroes. The Pocahontas story appeared in John Davis's *Captain Smith and Princess Pocahontas* (1805), and in a succession of plays. Even the lack of ivied walls and snowy summits old in story was compensated for when Washington Irving, setting about, one day, to poke fun at Mitchill's pedantic "Picture of New York," ended by establishing the Knickerbocker legend, and so supplied beauty to what had been regarded theretofore as unpicturesque American scenery.

During the period of the second war with Great Britain, American literature passed through the doldrums, but by its close there had developed a unified patriotic reading public. In fiction the growing vogue of Scott temporarily paralyzed native authorship, but that was only the dark before the dawn. With the overthrow of Napoleon, American interest in Europe languished, and with the settlement of the South and West the national character became more aggressive. Materials were at hand, and the public was ready for the rise of a new literature. The Indian and the Revolution had proved suitable to literary treatment, and native scenery, it had been discovered, could be invested with romantic appeal. The problem remained to adapt these native elements to the sustained method of treatment employed in the Scottish romances then so popular. This Cooper succeeded in doing, and with *The Spy* (1821) American fiction had its real beginning.

C. FENIMORE COOPER AND FRONTIER ROMANCE

Had J. Fenimore Cooper (1789–1851) been in any definite sense aware of the experiments with native material that had preceded him, he might well have entered with diffidence upon the task of writing an ''American'' novel. His had been a frontiersman's boyhood, followed, after two erratic years at Yale, by an apprenticeship at sea and a decade as a country squire, and it was only by merest chance that he fell into authorship. When his wife challenged him to write a better novel than the one he was at the time reading with disgust, he wrote *Precaution* (1819), a story of English life.

In *The Spy,* his first important book, he apparently borrowed the pedlar from Scott's *Antiquary,* and by making him a spy, utilized inter-

est in the well-known play *Andrè,* by his friend,
William Dunlap. To give the spy the best opportunity for his maneuvers, he staged the scene in
1780 on the "neutral ground" north of New York
City at a time when it was being overrun by the
various elements in the civil strife. Last, he introduced, after Scott's manner, a mysterious
stranger who proved to be none other than General Washington. By making the Wharton family a house divided against itself, and by allowing the spy to be persecuted by bands both of
Skinners and of Cowboys he supplied the element
of conflict, and in addition, that of suspense.
Cooper's distinct picture of the fratricidal nature
of the war is all the more commendable when it
is remembered that not until recently has the fog
of "patriotic" legend lifted from the tradition of
the Whig historians who misrepresented the Revolution as a united uprising against the mother
country.

The hearty reception of *The Spy* encouraged
Cooper to follow at once the career unexpectedly
opened up to him. But to do so required that
he draw upon material already at hand. His
acquaintance with Westchester county he had
used felicitously; there remained the memories of
his boyhood at Cooperstown, and his years at sea.
Affection for the pioneer village among the for-
est-clad hills surrounding Otsego pressed for
utterance, and Cooper improvised in *The Pioneers*
(1823) a series of sportsman's sketches not to be

outdone by the English sketches of Irving. The turkey-match, the shooting of myriads of wild-pigeons, the seining and spearing for bass, the deer-chase on the lake, maple-sugaring in spring, and sleighing-parties in winter carried the main appeal far more truly than the somewhat conventional and slight plot. The way of nature, embodied in the uncouth old hunter and his Indian friend, was obliged, however, to yield, in the end, to the stocks and to the fire brought by civilization, and the only escape in this tragic epic of the wilderness was a reluctant departure toward the setting sun.

In *The Pilot* (1823), Cooper drew upon his experiences at sea. Such adventures had ordinarily been discussed over a cob-pipe, on a wharf-barrel, or, at most, had got into chap-books; Smollett's sailors might have been stationed in a hotel, and Scott's *Pirate,* Cooper was sure, had been the work of a landsman. Cooper meant to leave no doubt as to the seamanship of his sailors. By choosing the northeastern coast of England as the setting for his story he had the two-fold advantage of exploiting sea maneuvers, which *The Pirate* lacked, and of complicating these with a love story in the castle that would be cherished by readers of Abbey romances. In the management of the story there was not so much that was new. The skirmishes of *The Spy* became chases between frigates and men of war; the devotion of Harvey Birch was changed to Long Tom Coffin's love for the sea; and an incognito Washington was replaced by an incognito Paul Jones. This repetition, with slight variation, not only of plot but of types explains Cooper's prolific production of novels. Such economy of creative effort was justifiable and perhaps necessary if Cooper was to lavish upon the details the interpretative sympathy that he was fitted to give. Thoroughgoing sailor that he was, he knew how good sea-dogs would thirst for a fight or boast of their prowess. There has been high testimony to Cooper's marinership. Among others, Joseph Conrad has been glad to acknowledge that Cooper taught him profound sympathy for the sea and artistic insight into its sublimity and mystery.

As the fiftieth anniversary of the battles of Lexington and Concord and Bunker Hill approached, the spirit of nationalism grew intense. Cooper, in the blush of popularity, conceived a plan for a series of historical romances on a national scale, to be called "Legends of Thirteen Republics," the scenes of which should be laid in the various colonies that had shared in the Revolution. For the first, *Lionel Lincoln* (1825), he undertook painstaking research; but he soon found irksome the attempt to blend with history his complicated plot of domestic intrigue, and shifted attention in the second volume to the melodramatic fortunes of his hero.

With *The Last of the Mohicans* (1826), Cooper returned to frontier material and a detailed study of the Indian. It was a stroke of genius not only to reintroduce, from *The Pioneers,* the aged hunter and his Indian comrade but to set them back nearly forty years, and to show them in the vigor of manhood undeniably the same individuals. The other characters in the story were redolent of the make-up box and the property-room. Cooper's "females" were the type then conventional. But the backwoods philosopher, Natty Bumppo, is, as Thackeray has said, "one of the great prizemen of fiction" and one of the few whom his country has contributed to the world of the imagination. The "pursuit-rescue" scheme the author managed with sufficient adroitness to display incidentally a great variety of Indian customs and traditions. As Cooper drew largely upon Heckewelder's idealized Indians he deserves credit for representing the red men as cunning and treacherous, and not merely noble. Of their traits he noted their acute senses, developed through woodcraft and warfare, their belief in omens and their tortoise and beaver worship, their mummery, their stoicism, their "gift" of revenge, their love of baubles, their respect for the feeble-minded or the aged, their chaste attitude toward female captives, the silence of the young, their funeral customs and deference to the mound for the dead, their councils of war and fierce tribal pride, and the craft and eloquence of their orators. Certain barbaric virtues were stressed no doubt in order to reflect by contrast upon the rude democracy of the author's countrymen. Yet, whatever the critics may say about Cooper's Indians—of late they have rather deferred to him—his conception of the red man has been impressive and is not likely now to be replaced.

In *The Prairie* (1827) Cooper hazarded a third venture with Leatherstocking, this time placing him on the plains beyond the Mississippi whither the popular mind had followed the removal of his prototype, Daniel Boone. In this novel the central figure, the squatter, is not heroic but lawless, and underhanded. There is an assault by Indians, a stampede by buffalo, and a prairie-fire; but on the whole the tone of the story is subdued. The author's brooding over the epic vastness of the plains makes this perhaps his most poetic romance. Cooper's imitators had directed attention, meanwhile, to early life in New England, and he turned in *The Wept of Wish-ton-Wish* (1829) to the period of King Philip's war. This work was a failure, because the author was unable to depict sympathetically the nature of the Puritans, and because he lacked the historical acumen of a Scott to make the past live.

Now, for a decade Cooper's work was largely controversial. *The Bravo* (1831), a skillfully executed tale of early Venice which he wrote while he was abroad, was, to be sure, pure tragedy; but in such caustic satire as *The Monikins* (1835) and *Home as Found* (1838) he gave full vent to his dissatisfaction with his countrymen. Not until after his return from Europe did he venture to continue what was becoming the Leatherstocking "series." In *The Pathfinder* (1840) he brought together his early successes, the Indian and the sailor; and, to crown all, he resurrected the aged hunter and portrayed him in love. In this admirable sylvan romance Cooper came under the spell of the contemporary school of sentiment. He continued in that vein in *The Deerslayer* (1841), a tale of adventure about his native Otsego, nearly, if not quite, his best work. After this Cooper also fell in line with the tradition to romanticize state history. *Satanstoe* (1845), the first of the Anti-rent novels, has proved one of the best documents of colonial manners in New York that we possess, but in the others his ardent republicanism which had grown truculent under Jacksonian democracy, impaired his art and clogged his narrative with propaganda. Of his numerous sea tales perhaps the best was *The Red Rover* (1828), though *The Crater* (1847) has qualities in common with *Moby Dick* and *Robinson Crusoe*.

Anyone can point out technical faults in Cooper's work. What he enjoyed was walking cross-country, and little he cared whether his boots were polished or no. He was prolix, but his very prolixity was a secret of his illusion. At his best his style had the rapid motion and color needed in a novel of action. He wrote far better than his

public required of him. For the epitome in fiction
of early American life one goes not to Irving or
Hawthorne but to Cooper; his representation of
it as the conquest of nature by the pioneer came
to be regarded as so characteristic of the American adventure that the novel as he conceived it
dominated the writing of American fiction up to
the eve of the Civil War.

To appreciate Cooper's outstanding work in
American fiction, one has merely to examine the
work of his contemporaries and imitators. During the 'twenties, novels of the Indian and the
Revolution came forward, many by women writers, but the work was feeble, encumbered with
supernatural machinery, and bent on a moral.

About 1830 a spiritual change came over America. Jacksonian democracy broke with traditional
politics. Reform movements of one sort or another, like the temperance movement, the femi-
nist movement and communistic experiments were
in the air. The lyceum flourished. Cities grew,
and acquisitiveness became aggravated. The age
of machinery was beginning to shatter old patterns of thought. East and West were at odds
over internal improvements and North and South
differed over nullification. The romances of the
period, while not great, were thoroughly indigenous, and are important in reflecting the taste
of the times.

While a poetic coterie in the North was laying its first fruits upon the national altar, the feudal South was dreaming of its heroic past. In *Horse-Shoe Robinson* (1835) John Pendleton Kennedy immortalized a homespun hero of the Revolution in South Carolina, and in *Rob of the Bowl* (1838), he depicted faithfully the beginnings under the Proprietary, of his beloved Maryland. William A. Caruthers in the *Cavaliers of Virginia* (1832), a tale of Bacon's rebellion, flattered his readers with the thought that Virginia's colonists had all been Cavaliers. But the most prolific novelist in the Scott-Cooper tradition was William Gilmore Simms of South Carolina. Conceiving of romance in terms of the epic, Simms achieved an enormous output of which only *The Yemassee* (1835), treating of the Indians in the early years of the Carolinas, *The Partisan* (1835), dealing with the campaigns of Marion and Tarleton, and *The Cassique of Kiawah* (1859), another pioneer romance, deserve to be remembered. Too often Simms was melodramatic, and the haste with which he was obliged to write in order to make a living too frequently caused him to transpose to his pages factual history without thoroughly imagining the situation.

During the early years of the republic, life on the "dark and bloody ground" of Kentucky appealed powerfully to the minds of men. Robert Montgomery Bird used it in his *Nick of the Woods* (1837), a most readable prototype of the dime novel that was shortly to enjoy its clandestine vogue. The realistic conception of Indians in this novel was in direct opposition to Cooper's idealization; the well-knit plot marked an advance in the art of native fiction. Realistic sketches had appeared in Kennedy's *Swallow Barn* (1832), and in the frontier episodes of Crockett's *Autobiography* (1834) and Longstreet's *Georgia Scenes* (1835).

More romantic was John Esten Cooke, who took his readers back to a sentimental Virginia with baronial halls and vast estates. In *The Virginia Comedians* (1854) he passed from the Governor's inaugural ball to the fox-hunt, the Jamestown races, and the theatre, and in its sequel, *Henry St. John* (1859), he made apparent on the eve of the Civil War that Virginia had always furnished her share of patriots—had, in fact, commenced the Revolution.

In the work of the aforementioned romancers the historical element was usually authentic but the fiction was often rather incongruously adapted to its background. Some of the writers had little acquaintance with the frontier. Yet compared with the early imitators of Scott and Cooper, they exhibited much originality, borrowing fewer of the supernatural agencies and giving larger place to realistic detail, as when, for example, they modified the scout of Cooper in conformity with various regional peculiarities.

In the section where Cooper had cultivated

American romance, only Paulding's *The Dutchman's Fireside* (1831), describing a settlement on the Hudson, and Hoffman's *Greyslaer* (1840), a story of the Revolutionary War, in the Mohawk Valley, attested a continued interest in this form of entertainment. New England was reading short tales, essays, and verse in the numerous "Tokens," "Annuals," and "Gift-Books" that appeared on every parlor table. Historical fiction was not to its liking when such distinguished sons as Bancroft, Prescott, Motley, and Parkman were supplying it with history "unvarnished." Yet romantic history like Thompson's *Green Mountain Boys* (1839), with its exploits of Ethan Allen and his democratic followers, stirred its sympathies, and not a few read repeatedly that rich store-house of backwoods manners in early Massachusetts, Sylvester Judd's *Margaret* (1845). Motley himself began writing with *Merry Mount* (1849), a conventional romance of Massachusetts Bay colony, and Parkman in 1847 directed attention to the Western frontier in the romantic realism of his *Oregon Trail*. Richard H. Dana, Jr., continued the tradition of fiction about seafaring in his vivid narrative *Two Years before the Mast* (1840). The novels of Hawthorne, and of Melville, were of course the most important fiction of this period, but their discussion has been reserved for a more appropriate place.

The conservative wing of New England thought found sympathetic presentation in Mrs. Harriet

Beecher Stowe's *Minister's Wooing* (1859) and
Oldtown Folks (1869). These transcripts of Puritan life supplied the cheerful and dynamic qualities of the Puritan which neither Hawthorne nor
other contemporaries seemed able to give. In
this field, Mrs. Stowe was thoroughly at home,
and pointed the way to the "local colorists" who
came shortly after. Without question, the most
widely influential novel produced in America
was her *Uncle Tom's Cabin* (1852). The larger
part of its popularity it owed to historical circumstances. When Webster and Clay proposed to
maintain the Union by means of the Compromise
of 1850 they antagonized both North and South.
Mrs. Stowe sought to remove the cancer in the
body politic by an operation. She pictured slavery as a system, with the tragic compulsions of
an "institution" and pleaded for its removal. As
a work of art, therefore, her novel suffered from
too specific a purpose. It is, moreover, highly
sentimental. But in its vivid tableaus, its admirable delineation of secondary characters, and in
its compelling narrative, the book has literary
claims much above those associated with amateur
theatricals.

By 1860 American fiction had become independent of the influence of Scott and Cooper, and,
while it owed some allegiance to Dickens in its
sentimentality, it manifested a constantly growing realism resulting in correspondingly more
vigorous and memorable work. On the whole,

surprisingly little art was displayed by the writers treating the romantic riches of the country. Sustained work seems not to have been exacted by a people materially prosperous but intellectually gross. With the rise of the magazine much talent went, of course, into the short story.

The dramatizing of novels had become popular, beginning with the work of Cooper and including many of his followers. A word must be said here concerning the early growth of the drama, since its pioneering had much in common with the novel. The stage had suffered, during the colonial period, from temperamental as well as theological opposition, and from the lack of leisure. Puritans and Quakers regarded mimic representation as trivial and expensive; in the South, however, Hallam's London Company of "Virginia Comedians" played Elizabethan and Restoration plays as early as 1752. By 1767 the first play to be written by an American for the professional stage, Godfrey's *The Prince of Parthia* (1759), was given at Philadelphia. Roger's *Ponteach* (1766), though not produced, was the forerunner of a number of plays on native material, notably the Indian. With *The Contrast* (1787), a comedy by Royall Tyler, the young nation protested the superiority of its honest Jonathan to the British fop, and prepared to enjoy a long succession of stage Yankees. William

Dunlap (1766–1839), the first professional playwright, wrote and adapted more than thirty plays,
of which only *Andrè* (1798) is now remembered.
His gossipy *History of the American Theatre*
(1832) is the first American stage record.   He
had the intrepidity of the pioneer, and though as
a producer he failed financially, he gave American drama a good start, one that unfortunately
was not followed up by such a worker in native
material as James K. Barker, or by an adapter
of foreign material like John Howard Payne.

In the second quarter of the century New York
replaced Philadelphia as the national theatrical
center.   Two important actors were now on the
stage: Joseph Jefferson, who popularized *Rip
Van Winkle,* and Edwin Forrest, who inspired
Robert Montgomery Bird to write for him *The
Gladiator* (1831) and *The Broker of Bogota*
(1834).   Only two other plays before the Civil
War deserve mention: Mrs. Mowatt's *Fashion*
(1845), a comedy of contemporary manners, and
George Henry Boker's *Francesca da Rimini*
(1855).   The latter depicts medieval Italian life
in musical verse in a way that compares most
favorably with the British poetic drama of the
period.   Neither of these plays led to anything
subsequent, however, and for the next thirty
years drama occupied a place of little importance
in American literary history.

III

THE ROMANTIC IMPULSE

THE literature considered in the previous division, while it reflected in varying degree the frontier frame of mind, was tinctured also by European tradition, a tradition that in one way or another dominated the work of the writers about to be discussed. It is a curious anomaly, but true, that the young nation, insistent upon its own experience, should yet in its major authors have imitated the romanticisms of England and Germany. It, too, cultivated the sense of wonder, the grotesque, the ego; was fascinated by the Middle Ages; had disciples of nature; and displayed enthusiasm for social reform. Interest in the national past, inspired by Scott, found its reflection in Cooper and his successors. Irving and the Knickerbocker writers, in conformity with foreign tradition, garbed the landscape of the Hudson in idyllic hue and Irving discovered old world picturesqueness. In a New England village, Emerson and Thoreau and others adapted from Coleridge and Carlyle the transcendental view and gave it currency. Longfellow and

Lowell, under the spell of German romanticists, stressed feeling and sentiment, an attitude which with Lowell and Whittier soon took the form of humanitarianism. Holmes tried to stand aside, critically, but could not keep entirely free from the prevailing sentiment. In Poe there was something of Byron and Coleridge, and it is only too obvious that the other lyricists of the South were disciples of the romantic poets of England. It is not to be inferred, however, that the writers now to be considered were merely imitative. They deserve to be read because in adapting a current tradition to American experience they left the unmistakable impress of their personality as well. So well did they do this that their era is frequently referred to as the "Golden Age."

1. IRVING AND THE KNICKERBOCKER SCHOOL

The life of Washington Irving (1783–1859) all but spans the richly creative period extending from the Revolution to the Civil War, a period beginning with practically no literature and ending with the most notable work done. Irving was the son of a New York cutlery merchant of Scotch Presbyterian stock. He studied law, but preferred taking his gun to Sleepy Hollow, or slipping off to the theatre. Before long he was writing papers in the manner of the *Spectator*. To check a tendency toward consumption, he was sent abroad. For a time the young man sky-

larked in Paris society, was almost persuaded in
Italy to become an artist, but continued his journey to Holland and England. Upon his return,
he tried his hand at the then popular periodical
essay, and dabbled a bit in politics. He and a
few congenial spirits promulgated *The Salmagundi Papers* (1807–1808), with their laughter at
the follies of the town. Everyone was amused by
the clever thrusts at society, the theatre, and politics. In the twelfth of these papers appeared
a hint of the author's next venture, a burlesque
on Mitchill's ponderous "Picture of New York."
By inventing a mythical Dutch historian as
author, and by making clever announcements of
the forthcoming work, Irving began to develop
the Knickerbocker legend. Not to be outdone by
its predecessor, this history proposed to go back
to the Creation; but, as the work advanced, its
author discarded the idea of parody, and by the
third book was describing in his own best comic
vein the reign of the illustrious Dutch Governor,
Wouter Van Twiller.

If *Knickerbocker's History of New York* (1809),
suffers from prolixity, and if the humor is occasionally too elaborate and prepared for, there
are also such breezy passages as the mock-heroic
one on the capture of Fort Christina. Quite incidentally, the book propounds theories of statecraft. Its fame it owes, however, to its introduction to the world of that curious mixture of wit
and nonsense, American humor. With true comic

art, Irving inserted it into the grave periodic sentences of his sustained narrative. The result was that the literal-minded were outraged, but others, like Sir Walter Scott, reported that their sides ached with laughter from reading the book.

After having lapsed into a period of graceful indolence, Irving was stirred by the death of his first love, Matilda Hoffman, to write some sketches of tender sentiment. They appealed quite as much to his early readers as had the less sad and more vivacious ones. Among the things he contributed to the *Analectic Magazine,* from 1814 on, were sketches of the Indians, and of other local matters of interest. Upon his return to England in 1815, he added to these his papers about the shrines and the holidays of the mother country. In this way Irving served to cement the friendship between two nations of a great common tradition. With the failure of the Irving firm in 1818, he devoted himself definitely to literature. He collected the following year the sporadic papers in which his talent for leisurely description and reminiscence, for humor and pathos, are best fused, and gave to this miscellany the title, *The Sketch Book* (1819–1820).

Here appeared such universal favorites as the Hudson River legends, "Rip Van Winkle," and "The Legend of Sleepy Hollow"; essays on British memorials, like "Westminster Abbey" and "Stratford-on-Avon"; tales with an old-time flavor, like "The Broken Heart," "The Wife," and "Christmas Eve"; the discreet, important paper concerning "English Writers on America," and that excellent parody on Gothic narrative, "The Spectre Bridegroom";—these, and many more. In some of the sketches the short story may be observed emerging from the essay. In style they exhibited a mingling of the old and the new; in them the mellowness of Addison and Goldsmith was blended with the sentiment and pathos that were gaining in vogue.

The most vital of the thirty-four sketches is "Rip Van Winkle." The story of Rip is based on a German legend, and owes its charm in part to its preservation of the qualities of a folk-tale; but owes it no less to the author's gift of selection and to his genial style. Its popularity was enhanced, further, by Joseph Jefferson's admirable dramatic interpretation. In the sketches of Westminster Abbey, Stratford-on-Avon, and those describing an old English Christmas, Irving wrote of England as an Englishman would like to have written about these subjects. At a time when America seemed prosaic, he invested old world subjects with an old world charm. By revealing England and America to each other in a period marked by misunderstanding he served as an international mediator. To many Americans, Europe is still Irving's Europe.

In his next work, *Bracebridge Hall* (1822), Irving elaborated the Christmas series which had been so much enjoyed. Some of the sketches in

this volume were rather thin, but "The Stout
Gentleman" and "Dolph Heyliger" made full
amends for the others. Irving, having met the
notables in England, now went into Dresden society, where he sought in vain the hand of Emily
Foster. He next drifted into a somewhat desultory life at Paris, where he helped John Howard
Payne revamp plays. In 1824 he published *Tales
of a Traveller*, brief narratives of the cruder
German sort, written in deliberate avoidance of
the popular full-length romances of Scott. "The
Italian Banditti" and "Buckthorne and his
Friends" are the best parts, although "The Devil
and Tom Walker" and "Wolfert Webber," from
the fourth section, are not far behind his best
sketches.

Needing a change, Irving next went to Madrid.
The Tales of a Traveller was to have been a German Sketch-Book, but he discovered that he had
been offering the public the same dish rather
often. For this reason, too, no doubt, he gave up
for the present a series of "American Essays."
In Spain he was attracted to Navarrete's heavily
documented *Life of Columbus*, which, instead of
translating, he proceeded to make the basis of
a readable life of America's discoverer. The
work enabled him to combine patriotism with his
love of the picturesque. At the time he was engaged on this task he threw off a historical romance, *The Conquest of Granada* (1829), which
purported to be the chronicle of a monk—a monk

none too well imagined. He also began an account of Mahomet, and projected into a cycle his knowledge of Mexican history. This project was never finished because he magnanimously resigned the material to the younger Prescott. The best product of Irving's residence in Spain and of his study of her chronicles was his Spanish sketch-book, *The Alhambra* (1832). He had enjoyed the freedom of the old governor's house, and was the only Anglo-Saxon who could then have written these tales. With rare sympathy and whimsy he produced a second "Arabian Nights," rich in both physical sensation and dream-like reverie.

At length, after seventeen years' residence in Europe, Irving returned home. Public dinners were arranged for the "Dutch Herodotus." He purchased "Sunnyside" for what he hoped would be retirement. But the popular clamor, asking that he exploit American material, could not be denied, and he set out for the frontier of the Southwest. He left by way of the Catskills, which he now explored for the first time, and then went across the plains west of the Mississippi as far as Fort Gibson in the present State of Oklahoma. His "Tour of the Prairies" appeared in *Crayon Miscellanies* (1835), alongside papers on Abbotsford and Newstead Abbey, and legends from Spain. Another work on the frontier which belonged to this period was *Astoria* (1836), a history of the enterprise on the Pacific Coast that had been begun by John Jacob Astor, the pioneer fur-trader. Irving's nephew compiled the facts and he himself brightened the account and added his name. As a kind of sequel, he made over, in *Adventures of Captain Bonneville* (1837), the diary of an army officer in the Rocky Mountains.

Political plums were now offered him, but Irving preferred to finish his *Life of Washington* over which he had been meditating for a score of years. One post he could not refuse, however, the ministry to Spain, which position he occupied four years. On his return in 1846 his career rapidly neared its close. He rewrote his graceful essay on Goldsmith, enlarged the earlier sketch of Mahomet, and finished, just before his death in 1859, his heroic legend of Washington. Always interested, as a chronicler, in the picturesque, and now, because of his advanced age, somewhat irked by intricate problems of Revolutionary strategy and party politics, Irving did not make his latest and longest work as scholarly and sound as it might have been, but he did succeed in giving a much more lifelike portrait of the Father of his Country than had any of his predecessors.

Irving was never robust; hence his work is rarely intense. The perplexities of his contemporaries disturbed him little. The democratic ferment gave him no inspiration. He was urbane and good-natured rather than strenuous and provincial. He delighted in exercising the fancy rather than the imagination. For some his old-fashioned style has not enough preciosity, his ideas seem obvious, and his sentiment lacks distinction. This age prefers a more incidental or dramatic rendering of pathos. Perhaps it lacks the leisure to enjoy the Knickerbocker flavor of writing. Irving's contemporaries thought his work, in contrast to the prevailing allegories, realistic enough. Unquestionably he had a fine sense of form: simple structure, nice gradation of tone, discreet length, and a middle style, fusing the witty and the metaphorical; and, as his natural idiom, mellow humor. His humor and his style are indeed Irving's chief claim to consideration. With them he cast a spell of romance over the Hudson and lingered with dream-like reverie over the Alhambra and other old-world shrines. In contrast to the nervous, journalistic style of the present day he offers serenity and charm. His appeal is somewhere between that of Lamb and of Dickens.

Irving's influence on lesser writers was considerable. The immediate Knickerbocker Group —Paulding, Bryant, Willis, Halleck, Drake, and Dana—came in most direct contact. Joseph Rodman Drake was the author of the spirited poem "The American Flag" and of the once popular poem "The Culprit Fay." Fitz-Greene Halleck is known for his elegiac lines on Drake beginning "Green be the turf above thee," for the over-declaimed ode "Marco Bozzaris," and for the humorous and satirical "Croaker Papers," on which he and Drake collaborated. Of James K. Paulding, co-author of *Salmagundi,* it has been said that he had Irving's glee without his grace. He is best remembered for his story of the Hudson settlement, *The Dutchman's Fireside* (1831), and for a tale of Kentucky entitled *Westward Ho!* (1832). Somewhat nearer Irving's manner is the leisurely and genial romance, *Wilderness and Warpath,* by James Hall, interpreter of the West to the East. John Pendleton Kennedy's *Swallow Barn* (1832), with its fine grace and culture, is a Virginian *Bracebridge Hall,* even to certain incidents and characters. Mexican romances, like Timothy Flint's *Francis Berrian* (1826) and Robert Montgomery Bird's *Calavar* (1834) and *The Infidel* (1835), recall the interest in Spanish civilization awakened by Irving.

In the field of the essay Irving's romantic vein was continued by Nathaniel P. Willis in his jaunty *Pencillings by the Way* (1835), by Donald G. Mitchell ("Ik Marvel") in the somewhat cloying sentiment of *Reveries of a Bachelor* (1850) and in *Dream Life* (1851), and by George William Curtis, editor and orator, in *Prue and I* (1856). Charles Dudley Warner likewise owed much to Irving.

2. Transcendentalism in New England

In passing from Irving to the Transcendentalists, the background shifts from liberal New York to conservative New England. When the Mather idea of a theocracy had faded out, largely because of a growing prosperity, intellectual stagnation had set in. But the religious temper was merely inert, not crushed. In the ferment of the 'twenties came the Unitarian revival in eastern Massachusetts, an impulse which dropped the central philosophy of Puritanism but kept its ethical interest. When the separation of church and state pushed the problem of religion into the bosoms of individuals, man's salvation was sought no longer in an institution but in the perfectibility of the individual. The stress was shifted from the total depravity of man to the innate nobility of human nature. This change in point of view was accompanied by a spirit of optimism; the pressure of dogmatism having been removed, and comfort having replaced hardship, a liberal criticism of life followed.

For the first time in the intellectual history of the country were people ready for the speculative outlook on life. Knowledge derived through the senses alone seemed inadequate to compensate for the breakdown of faith; therefore thinkers like Emerson turned to the idealistic philosophy of Kant that had come to them by way of Coleridge and Carlyle. Unitarianism as thus modified by European idealism became known as Transcendentalism. As defined by Frothingham, Transcendentalism is a system of thought "based on the assumption of certain fundamental truths not derived from experience, not susceptible of proof, which transcend human life, and are perceived directly and intuitively by the human mind." The idealistic basis of Transcendentalism is to be found, of course, in the teaching of Plato; but its immediate provocation was the rapidly growing materialism of the country.

The intellectual awakening took different doctrinal form in different individuals. Perhaps the most eccentric representative of the movement was A. Bronson Alcott (1799–1888). He was a lifelong vegetarian, an educational reformer, an advocate of feminism, a founder of the Transcendental Club in 1836, and an idealistic experimenter with a farm, Fruitlands. He was an incessant talker, whose "Orphic sayings" could not all be comprehended even by the initiated. His daughter Louisa, author of *Little Women* (1867), was obliged to support the family. He left some personal poems and the reminiscent *Concord Days*. Margaret Fuller (1810–1850), the most intellectual woman of the period, was the first editor of *The Dial*, the literary organ of the movement. Later, as literary editor of Horace Greeley's *Tribune*, she wrote some excellent critical papers, collected and published in 1846 as *Papers on Literature and Art*. On her return from Italy with her husband, the Marquis d'Ossili, she perished in a shipwreck. George Ripley (1802–1880) was the leader of the Brook Farm venture in communistic living. Jones

Very (1813–1880) and Christopher Cranch (1813–1891) wrote exquisite verse, mostly sonnets of a mystical nature, as did Ellery Channing, nephew of William Henry Channing, Unitarian leader, and cousin of the anti-slavery orator, William Ellery Channing. In the humanitarian field, Theodore Parker (1810–1860) and George William Curtis (1824–1892) carried on the later ideals of the group.

The literary outlet of the Transcendental Club was *The Dial*. It appeared from 1840 to 1844, and disseminated largely German and oriental philosophy. Most of the persons just mentioned, as well as Emerson and Thoreau, contributed articles and poems to it. When Margaret Fuller left the editorship in 1842, Emerson, together with Thoreau, had charge of it. As an expression of the return to nature and the simple life some of the Transcendentalists established in 1841 at Brook Farm, on the outskirts of Boston, a communistic society. In England, Coleridge and Southey had indulged in pantisocratic notions, and in France, Saint-Simon and Fourier were advocating communism as a solution of some of the problems raised by the industrial revolution. In America, the best known of some thirty ideal communities established by 1840 was Brook Farm. Here men and women worked for a few hours a day for their sustenance and spent the rest of the time in intellectual discourse. Besides Ripley, such literary men as Hawthorne,

Dana, and Curtis were for a time connected with it. Emerson, Margaret Fuller, and Horace Greeley, though interested in the undertaking, were not members. In all there were about 150 members, and an annoying number of visitors. When in 1844 the experiment came under the influence of Fourier it began to disintegrate, and, with the destruction of the main building by fire in 1846, the project soon came to an end. Some of the idealism now spent itself in humanitarian endeavor in the political field by opposition to the institution of slavery. The main effect of the movement, so far as literature is concerned, was to quicken and bring together such intellectual leaders as Emerson and Thoreau, and, less directly, Hawthorne and Melville.

a. RALPH WALDO EMERSON (1803–1882)

In Emerson, two centuries of Puritan aspiration come to flower. He is without question the outstanding thinker in American letters. He is hardly a philosopher—for that term implies a system of thought—and Emerson was not syllogistic, but intuitional. In the spiritual growth of America he personifies the break with Puritan determinism and institutionalism in favor of a mystical optimism based upon the evidences within the individual self. His mind garnered the wisdom of the ages and reminted it for the uses of his generation and ours. Divesting things of their associations, he put them to fresh application in the light of new experiences and thus liberated the mind. By flashes of insight here and there he bade his countrymen trust themselves, for democracy, he taught, comes only with the ideal development of the individual. So responsive have the American people been to his ideas that he is regarded as the most characteristic as well as the greatest American mind.

The outward facts of Emerson's life are quickly told. His was a home that practiced plain living and high thinking. "Heredity slept strong in the boy." An important formative influence was an aunt who rather forced his educative process. At Harvard he was not brilliant, but a fair scholar, somewhat formal. Amid clerical surroundings, in Boston, he naturally took up the art of preaching. Then, at twenty-nine, came the most decisive act in the whole career of this serene man. Partly because of ill health, but mainly because he could not conscientiously administer the sacrament, he left the Unitarian ministry to become lay-preacher to the world. First, he went abroad. In his travel in the old world, his mind was on his own ideas as may be seen in his lines "Written in Naples" and "Written at Rome." He met Landor, Coleridge, and Wordsworth but seems to have been impressed only by Carlyle, with whom he formed a memorable friendship. Their *Correspondence* makes profitable reading. On Emerson's return, he settled at

Concord, leaving his home only for his lecture engagements—which, by the way, helped make the lyceum an institution—and for a second and a third trip to Europe. The biography of Emerson is truly to be found in his successive publications as they variously unfold his thought.

The essence of what Emerson had to tell his generation he set forth in a pamphlet entitled "Nature" (1836). In it he considered the relation of the soul to Nature and to God. "Every soul," said he,[1] "is of the divine essence, and may have communication with all that is divine in the universe; and since all things and all actions are manifestations of the divine, it may read a spiritual lesson in every work of nature or of art." The individual soul is dignified by the utility, beauty, and discipline offered by Nature and is lifted Godward. This faith in the self-sufficiency of the individual constitutes the rhapsody of the mentor of the Transcendental movement.

In his next utterance, "The American Scholar" (1837), the new leader sounded the nation's cultural declaration of independence. Emerson, said Lowell, first "cut the cable that bound us to English thought and gave us a chance at the dangers and glories of blue water." "The Man Thinking," with new data in new surroundings, was placed before the world. On its converse side, this Phi Beta Kappa address at Harvard

[1] As summarized by W. B. Cairns: *A History of American Literature* (1912), p. 232.

revealed the narrowness and poverty of contemporary thinking. When the high appeal of this message was repeated the following year in the "Divinity School Address," there were many who shook their heads. The implication to short-cut historical Christianity and the injunction to look into one's own soul and acknowledge what one sees there appeared blasphemous, and for a generation his *alma mater* spurned him.

There followed now the first series of his *Essays* (1841), and, three years later, the second series. In these the ideas set forth in "Nature" had ripened through contact with the world. Matthew Arnold put them alongside Wordsworth's poems as the best work of the century. Among the outstanding essays are "Self-Reliance," "Compensation," "The Over-Soul," "Fate," "Power," "Culture," "Worship," "Illusions." The ideas in them are thrice-distilled. They had been gathered by random reflection and first noted in the *Journals;* next they had been developed as lectures; and finally they were refurbished as essays. No wonder they are richly suggestive and stimulating to one's ideals!

The central idea behind all the essays is the Platonic doctrine of the Over-Soul. The Over-Soul is that great nature, he says, "within which every man's particular being is contained and made one with all other." It abolishes time and space. At moments when we are receptive to it, it lifts us through the intellect to genius; through the will, to virtue; through the affections, to love. Such moments do not come when we are in society but when we are in solitude. As the soul is the selfsufficient perceiver and revealer of truth, the author naturally deduces the doctrine of self-reliance. The union of each and all, on the other hand, argues for friendship on a high and comprehensive plane. Nature, since it helps establish harmony between our best selves and the Over-Soul, takes on new dignity and significance. History and geography are made vital through a sense of the immanence of God. Art becomes an expression, even though fragmentary, of eternal beauty. Revelation is not something that happened historically but that which continues in each passing hour. Such a brief summary of the tenor of Emerson's thought in the essays gives no indication, of course, of their candor and their ingratiating personal qualities, their flashes of poetic description, their epigrammatic good sense.

When Emerson went abroad a second time, in 1847, he gathered his observations in a work called *English Traits* (1856). In his London lectures, *Representative Men* (1850), he seems to have followed the general plan of his friend, Carlyle, in his *Heroes and Hero-worship*. Such happy portraitures as those of "Montaigne" and "Napoleon," as well as the half-humorous one of Socrates in his "Plato," reveal the author's powers as an ethical critic. The essay on Thoreau is equally clear-cut, but most of his later essays add little to his fame, with the exception of *The Conduct of Life* (1860), in which he set his conception of patriotic idealism before his countrymen.

In rewarding contrast to the later essays, are Emerson's *Journals*. Many germinal ideas were first conserved in this "savings bank," as he called it. It contains his candid judgment upon men, books, and public events, and gives some of his personal ecstasies. It is the record of a "New England conscience deprived of its concrete deity, buoying itself on gleams and suggestions of eternal beauty and holiness." [2] For those who do not have access to the entire set of *Journals* there has been made available *The Heart of Emerson's Journals* (1926).

The poems of Emerson originally appeared, for the most part, in *The Dial*. They may be described as reverberations of his essays. Indeed, many of the poems were prefixed to the essays and state the same theme in somewhat more compact and universal form. For example, "Each and All" suggests the philosophy of "Compensation"; "The Rhodora" points to the ideas of "The Over-Soul"; and there are strong analogies between other poems and essays. Like the essays, the poems are sententious; their strength lies in a phrase, or passage, rather than in the poem as a whole. Their author is a "seer" rather than

[2] P. E. More: *Shelburne Essays,* XI, p. 73.

a "maker." He lacks temperamental ardor; therefore his poems are not sensuous. He is somewhat tone deaf; therefore, his poems are deficient in melody. Yet if they are seldom, in Milton's sense, "simple, sensuous, or passionate," they are none the less memorable. Such concentrated bits of thought as "Days," "Brahma," "The Rhodora," "The Problem," "The Concord Hymn," and "Terminus," not to mention such aphorisms as the ones beginning, "So nigh is grandeur to our Dust," and "Though love repine and reason chafe," have found a permanent place in literature. Their influence is traceable in modern verse.

In passing from a consideration of Emerson's poems to a study of his prose style, it becomes apparent that the prose is somewhat richer in metaphor and analogy. It has something of the ejaculatory eloquence of the lyceum. It is a bland style, not so much gauged for the reader —more as if the author were talking to himself. It is noble in passages, but lacking in continuity of thought. For complete unity of thought Emerson's vision was not opulent enough, though a sufficiently wide reading of his work lends it an inner logic. "A rhapsodist and psalmist," Emerson has been called, and here, without question is where he belongs—with Epictetus and Marcus Aurelius, with Montaigne and Sir Thomas Browne, the wisdom writers of the ages. Even those who find it hard to be in sympathy with his thought feel in his work the presence of a great mind. Arnold spoke truth when he called him "the friend and aider of those who would live in the spirit."[3]

Emerson's aloofness from "movements" and institutional life generally impairs to an extent his message for an age such as this in which social problems are paramount. A world living in the realm of the senses finds it hard to warm to Emerson's impersonal deity. His philosophic utterances do not offer the spiritual consolation which religion affords through the tremendous reality of its sense of evil. He has been charged with being a too facile optimist. His ethical concepts rest on bases belonging to the sentimental, prescientific era. Yet his doctrine of self-reliance is tonic, particularly so for an over-organized, machine-bound age. More than any other of his countrymen, he has made apparent "the happiness eternally attached to the true life in the spirit." A thoroughgoing democrat and liberator, he has been "the most powerful and stimulating ethical teacher that the nation has produced."[4]

b. HENRY D. THOREAU (1817–1862)

Thoreau was for his generation a mystery, a comparatively unregarded satellite of Emerson.

[3] Matthew Arnold: *Discourses in America,* essay on "Emerson."

[4] W. B. Cairns: *Op. cit.,* p. 238.

Yet he was unquestionably original, not to say eccentric. Stoical, solitary, "wild" he was, but he had also affection and grace. His letters show that the solitude he esteemed was a solitude of the soul. Thoreau was provincial only in the sense that Concord was at the time the habitat of his body; he traveled, as he himself said, "a great deal—in Concord!" His culture was more solid than Emerson's, and in his stalwart socialism he was more forward-looking. His tonic simplification of life is giving him a fresh vogue, and it seems that the village crank who wrote with aboriginal vigor is at last coming into his own.

After a four-year period of browsing at Harvard, Thoreau for a time engaged in teaching, a task which he soon gave over in order, among other things, to lecture for the Lyceum. From his lectures as well as from the jottings in his surveyor's notebook, he later made his essays. A trip with his brother John developed ten years later into his first book, *A Week on the Concord and Merrimac Rivers* (1849). This work is a miscellany, consisting of observations upon nature and reflections on books and on life. In the essay on Saturday, the echoes of civilization still reach the voyagers; on Sunday, there is a discussion of Hindoo and Greek philosophy and of books; then follows a masterful discussion of style; the marvelous daybreak of Tuesday next holds attention; on Wednesday there is a notable sermon on friendship; next comes the story of Hannah Dustan among the Indians, followed by a discourse on epics; by Friday the reflections shift to Ossian, and thus is concluded a week covering ages of human thought. Throughout the voyage there are glimpses of an America that had been omitted from the *Sketch Book*. There are poems, too, and papers from *The Dial* that he had pitch-forked together with passages from the journal.

When the publishers were unable to dispose of the book, Thoreau carried home most of the edition, saying with fine gallantry, "I have now a library of nearly nine hundred volumes, over seven hundred of which I wrote myself." After this came two years as Emerson's man-of-all-work, years mutually impressionable to the two men. A season of tutoring in New York followed, after which he resorted at odd times for years to the family's business of pencil-making, and to surveying.

It occurred to Thoreau that by six weeks' manual labor he could support himself a year. To prove his contention, he became for two years, while still in his twenties, an amateur hermit on the edge of Walden Pond. Here he possessed his soul far more absolutely than would have been possible either in Concord or with such a group as that at Brook Farm. Regarding his purpose he said in *Walden* (1854), the record of his experience: "I went to the woods because I wished to live deliberately . . . and not, when I came to die, discover that I had not lived." The experiment was, in brief, a protest against the type of man that the growing industrialism was producing. It was life, not things, that Thoreau went to possess. His venture was not a pose for "copy": what others preached, he lived.

Though his adventure in spiritual perfection was not successful, as the allegory of the hound, the bay horse, and the turtle-dove in *Walden* pathetically admits, there is no question that he thoroughly enjoyed the experience of "camping." And his book, because it is an honest book, appeals in its buoyant record of actual experience much as *Robinson Crusoe* ministers to man's primitivism. It is a wise, refreshing book that for beauty, precision, and indigenousness has perhaps no equal in American literature.

Thoreau was a poet rather than a naturalist. He was not an impeccable observer; he did not measure minutely; rather, he possessed the imagination and reflection of a poet. He was an out-of-doors man with a heavenly gift of expression. His journeys to Cape Cod, to Canada, to Maine, up the Monadnock, and out to Minnesota each took in the aroma of field, mountain, and stream. What he wrote was couched in the most sinewy prose style, at once easy and sententious, that America has yet produced. Its very sand and grit admirably reflect the awkward, blunt man who loved the singing of the wind in the telegraph-wires and despaired to match it in his writing. It is true that he never quite forced his form beyond the sentence, and it may be admitted that his sentences are seldom finely turned. Yet there is a gnarled, homely beauty about them that lifts his expression far above the perfunctory, cataloguing qualities of most out-door literature. His essay on "Wild Apples," for example, shows how the gusto of his enjoyment fashions beauty out of the plainest materials. What he says is "as fragrant and pungent as a hemlock pillow." There lurks behind his phrases a sly, sardonic humor that lights up details with the author's inexplicable genius. Whence came this style? It came from the Hindoo literature a London friend sent him; from the classics, which he knew in the originals; and from such seventeenth century men as Herbert and Milton; a glorious compound strained carefully through the Concord microcosm. The bookish flavor of this man's celestial homespun may in the end prove his greatest charm.

But however much Thoreau was the master of his medium, no consideration of his work can end with evaluation of his style. As a thinker and writer he had something to say to his generation and to ours. As Emerson's ideal man in action he tried to make his intuitions of spiritual life co-ordinate with nature. He said, "I am a mystic, a Transcendentalist, and a natural philosopher." He sought to detect in nature some trace of the ineffable. Romantic wonder with him was transformed into awe. From his communion with nature came his negative attitude, his setting up of the individual against government and law. If man is divine, he argues, why must he then cripple himself with stupid laws and outworn observances? In his *Journals*, the "heart" of which is easily available,[5] one may find the completest expression of this rugged man's philosophy. If Thoreau was an ascetic, he was, as Stuart Sherman has pointed out, "an ascetic of the Epicurean sort. He dieted his senses only in order to make them more acute. He boiled the water out of his life for the sake of the sugar at the bottom of the pan, and he got the sugar! . . . What Thoreau set out to explore was the capacity of the human will to accomplish whatever it was set to perform: whether to walk forty miles, eat a fried rat or a keg of nails, read Oriental philosophy, sleep under boards, or write the most sinewy prose in America. . . . He explored the powers of a minority of one, and he found them considerable."[6]

C. NATHANIEL HAWTHORNE (1804-1864)

Hawthorne was a reflective Puritan reinspired by the ideas of Transcendentalism. However liberal he may have been doctrinally—and he was in no sense a reformer—temperamentally he was a Puritan. To this ancestral strain he owed his

[5] *The Heart of Thoreau's Journals*, ed. by Odell Shepard (1927).
[6] Stuart Sherman: *The Main Stream* (1927), p. 45–46.

obsession with the problem of evil. Human nature under circumstances of sin was his favorite study, and the Calvinistic order of his forefathers furnished him the artistic setting. For this retrospect he was born most opportunely. He came just as the moral ideas of New England were passing from the conscience to the imagination and before the decay so ably depicted in the impotent characters of Mrs. Wilkins-Freeman set in. When the once alluring faith of Jonathan Edwards had paled, says Paul Elmer More, there was ready for Hawthorne's art, anguish and bereavement and loneliness. Not only did Hawthorne depict the decaying culture of his fathers; he also directed his scrutiny to the Transcendentalists, who after rejecting Puritanism were substituting for its doctrine of sin, self-reliance; for hell or heaven, compensation; and for authority, freedom of thought. He was a Transcendentalist only, therefore, in a critical sense.

Born in Salem, where the gray mist of the seaport settled upon him, he inherited from seafaring ancestors a solitariness redeemed only by his physical vigor. For all his trenchant independence on occasion, he could and did mingle with men of all stations. As a youth he read widely, including Scott, Rousseau, the *Newgate Calendar, Caleb Williams,* and the *Faerie Queene.* Then he attended the rustic Bowdoin College, where he gained a few life-long friends like Horatio Bridge and Franklin Pierce, and from which he was graduated in 1825 with Longfellow. For the next dozen years he lived the life of a recluse and fatalistic drifter. He published *Fanshawe* (1828), a romance revealing indebtedness to Scott, which proved a failure. During his taciturn period, when the literary fashion changed to American themes, his imagination harked back to the early chronicles. From time to time there appeared from his pen in fugitive magazines and annuals, tales which he described as "pale-tinted flowers that blossomed in too retired a shade." These were collected by his friend, Bridge, and published as *Twice-Told Tales* (1837; 1842).

The hundred or more tales contained in this collection and in *The Mosses from an Old Manse* (1846) and *The Snow Image* (1851) afford the best approach to the peculiar genius of Hawthorne. In them a painstaking artistry is already apparent. They may roughly be classified as historical sketches, allegories, and studies in personality. In such historical sketches as "Endicott and the Red Cross" and "The Gray Champion," Hawthorne selects for his story the dramatic moment when the old order changes to the new. In allegories like "The Great Carbuncle," "The Minister's Black Veil," and "Rappaccini's Daughter" he writes with the largeness of a poet. In "Wakefield" and "Ethan Brand" he probes into the recesses of the human heart; and in "The Great Stone Face" and "The Ambitious Guest" he touches the new romanticism with morals. In

the earlier tales, perhaps owing to the influence
of Irving, the essay form predominates. In a
few, as in "Mrs. Bullfrog," he exercises his
satiric powers. In others, material facts serve as
symbols of spiritual meaning, and the fancy plays
on the borderland between the two. Motifs recur
in different stories. An episode in "Endicott and
the Red Cross" and the whole of "The Minister's
Black Veil" foreshadow *The Scarlet Letter.*
Some of the devices which Hawthorne uses over
again are: the conception of herbs or flowers as
having mystical potency; viewing life as a proces-
sion; the tolling of bells; a bloody footstep; a veil;
the quest for the elixir of life. Indeed there is
some justification for regarding the tales as notebooks. The material in many of them, it is apparent, did not rouse his intellect sufficiently to trans-
form them into concrete wholes. When they are
studied in conjunction with the three *Notebooks,*
with their carefully phrased entries extending
over many years, the question arises why so few
fragments of his rich imagination were ever finished. However that be, the delicate beauty with
which the tales were imagined was evidence that
an artist of the first order was at hand. They
belong, with the short stories of Poe, to the pioneers of the *genre.*

After a few years in the Boston Custom House,
Hawthorne had a brief sojourn at Brook Farm
that did not appeal to him. Shortly after, followed his happy marriage and residence in the

Old Manse at Concord. Here, on the edge of the
village, he lived in idyllic content, making an occasional call on Emerson, Thoreau, or Channing.
In four years he was back at Salem, the town of
his birth, as surveyor of customs. The routine
of this life he described in the admirable essay
prefixed to *The Scarlet Letter*. When, through a
change of administration, he was shortly turned
out by his political opponents, he did not fret for
now he had leisure to finish what was to prove
his masterpiece.

The Scarlet Letter (1850) deals with the New
England past which he knew thoroughly. Its effect turns upon the Puritan conception of life.
Underlying the story is the Puritan reverence for
physical purity. Adultery is conceived of, not as
an affair of the civil order, but as a problem of
the immortal soul. It has been well said that a
Frenchman might have painted Dimmesdale
with his forbidden mistress; an Italian would
probably have traced the fierce course of Chil-
ingworth, the outraged husband, to a justified
revenge; and a German might perhaps have exhibited Hester, the offending wife, as actually
achieving an outward freedom to match the one
within. Hawthorne puts the whole matter on a
different plane. Instead of singing the pleasures
of the flesh, he emphasizes the inexorable judgment, and thus lifts his story from one of adultery
to one of the trials of the spirit when it seeks
to conceal sin. He makes use, moreover, of the

Puritan reverence for the minister and for the magistrate, both of whom he humbles. Such an attitude as is maintained toward these worthies by the populace is likely only in a community that is preoccupied with the life of the soul. Throughout the book it is evident that the Calvinistic preoccupation with evil is viewed through the not too sympathetic eyes of a son of the seventh or eighth generation of Puritans. Nevertheless, it is the ancestral strain in Hawthorne that makes him the final historian of Puritan New England. *The Scarlet Letter,* apart from its service as a transcript of that life, has artistic excellence of the highest order. The dramatic action of this New England *Faust,* with its crisis in the forest scene in which freedom is offered, only to be followed by the expiation scene, is unmatched for depth, tensity, and style in American prose fiction. It is an inexorable study of society and the validity of its conventions. To read it is to quicken one's sense of the reality of spiritual things.

So well was *The Scarlet Letter* received that its author, who had been depressed by the failure of *Fanshawe* and by his lack of progress beyond apparently fugitive tales, could look into the future with more self-confidence. In the Berkshires, in the company of Herman Melville, he set to work on a romance of heredity, *The House of the Seven Gables* (1851). Hawthorne's delineation of the problem of ancestral guilt, though almost as powerful as that of the sin of concealing sin, is less harrowing than that of the ordeal in his previous romance. For one thing it is a love story; there is lightness in the handling of Hepzibah, and the ending is happy. But a story of terror is combined with it—the curse of Maule is upon the house. There is a concealed stairway, and there are concealed papers. Judge Pyncheon's swaggering respectability, bent on selfish triumphs of aggrandizement, meets a tragic doom. Little Phoebe is an affecting repetition of the Pearl-motif of the previous book. Clifford haunts the reader most of all. The threshold of the story is realistic; thereafter the murkiness increases with the latitude claimed by the author in the Preface, in which he stated the important distinction between the nature of the romance and the novel. Though the physical tragedy in the story does not quite blend with the moral tragedy, the author admirably fuses charm and power in illustrating the Emersonian doctrine of Compensation.

There followed *The Wonder Book* (1851), with its classical legends freshly retold for children, and then came *The Blithedale Romance* (1852). This story is free from the supernatural, having been based upon the author's Brook Farm experience. Romance and realism mingle as the mystery surrounding the seamstress is followed by the search for the drowned body. Zenobia apparently represented Margaret Fuller, whose forwardness offended Hawthorne's latent Puritan-

ism. She and the old farmer appear to be the
only human beings among the phantoms of this
Utopia. Hawthorne was not greatly in sympathy
with social reform movements; as a consequence,
he exhibited much shrewd irony in the emotional
devastation of Hollingsworth.

For writing a campaign biography of his friend,
Franklin Pierce, Hawthorne was appointed Consul at Liverpool. From this contact with the
English public came *Our Old Home* (1863), still
a readable description of English places and manners. But travel came too late for Hawthorne
to derive from it new elements for his art. He
was ever the sturdy provincial. When he wrote
the Preface to *The Marble Faun* (1860), he seems
to have felt that he had exhausted the romantic
material in American life. He therefore lavished
upon a work with a foreign background the ex-
uberance of a first tour of Europe, especially of
a visit to its art treasures. The Faun of Prax-
iteles suggested the germ of the romance. The
theme of the transforming power of evil in developing the soul illustrates Emerson's theory of
"Circles."

Donatello is a creature trying to develop a soul.
Paradoxically, the faun becomes humanized
through the murder he commits at the instigation
of Miriam. Now the common heritage of knowledge and sorrow becomes his; the wood-creatures
will have no more to do with him. On the other
hand, Miriam, on whose behalf he committed the

crime, is spiritually united with him henceforth.
As sin's mysterious transforming power unfolds
in the course of the romance, its shadow falls upon the innocent Hilda, but because of her New
England conscience it falls with the ennobling
power of absolution. The description of Italian
art, scenery, and antiquities are not the least
notable part of the book.

When Hawthorne returned to America he was
seriously perturbed over the country's impending
civil strife. He worked with waning powers on a
romance attempting to connect crime in an ancestral hall, a physician's secret, and the quest for
immortality. *The Ancestral Footstep, Dr. Grim-
shawe's Secret,* and *Septimius Felton* appear to
have been successive efforts to handle material
that he tried to embody in *The Dolliver Romance*
when death cut him short. The end came while,
in the company of ex-President Pierce, he was
on a journey to the White Mountains.

Like Hamlet, to whom he has been compared,
Hawthorne had a feeling of isolation, a fondness
for speculating on the mystery of life, a sense of
leaving at his death an unfinished task. His
sense of solitude has its direct counterpart in his
work. It appears in the isolation of "The Gentle
Boy," in the minister who wears the black veil,
in the main characters of *The Scarlet Letter* and
The House of the Seven Gables, and even in the
unfinished fragment of *The Dolliver Romance.*
Accompanying this sense of isolation was a tend-

ency to brood on the moral implications of a given situation. In "Ethan Brand" and "Rappaccini's Daughter," the problem is one of developing intellect at the expense of the soul; in *The Scarlet Letter,* it is the penalty attaching to hidden guilt; in *The House of the Seven Gables,* it is the meditation on ancestral crime; in *The Marble Faun,* the influence of sin upon the development of character. Hawthorne's moral preoccupation is not narrowly didactic, however; it is expressed in terms of symbolism. It is in this connection that his transcendentalism is most apparent. In his earlier work he had been inclined to brood so long over a problem that the symbol became fanciful. Gradually, however, his imagination triumphed more and more, until in *The Scarlet Letter* only the legerdemain of the letter A in the heavens at night remained. In addition to their symbolic nature, nearly all Hawthorne's characters are seen through a haze. Frequently the haze is produced by distance in time. It is when he deals with the New England past which he knew thoroughly, that he does his most memorable work.

Hawthorne wrought in a sad sincerity: his art stooped to no tricks or compromises. His was the realm of the fancy—the darker phases of life's interior drama interested him. For him there was more in heaven and earth than was dreamed of in the philosophy of the utilitarians. As one of the contemplative school, he looked in his romanticism to the past, linking it with the present; unlike his German contemporaries, however, he stayed close to reality. In a period of didacticism he emerges the true artist. In him the style is truly the man. Without a false note, his style shifts readily from the concrete to the symbolic, from humor to pathos, from irony to pity. It is clear, elevated, and musical, and in perfect taste. America has produced no greater master of the art of fiction than Hawthorne.

d. HERMAN MELVILLE (1819–1891)

Hawthorne's close friend Melville was like him an isolated figure, proud and sensitive, all his life living inward, his ego in fierce rebellion. When his transcendental speculations came into contact with the hard life of the forecastle, the natural result was pessimism. His generation, immersed in things, could not understand his trouble about life, and spurned him as he spurned it; but his genius could not remain hidden and now bids fair to be appreciated.

Melville was born in New York of New England and Dutch stock. He was largely self-educated. He tried teaching for a time, but early his adventuresome spirit lured him to sea. After serving on a sailing vessel bound for Liverpool, he went in 1841 with the off-scourings of humanity on a three-year whaling voyage into the South Pacific. Thrilling adventures on this trip furnished the basis of material for his noteworthy romances. In *Typee* (1846) he "fictionized" the four months he was "indulged" by cannibals of Marquesas before he was rescued by an Australian whaler. In *Omoo* (1847) appeared further adventures with the islanders, romanticised somewhat. *Mardi* a satiric fantasy, and *Redburn* followed in 1849; *White Jacket* (1850), with its diatribes on seamen's flogging, recurred to his life on a warship. Just before Melville became preoccupied with metaphysics he wrote his masterpiece, *Moby Dick* (1851), in which he united his whaling experiences and speculation on the mystery of existence with a power hardly equaled in American romance. For forty all but silent years the author lived on, publishing *Pierre* (1852), a not well understood reference to his unhappy childhood, and *Israel Potter* (1855); but remained for the most part a disillusioned recluse, his work almost forgotten; only in recent years, with a revival of interest in the sea by men like Conrad and Masefield and Kipling, has Melville received the consideration due him.

Moby Dick, the story of the White Whale, is much more than a nautical romance, and easily outstrips its author's other work. That is not to say, however, that the idyllic *Typee,* with its languorous atmosphere and color and dusky beauties in their Utopian surroundings, its repudiation of progress and glorification of the primitive, is not without its power to cast a spell still. But

Moby Dick is an epic of the human spirit and
its eternal feud with the sheer brute energy of
the universe, told in the form of a story of a
great white whale pursued with implacable hatred
by Captain Ahab for having bitten off one of the
seamen's legs:

Ever since that almost fatal encounter, Ahab had
cherished a wild vindictiveness against the whale, all
the more fell, for that in his frantic morbidness he at
last came to identify with him, not only all his bodily
woes, but all his intellectual and spiritual exasperations.
The White Whale swam before him as the monomaniac
incarnation of all those malicious agencies . . . all the
subtle demonisms of life and thought.

Like Lucifer's proud hatred of the Almighty is
this antagonism between Ahab and Leviathan.
So vivid are the details of the chase and so in-
fernal are the accumulating terror and grandeur
of nature that doom man to defeat in the struggle
that, despite devious turns in the narrative and
excrescent chapters that seem to belong in an appendix but give the epic its ballast, one follows
this chaotic tale to its irresistible end. The very
irrelevancies aid somehow in bringing out the
diversity and terror of the whole thing.

Not a little of the charm lies in the racy style.
Moby Dick is poetry in as true a sense as the
King James Bible. The richness of early seventeenth century prose abounds here. Such phrases
as "gay fowl softly feathering the sea," "the
water in his vengeful wake" exhibit the subtle

secrets of the art of alliteration; metaphors like
"A whole hour now passed; gold-beaten out to
ages" and the ocean "seemed a noon meadow, so
serenely it spread" are constant features of Melville's rich prose. There is personification: "The
day was nearly done; only the hem of his golden
robe was rustling"; there is biblical and classical
allusion, the use of forceful adjectives, and, no
less striking than imagery or vocabulary, rhythm.
A short passage from Chapter CXXXII will suf-
fice to illustrate most of these qualities:

It was a clear steel-blue day. The firmaments of air
and sea were hardly separable in that all-pervading
azure; only, the pensive air was transparently pure and
soft, with a woman's look, and the robust man-like sea
heaved with long, strong, lingering swells, as Samson's
chest in his sleep.

There are faults, of course, but they are faults
of strength rather than of weakness, and in so
vast a theme hardly out of keeping. In poetic
rhapsody and sweep of the imagination American
literature has not its equal. The day is at hand
when this powerful allegory will take its rightful
place beside the *Faerie Queene, Pilgrim's Progress,* and *Paradise Lost.*

3. EDGAR ALLAN POE (1809–1849)

While New England writers occupied themselves with a transcendental conception of nature,

Edgar Allan Poe, the leading writer in the South, domesticated the "mystic mid region of Weir." Poe owed more to the influences of his time than has been generally supposed. The conception of him as a lonely exotic, while it sets him off against an increasingly commercial and unintellectual world, does not take into account the services he rendered to his generation as critic and editor. Nor does it consider the fact that as romancer and poet he belongs to the Gothic movement—the school of surprise and terror—of which he was the curious "terminal moraine."

The career of Poe is a story of continuous disappointments. It is a melancholy tale of outer and inner maladjustments, this story of the seraph Israfel doomed to carking, persistent poverty. Born in 1809, in Boston, of strolling actors who died before he was three, the waif early experienced his one bit of good fortune: he came to the attention of the childless wife of a Richmond merchant, by the name of Allan, was adopted by the Allans, and enjoyed excellent tutoring both in Stoke Newington, England, and in private schools at home. The lad showed proficiency in Latin, in sports, and in versifying. His need for feminine sympathy appeared early, and must explain his nightly haunting the grave of a Mrs. Stanard who had befriended him. She is the subject of the remarkable poem, "To Helen."

The scale of living to which the foster father

of the proud and sensitive young Virginian had accustomed him made the poverty of Poe, after Allan withdrew his favor, calamitous. The young man's willfulness, too, helped frequently to undo him. He left the University of Virginia after a year to try army life for a time, always hoping for reconciliation with his foster parent, yet unwilling to forsake his literary ideal for a tradesman's life.

After publishing *Tamerlane and Other Poems* (1827) in Boston, he came to Baltimore, where his short story "MS. Found in a Bottle" won a prize, and, more important still, gained him the friendship of John Pendleton Kennedy, the novelist. Through Kennedy's assistance Poe secured his connection with the *Southern Literary Messenger*. Poe's discerning reviews put the magazine into the front rank of American periodicals. For a time things went better. There was opportunity to publish his tales and to re-publish them. Soon, however, his irregular habits lost him position after position. In New York he published the lengthy South Seas horror, the "Narrative of Arthur Gordon Pym," but, finding no employment, he moved with his fragile girl-wife, his cousin Virginia Clemm, to Philadelphia. Here for six years he served in various capacities, as editor, contributor, and hackwriter. From *The Gentleman's Magazine* he went to *Graham's,* to which he contributed some of his best work; but his articles remaining for long unaccepted, and his wife's health failing, he sought better fortunes in New York.

His publication of "The Raven" in the *Evening Mirror* in 1845 brought him fame at last, but it was only four years before the end. For a time he was co-manager of the *Broadway Journal;* then he contributed to *Godey's Lady's Book;* but reverses came thick and fast, driving the neurasthenic frantic. He had early admitted writing down to his public and he now resorted to one device after another to fool it. His brief successes had been but flashes in the pan—enough, it is true, to haunt him with the idea of founding a national magazine. But when his wife died, not even his success at hoaxes enabled him to sustain faith in himself, and his abnormalities soon culminated in the final episode at Baltimore.

It is the most pitiful tale in our annals. But what concerns the student of literature is how this solitary, embittered craftsman could create, out of disordered fancies and dreams of physical horror and strange crime, structures of imperishable beauty. It is one of those miracles that transcend explanation. A new land was added by him to the empire of the imagination, a fascinating, terrifying land where no didacticism enters in and sheer artistry holds sway.

Poe's consuming ambition was the editing of magazines. It has already been observed that it was as journalist and critic that he commanded the attention of his contemporaries. Much of his criticism, it is true, has sunk into oblivion with the ephemeral works upon which it was wasted, yet enough of his principles have endured to rank their author with Lowell as the outstanding American critics. His review, for example, of Hawthorne's "Twice-Told Tales" contains the accepted essentials of the short story. In "The Poetic Principle," likewise a widely known essay, he stated his theory of poetry as "the rhythmical creation of beauty." Pleasure was to be the objective, rather than the then prevalent enforcing of a moral. Since intense, pleasurable emotion cannot be sustained for long, he argued that a long poem is a "contradiction in terms." In still another critical essay, "The Philosophy of Composition," Poe analyzes his composition of "The Raven." His *ex post facto* analysis is now regarded as a hoax of his puzzle-loving mind; nevertheless it gives the clue to the choice of his favorite materials.

As a critic Poe brought to his task a keen, analytic, and independent mind. In scrutinizing the workmanship of others he was inclined, usually, to find fault with an author's craftsmanship or with his lack of originality. Probably because his acquaintance with literature was limited, he seldom extended it to an examination of what is more important—the author's philosophy. Poe's criticisms were weak when they went beyond a defensive rationalization of his own taste. Upon female poets he was apt to bestow fulsome praise, and he was rather partial to writers of the South as compared with writers from New England. Yet his more important judgments have been upheld. He winnowed the good from the bad in Long-fellow and Hawthorne, and his views of Macaulay, of Bryant, and of Dickens have been sustained. He rescued criticism in this country from mutual commendation by authors and, more important still, from subserviency to contemporary English criticism.

If some of Poe's judgments were bestowed upon unworthy writers, it must be remembered that he felt it his duty to expose mediocrity as much as to discover genius. His romantic point of view in criticism he owed in part to Coleridge, but his judgments were essentially his own. Even now his "Marginalia" and "Literati" as well as the more generalized statements of his criticism, already referred to, are piquant and suggestive reading. And to Poe belongs the credit of being the first of American authors to feel aesthetic problems keenly enough to try to formulate the principles.

As a poet, he possessed to a rare degree the fundamental requisites of melody and imagina-tion. Words like "Auber" and "Yaanek" and "never-more" are melody incarnate, and Poe uses them and others like them to produce the rarest music. Refrains, repetends, alliteration are used in varying profusion, baffling analysis, yet haunting the memory with their unearthly

chords. Combined with these is an imagery that
is illumined by a spectral light that no one but
Poe could have imagined. The reader comes
nearest it in the poetry of Coleridge, and occasionally in Shelley.

The range of Poe's verse is not great, being
confined to the short lyric; but within this form
he did some of the most exquisite work that has
been done by an American. "To Helen," "Israfel," "The City in the Sea," "The Haunted
Palace," "Annabel Lee," "The Raven," "Ula-
lume," "The Sleeper," "For Annie," and the
beautiful reverie, "The Valley of Unrest," have
the originality, the rare beauty, and finish that
belong to great poetry. The substance in these
is slight: one does not seek in them a "criticism
of life." But in these haunting melodies of re-
gret and of escaping beauty, poetic souls find
supreme pleasure.

In his prose tales, Poe bestowed on an even
wider range of materials the romantic glow and
burnish of his vividly imagined sensations. When
Poe and Hawthorne began to publish their short
stories in 1835, only the loose sketches of Irving
and lesser writers had been before the public.
While Hawthorne kept close to the essay form
from which the short story emerged, Poe ventured to raise to the nth power an old principle
of narrative art, suspense. He could begin a
story with superlatives, yet somehow hold attention to the end.

Perhaps what helped most of all was the fact that he maintained one dominant impression. His theory of singleness of effect he set forth in 1842 in the oft-quoted passage from his review in *Graham's Magazine,* of Hawthorne's *Twice-Told Tales*:

A skilful artist has constructed a tale. If wise, he has not fashioned his thoughts to accommodate his incidents; but having conceived with deliberate care, a certain unique or single *effect* to be wrought out, he then invents such incidents—he then combines such events as may best aid him in establishing this preconceived effect. If his very initial sentence tends not to the outbringing of this effect, then he has failed in his first step. In the whole composition there should be no word written, of which the tendency, direct or indirect, is not to the one pre-established design. And by such means, with such care and skill, a picture is at length painted which leaves in the mind of him who contemplates it with a kindred art, a sense of the fullest satisfaction.

"The Fall of the House of Usher" will be found to conform admirably to the foregoing principle.

More clearly than anyone else, Poe saw the large variety of topics which the short story might handle. The subject-matter of his stories varies so much indeed that most attempts to classify them on this basis have been unsatisfactory. There are stories of mystery and terror, such as "The Masque of the Red Death" and "The Pit and the Pedulum"; there are analytical or detective stories like "the Gold-Bug" and "The Purloined Letter," in which field Poe was a pioneer; and there are poetic prose tales like

"Eleanora" and "Ligeia," and such studies as "Shadow" and "Silence" that mark Poe, like DeQuincey, a master of style.

These stories are Poe's adaptation of the three-volume Gothic romance to the magazine. Tales of the grotesque and the arabesque they are. In motif, in phantom hero or heroine, in mood and cadence, they are at one with the stories of Hoffman, the late English romantics, and our own earliest romancer, Charles Brockden Brown. Poe-land is indeed a counterfeit world, the dextrously fabricated world of a dreamer, who knew how to use such artifices as the first person method, an intense rhetoric, a weird setting, bloodless characters, and a carefully ratiocinated plot to wring the reader's sensibilities rather than to charm them.

As an artist Poe was limited by his own subjectivity. His work lacked healthy humor; he was unable to penetrate beneath the gloom and terror of his story to arrive at the springs of action. Character he could not depict, nor was he able to do a sustained piece of work. He was uncannily inventive, but his imagination provided a neurotic sensationalism rather than love and ideality and heart. He did possess, however, the rare power to make the reader see the mysterious and the beautiful. Of all American writers he was the first to whom art meant more than either subject or moral. He gave writing in this country a sense of form and structure that it badly needed. As their culture approaches the sophistication of Europe, Americans are coming more and more to realize that of all their writers Poe was the absolute artist.

4. HENRY WADSWORTH LONGFELLOW (1807-1882)

The most representative poet of the period was Longfellow. When the vigor of the Romantic Revolt in England had begun to wane, a resurgent sentimentalism set in. On this side of the water Irving had exhibited this strain in some of his sketches, and female writers, on the high tide of the popularity of Dickens, had continued it. It was a by-product of middle-class prosperity, and Longfellow gave it popular expression in verse. Like Irving, he interpreted for a busy and unlearned generation the alien treasures of European culture, and became thereby a potent civilizing force. For a period of unrest he supplied poems of comfort. The same philosophic strain that made Emerson a transcendentalist, Hawthorne a solitary, and Thoreau a mystic made Longfellow an apostle of beauty. For the bare New England home he cultivated the romance of sailing ship and countryside and interpreted the charm of old cities beyond the sea.

Longfellow was born in 1807 in the harbor-town of Portland. Naturally, the sea stimulated his imagination. But he was not to choose the life of those who go down to the sea in ships. He was to see life through study-windows. He

attended the neighboring college of Bowdoin, in
Maine, graduating in the class with Hawthorne,
but forming no intimate acquaintance with him.
Indeed, his college life served mainly to widen
his opportunity for knowing books. Upon his
graduation, his *alma mater* called him to the
newly established chair of romance languages.
In order to prepare himself for his duties he was
privileged to travel for three years in the old
world. With travel came comparisons, and perspective. The romance of town and tower and
storied stream stamped itself indelibly on his impressionable nature.

On his return, he published Irvingesque sketches
of the Latin countries in a volume to which he
gave the name *Outre-Mer* (1834). Harvard now
invited him to a professorship, and he made a
second journey abroad, this time adding to his
equipment a knowledge of Germanics. In Holland his wife died. The saddened man went to
Heidelberg to find solace in the sentimentalism
of his beloved Jean-Paul Richter. The sentimentalism of German writers touched "The
Golden Legend," and poems like "The Voices of
the Night" and "The Footsteps of Angels"; it
was also reflected in the autobiographic prose
romance, *Hyperion* (1839). Two other influences
shaped Longfellow's thought, Norse mythology
and Spanish romance. Both of these he knew
thoroughly. In all, he published translations
from no less than nine languages.

Not until after a decade of teaching did Longfellow find fame as a poet. Then "The Psalm of Life," "The Reaper and the Flowers," "The Wreck of the Hesperus," "The Skeleton in Armor," "The Village Blacksmith," "The Rainy Day," "Maidenhood," and "Excelsior" followed each other like song-birds at dawn, and everybody listened. The poet had the rare gift of making his readers feel that here were their daily thoughts and emotions set to music. Lines like "The tide rises, the tide falls" sang themselves inevitably. The ballads attested a poet's sense of rhythm. The metaphors, peculiarly varied and ingenious in the poems about night, still further exhibited his skill and endeared his early lyrics to his widening public.

From the political thought of his day the poet at Craigie House was free, compared with contemporaries like Lowell and Whittier. His poems on slavery lacked the vigor of his "Arsenal at Springfield" or the happy blend of the dramatic and the dynamic in "The Building of the Ship." But underneath the European surface it was becoming apparent that his native strain was about to emerge and express itself. Legendary subjects like those on which he was to base "Evangeline," "Hiawatha," "The Courtship of Miles Standish," and "The New England Tragedies" responded naturally to the romantic cast of his thought. He was to become popular through these longer poems.

In "Evangeline" (1847) the poet took his readers into the colonial past when the Acadians through an act of official stupidity were forced out of their pastoral environment and scattered as far south as Louisiana. The germ of the story Longfellow had from Hawthorne, but he had drawn also on Haliburton's account of the Acadians and on other sources. In unhurried hexameters, the narrative leads through strange regions and harrowing experiences. The poet muses on the ruthless parting of the lovers, recalls the bayou by the Red River where they unknowingly pass each other, and ponders the final scene in the Quaker city with its note of serenity after the long fruitless search. In execution the work is rather uneven. The imagery is vivid, and there are scenes of much beauty and poignancy; but the author's frequent lapses into the sentimental impair the narrative, particularly in the second part.

In "Hiawatha" (1855) Longfellow used the legends and myths of the Indians, as recorded by Schoolcraft and others, for a poem that may be regarded the nearest approach in America to the genuine epic. With the aid of a primitive measure, the use of parallelism, and cumulation, he skillfully reproduced the childlike outlook of a race and the color and freshness of the forest which they inhabit. If the Manabozho of the Ojibways was a more malicious trickster than the hero gave indication, and if some situations follow, not remotely, the Finnish epic, "Kalevala," nevertheless, "Hiawatha" has been the most successful attempt to immortalize Indian life and legends that our poetry affords. When Hiawatha departs in sunset splendor the work of the American King Arthur is done, the glory of his people has departed with him. But the children of palefaces still treasure the undeniably human types of this romantic legend, while their elders read behind the symbols the common history of the race.

In "The Courtship of Miles Standish" (1858) Longfellow draws upon family tradition from the days of Plymouth Colony. When Miles Standish sends an attractive Launcelot, in the form of John Alden, to woo the demure Priscilla, the poet takes opportunity to bring out the lighter side of Puritan life that historians and a romancer like Hawthorne had been prone to overlook. The darker side appears in the "New England Tragedies" dealing with the Quaker persecution and the witchcraft hysteria.

After the tragic death of Longfellow's second wife, he occupied himself with a translation of Dante's *Divine Comedy.* It is a fairly faithful version, whatever it may lack in poetic grace or fire. It set a high standard for American translations that were to follow, like Bryant's of the *Odyssey* and Taylor's of *Faust.* In the "Tales of a Wayside Inn" Longfellow could again rely on a prop. The expedient of fitting together stories associated with an inn had been anticipated by Chaucer and by Boccaccio. For the various narrators he used Boston friends. Only the landlord's tale, "Paul Revere's Ride," and the concluding one, "The Birds of Killingworth," seem to be generally known. The latter suggests comparison with Lowell's half-humorous poems of country life.

Of his late poems it suffices to recall the imagistic "Keramos," the delightfully reminiscent poem, "The Hanging of the Crane"; poems of friendship like the tender greeting to his neighbor, Lowell, in "The Herons of Elmwood," and the lovely elegy for Hawthorne; and what is perhaps the most noble of his "occasional" poems, "Morituri Salutamus."

Choicest of all Longfellow's work are his sonnets. In richness and variety they challenge comparison with the better sonnets in the English language. Some of the best grew out of his long acquaintance with books: "Chaucer," "Milton," "The Divine Comedy," "Shakespeare," "Keats," and "My Books." The sonnets to "Three Friends of Mine" reveal his rich gift for friendship. There are exquisite sonnets about nature, the most notable being "The Sound of the Sea" and "Nature." Finally, there is that masterpiece to his wife, "The Cross of Snow." These are secure among the imperishable treasures of American literature.

It has been the fashion to scoff at Longfellow

as the "poet of the obvious and the humdrum," the poet of the immature. It is true that of all our writers he has best deserved the name, "the household poet." Such laureateship, however, significant though it is in American literary history, does not necessarily crown the highest order of poetry. To answer whether, after all, he was an important poet one must take into account the whole body of his work. It is necessary to read other poems beside childhood favorites. Much that he has written is *cliché* without a doubt.[7] His simplicity of manner borders at times on guilelessness. The Puritan strain in him made him somewhat overanxious to point a moral; that is not very flattering to one's intelligence. Then, it must be admitted that for a long time he did not free himself from the all but prevailing sentimentalism of his day; the expression of such indulgence of feeling that does not issue in action is in modern ethics considered a form of mental dissipation. Yet three generations of readers have found Longfellow a vital force in their lives; and it seems safe to predict that as long as simplicity and reverence are valued the people will read him gladly.

5. James Russell Lowell (1819–1891)

Lowell had in common with Longfellow, to whose professorial chair he succeeded, certain

---

[7] Not all, however, is *cliché*. For extracts that might be thought to come from contemporary poets see G. R. Elliott's "Gentle Shades of Longfellow." *The Southwest Review*, April, 1925.

inherited Puritan qualities and a bookishness
nourished on European culture. Like his Cambridge neighbor, he disseminated what he had received abroad, and sought, also, to foster an
avowedly native literature. Lowell was more responsive than Longfellow to the changing interests of American life. In his work the civic note
was dominant. "Patriot, scholar, poet, orator,
public servant" reads the legend of Lowell.

Lowell was descended from a prominent New
England family; he was the son of a learned
clergyman and a ballad-loving mother. He early
browsed in many books at Elmwood, pausing at
times to rest his fancy on the dandelions that
dotted the lawn or to listen to the herons in the
wood. At Harvard he read all books but "pre-
scribed" ones. In his senior year for infraction
of some rules he was "rusticated" at Concord.
The Transcendentalists there were not to his liking, nor, for that matter, was the practice of law,
which he undertook on leaving college. He had
been class poet, and he continued to write, under
the influence of the English romanticists, notably
Keats, poems of love and poems of contemplation
on New England landscape.

In Lowell's work, the native pastoral quality
was fairly pervasive. "An Indian Summer
Reverie" and "To the Dandelion" reveal it early,
and the June passages of "The Vision of Sir
Launfal" and "Under the Willows" reflect it
later. In "Rhoecus" he glorifies primitivism;

in "The First Snowfall" and "After the Burial"
he connects nature with bereavement and longing.
Though the poet's naturally buoyant spirits
triumphed at the time, the battle with doubt as
indicated by "A Mood" and by so late a poem
as "Credidimus Jovem Regnare," was for him, as
for Arnold, one that continued throughout his life.

Lowell also wrote verse of a political and social
nature. His feeling for the prophetic task he indicated in the "Ode" (1842). Then, in the
"Stanzas on Freedom" he stirred the indifferent
among his generation when the annexation of
Texas was under discussion. His earnestness
reached its highest pitch in "The Present Crisis."
So universal is the application of its best lines
that they are quoted now without reference to the
occasion that gave them birth. Lowell's marriage
in 1844 to Maria White, an abolitionist, added impetus in the direction of humanitarian movements
toward which his mind had been tending. In 1846
he began publishing a series of papers in the *Boston Courier* that were to constitute his most important venture into political satire, *The Biglow
Papers* (1848; 1866). The dialect poems in
these papers purported to come from a young
rustic poet, Hosea Biglow, and were introduced
by letters from Parson Wilbur, his counselor.
The remarks of the pedantic parson neatly offset
those of the waggish Hosea. In the first series,
published at the time of the Mexican War, the
author furnished a wholesome antidote to the

slogan, "Our country right or wrong"; and in the second series, with feeling more tense and humor more grim, he directed the popular mind toward the preservation of the Union. In the *Biglow Papers* Lowell was in his element. Here his love of the pastoral and his mother-wit fused admirably with his didactic instinct. Here he could turn suddenly from the playful to the scornful, and back again. His observation of human nature and his sense for local peculiarities of speech enabled him to achieve such masterpieces in Yankee dialect as "The Courtin' " and "Sunthin' in the Pastoral Line." The election ballad, "What Mr. Robinson Thinks," was soon on everybody's lips, and other political satires in the series were well known. Satire is not a high order of poetry, but so well did Lowell let himself go in these lines in the vernacular that they are among the most successful political poems of modern times.

The supreme note in Lowell's patriotic verse was struck in the "Ode recited at the Harvard Commemoration" (1865) at the close of the Civil War. This Ode, sonorous and dignified, yet readily intelligible, is one of the noblest expressions of patriotism in the language. Written to commemorate the Harvard men who had fallen in the war, some of them the poet's own kinsmen, it had its inception in those peculiar conditions which made Lowell a successful writer for "occasions." Some strophes are naturally more ex-

alted than others. Most felicitously expressed is
the tribute to Lincoln, a tribute which, though
added later, is the more remarkable for coming
so early and from a man of the Brahmin caste.
The author's essay on Lincoln, written the previous year, may well be read in connection with it.
"Under the Old Elm" expresses less affection for
Washington, and is perhaps not simple and sensuous enough on the whole, but rises in its final
strophe to such height of power as to warrant its
classification among the nobler American pane-
gyrics. The tribute to Agassiz is a later ode to
a personal friend.

The year 1848 was Lowell's *annus mirabilis.*
Besides publishing the first series of the *Biglow
Papers,* he brought out also "The Vision of Sir
Launfal" and "A Fable for Critics." "The
Vision," with its confused imagery and obvious
moral, has been overpraised; the "Fable" is still
much quoted. In its rollicking lines on contemporary authors represented in Griswold's *Poets
and Poetry of America,* Lowell uttered surprisingly sound critical judgments for a contemporary. They have not the bitterness of *The Dun-
ciad* or *English Bards and Scotch Reviewers.* Not
only are the judgments remarkably discriminat-
ing, but they concern for the most part writers
whose reputation subsequent criticism has upheld.
In these lines the author's overflowing energy and
gift for improvisation issued once again in the
good-natured satire of which he was a master.

Lowell's relation to other writers may not be understood without a review of his connection with various magazines. In 1843 he had founded the short-lived magazine, *The Pioneer,* to which Poe, Hawthorne, and Whittier contributed; then, for a time, he wrote essays for various magazines that have since disappeared. At the age of thirty-six, after his second trip to Europe, he succeeded Longfellow as Professor of Modern Languages at Harvard. In the same year, 1857, he became the first editor of *The Atlantic Monthly.* This connection enabled him to render a unique service in the cultivation of the American mind. He gave encouragement to young writers, and furthered realistic writing. After four years on the *Atlantic,* he helped Charles Eliot Norton edit *The North American Review.* Lowell was connected with the *Review* until 1872. To it he contributed his best critical, social, and political essays. Through his own appreciation of the great figures in world literature and his understanding for international politics he developed similar interests in his countrymen.

Despite certain shortcomings Lowell has been the most distinguished of American critics. In contrast to Poe, he praised the indisputably great writers—Dante, Chaucer, Dryden, Wordsworth, Shakespeare, Emerson—preferring to discover new beauties in them rather than make known meritorious authors of submerged reputation. So wide was his acquaintance with literature that his

essays form a critical history of the most important figures from Dante to his own day. As a
critic Lowell was a disillusioned romanticist, but
he lacked intellectual impetus to push beyond im-
pressions to universal principles. The amorphous nature of Lowell's essays was attributable
to his life-long habit of jotting down marginal
notations on his reading which he later transferred to his pages. As a consequence, there are
felicitous judgments here and there but the essays
lack somewhat the clarified central conception of
one who has thought matters through. Nevertheless, they are enjoyable to the educated reader,
stirring the imagination by tricks of phrase and
flashes of genuine insight. By following his brilliant talk on writer after writer, the reader may
develop an appreciation for literature not to be
obtained from reading a formal treatise or by
studying merely the literature of one country.

Besides the literary essays, Lowell wrote on
such topics as "My Garden Acquaintance," "On
a Certain Condescension in Foreigners," and
"Democracy." The last two are perhaps his best
known essays. Not a little of the condescension
practiced by foreigners had been invited, Lowell
asserted, by the deference of Americans; but now
he shrewdly bade his countrymen stand on their
own merits.

Lowell had been drawn into politics, first in
a minor and local way, but, at length, to serve
his country as minister, from 1877 to 1885,

first at Madrid and then at London. In this capacity his social charm and innate tact attained their greatest usefulness. Through his adaptability, cultural associations with the old world became established. The English, after the Civil War, he found to be strangers, but he left them cousins.

In "Democracy," delivered originally as an address at Birmingham in 1884, Lowell asserted his life-long faith in the democratic principle. Because of certain Tory sympathies in his nature he was able to make clear to the British what constitutes the American experiment in government; at the same time he refuted those at home who doubted his loyalty. So adequately did he sum up the achievements of democracy and outline the perils, that this essay has become a classic to be read by every American. During his last years, when political corruption was rampant, Lowell was somewhat more dubious concerning the manifest destiny of democracy than he had been in his earlier essay; in "The Place of the Independent in Politics" he questioned the efficacy of the two-party system in times of national duress. American culture has needed and still needs his fearlessness and his urbane exposition of the democratic idea.

Lowell's tendency toward diffuseness, observed in his essays, and his genius at improvisation, noted in his verse, combined to make him an outstanding writer of letters. In his familiar letters his wit sparkles. Those qualities of poise, cleverness, and personal charm which were his to a rare degree as an after-dinner speaker also characterize the letters and make them worthy successors of the English masterpieces of epistolary art of the preceding century.

When the work of Lowell is passed in review, there is observed in it the mark of a versatile mind. Unquestionably he was as well read as any man of letters that this country has produced. He touched life at many points and he always had something to say. Yet his work lacks something which men of narrower range but greater concentration have overcome. He had the zeal of the scholar but he allowed social demands to cripple the artist. It would seem that Lowell was a dilettante. He dipped into poetry, into prose criticism, into public affairs. He was, however, an American dilettante: he carried into each of these fields a distinct, energic style; at home and abroad he was a respected man of affairs.

Most of his life Lowell was a romanticist: but he was a little too late for the enthusiasms of the romantic revolution, and too early to adjust himself to the scientific age. The English writer with whom he may most readily be compared is Matthew Arnold. Both are in their verse concerned with the religious perplexities of an age of unrest, though Lowell is the less heavy-hearted of the two. Both are impressionistic critics. Much of Lowell's contemporary reputation he undoubtedly owed to whimsical elements in his personality, to the sparkle of his good-natured wit and the dash of his satire. In the process of the years much of his improvisation has lost favor, not having been carefully enough wrought to endure. Nevertheless, his work still inspires those who would live the well-rounded life. His country has produced no more distinguished humanist than he.

6. OLIVER WENDELL HOLMES (1809–1894)

The "last leaf upon the tree," Lowell's Boston neighbor, Holmes, was also at his best in the lighter vein, in familiar verse, and in the light personal essay. He was in many respects a survival of the eighteenth century wit. His essential urbanity he owed to a long and distinguished line of ancestors. For him Boston Statehouse was naturally "the hub of the solar system." In that city's "Brahmin caste," as he called it in the first chapter of *Elsie Venner,* he was a fellow of infinite jest. But he did more than scintillate among his group at the Saturday Club—he purged New England of its sourness. His wit and his eager rationalising distinguished him from his romantic brethren at Cambridge, and made him, despite some lapses into the sentimental, a critic of romanticism.

When Lowell became the first editor of *The Atlantic Monthly,* the organ of the new literature

that had arisen since the demise of *The Dial,* it
was on condition that Holmes should contribute
regularly. For this Holmes was well qualified.
He had been bred among books, had been graduated with the "Boys of '29" at Harvard, had attained fame at twenty-one with the spirited lyric,
"Old Ironsides," had given up the law for medicine, and had produced a handful of light verse.
Of this early verse, "The Last Leaf," with its
delicate blend of humor and pathos, was destined
to become his most memorable poem. Other verse
of a humorous nature appeared from time to
time, including "The Height of the Ridiculous,"
"The Ballad of the Oysterman," "My Aunt,"
"The Poet's Lot," and "On Lending a Punch-
bowl." The young physician who had gayly announced that "the smallest fevers would be cheer-
fully received" was making his shrewd observations in his own way, as may be inferred from his
jolly ballad, "The Stethoscope Song." Accordingly, when in 1857 he contributed to the *Atlantic*
the first of his Breakfast Table series, he was no
longer a novice in the study of human nature.
He was drawing upon the rich experience of a
man about fifty.

The Autocrat of the Breakfast Table made
Holmes a man of more than local reputation; it
became his "visiting-card to posterity." It was
clever to use for the setting of his discussion a
boarding-house, since talk there may turn to any
subject, as this or that person takes it up, yet is

usually dominated by one person, whose whims may be challenged from time to time, but to whose ideas the boarders for the most part defer. To get the complete symbolism of the picture, the social historian must connect the audacities of the "Autocrat" with the opposition of the angular female in black bombazine, and note the reaction of other "boarders" as they exemplify an age passing through the throes of didacticism and the cult of the obvious.

Indeed, the "Autocrat," who smiled so benignly over the teacups and suavely declined to take the dogmas of his day seriously, was once under the ban for his freedom of thought. "Every real thought on every real subject," said he, "knocks the wind out of somebody or other," and he refused to utter thought-stopping conclusions about anything. From time to time he offered sly digs and side slaps at the doctrines of foreordination, infant damnation, and other barbaric notions. But always he steadied his thrusts with "probably" and "it seems," and through such gentle satire as that in "The Wonderful One-Hoss Shay" he smiled down the vestiges of Calvinism. At the same time, in such a lovely parable as that of the stone with the grass growing around it, he offered genuine inspiration to unaffrighted inquiry.

There is a pleasant, unaffected egotism about the "Autocrat." His monologue sparkles with epigrams; for Holmes was a born proverb-maker.

Here are some of his terse sayings—meaty as hickory-nuts:

Put not your trust in money, but put your money in trust.

Knowledge and timber shouldn't be much used till they are seasoned.

All men are afraid of books, who have not handled them from infancy.

Sin has many tools, but a lie is the handle which fits them all.

The world has a million roosts for a man, but only one nest.

The clergy rarely hear any sermons except what they preach themselves. A dull preacher might be conceived, therefore, to lapse into a state of *quasi*-heathenism, simply for want of religious instruction.

A thought is often original, though you have uttered it a hundred times.

Any new formula which suddenly emerges in our consciousness has its roots in long trains of thought; it is virtually old when it first makes its appearance among the recognized growths of our intellect.

Man has his will—but woman has her way.

In this book are comments on many subjects. Men, books, customs, superstitions, pugilism, trotting horses, trees, religion, table manners, pronunciation, medicine, locutions, topics of the morning—the author toyed with them all and made them all piquant and instructive. Poems embellish the *Autocrat*. "The Chambered Nautilus," which Whittier said was "booked for immortality," appeared in it, as did the ironic lines of "Contentment," and that "logical story" in Yankee dialect, "The Deacon's Masterpiece, or

the Wonderful 'One-Hoss Shay.' " There is
vivacity in the *Autocrat;* it has the flavor of the
spoken word; and, as a liberating book, it is still
timely.

With the other work of Holmes, the winnow-
ing process of time has not dealt so kindly. In
The Professor at the Breakfast Table (1859),
The Poet at the Breakfast Table (1873) and *Over
the Teacups* (1890) there are further thrusts at
dogmatism and bigotry and further instances of
shrewd sagacity; there are solicitations to keeping an open mind and to cultivating good manners, but they are less varied and less spontaneous than formerly. The novels, *Elsie Venner*
(1860), *The Guardian Angel* (1868), and *A Mor-
tal Antipathy* (1885), all dealing with phases of
the problem of heredity, have been called "medi-
cated fiction" by the author himself, and it is
generally conceded that he was not a born novelist. The better work of Holmes appears to include, besides the *Autocrat* and the poems already
mentioned, the beautiful elegy, "The Voiceless,"
the quaint "Dorothy Q.," two class poems, "The
Boys," and "Bill and Joe," together with a few
hymns, notably the one beginning with "Lord
of all being! throned afar."

Much of his poetical gift Holmes devoted to the
post-prandial entertainment of friends; and,
since more than half of his verse was written for
occasions, its appeal has naturally been limited.
In style his verse was distinctly of the eighteenth

century, belonging with that of Prior and Gay.
His prose style was that of a more kindly Sterne.
But in thought, Holmes belonged to the nine-
teenth century. Though he could not keep entirely out of his work the mid-Victorian zest for
reforms, he was one of the early reactionaries
against the sentimentalism of his age. His scientific training no doubt made him skeptical of
dogma. His kindly wit civilized at a time when
good manners were badly needed. He opposed
romantic equalitarianism because he realized that
society would tend to stratify anyhow, and he was
a thorough believer in the life of cultivated
leisure. As America's chief discursive essayist,
Holmes did more than make thinking in public
decorous; he made humane living inviting and
thoroughly desirable.

7. JOHN GREENLEAF WHITTIER (1807–1892)

The work of Whittier, like that of Lowell,
marked a humanitarian advance in American annals. Unlike his New England contemporaries
except Thoreau, Whittier was a product of the
soil. He was, therefore, representative of a
larger portion of the American people than was
any other of the elder poets. Though he gained
renown by opposing slavery, the pastoral quality
in him seems likeliest to survive.

Whittier was born of sturdy Quaker stock on
a farm in northeastern Massachusetts. He was

reared in an atmosphere such as he has pictured inimitably in his masterpiece, "Snow-bound." The slight schooling he enjoyed at Haverhill Academy he paid for with his own hard earnings as a shoemaker. He was not only poor and untaught, but frail. Two influences effected his self-discovery: a stray volume of the poetry of Burns, and contact with Garrison, the abolitionist. Burns made him a neighborhood poet, and Garrison gave him courage to voice a love of freedom that had long been inherent in his stock. In 1833 he enlisted his practical idealism with the Abolitionists, and after a short period in the legislature, went to Philadelphia to edit the *Pennsylvania Freeman.*

In his writing, Whittier was early attracted to history and Indian legend; besides his verse on colonial life, his one piece of memorable prose, *Margaret Smith's Journal* (1849), treated of colonial traditions. With full understanding the poet undertook to sing the songs of labor—of shoemaking, lumbering, and cornhusking. Incidentally, he pictured the Merrimac countryside he knew so well. He even ventured to meditate on bits of foreign lore. He wrote anti-slavery poems. But not until he was stirred to write such a summons to action as "Voices of Freedom" (1841) was he transformed from a local and imitative poet to the impassioned spokesman of a national cause.

In his opposition to slavery, Whittier made it

clear that his enmity was not against slaveholders but against slavery as an institution. In this he was perfectly sincere. He had studied Milton and Burke, the great spokesmen of English liberty, and to him the emancipation of negroes was but a single phase in universal liberalism. Of the anti-slavery poems, the more impassioned were: "Massachusetts to Virginia," with its hint of a limit to tolerance; "Ichabod," burning with indignation at Webster's compromise in the famous "Seventh of March Speech" (1850);[8] and, when the long struggle was at last over, the paean, "Laus Deo." Much of Whittier's verse during the period before the war was written for newspapers, and altogether too many of his utterances were the declamatory rhetoric of prejudice. They delayed his arrival as an artist; yet perhaps he needed the delay, to judge by the poise and finish of his later work.

While Whittier was laying what he deemed his best gifts on the shrine of freedom, he found time to write the songs and ballads that have found more abiding favor. "Cassandra Southwick," dealing with the persecution of the Quakers, shows ability to tell a story with vigor and picturesqueness; "Barbara Frietchie" is not so successful, being rather melodramatic; "Maud Muller" brought together on a common level and in a sentimental way such social extremes as a

---

[8] The poet modified this statement in a calmer hour in "The Lost Occasion" (1880).

city judge and a country girl; in "Amy Went-worth" the author reversed the social relation when he depicted the love of a high-born lass for the hero of a fishing smack. His most artistic work in ballad form is "Skipper Ireson's Ride." It moves faster than the others and stops when it is through. Where some of the others tend to be too homiletic, it allows the moral to emerge naturally. It matters little whether the captain was to blame or the crew for the abandonment of the ship off Marblehead for which he was tarred and feathered and drawn through the town in a cart by the indignant women of the town; the poem has the rhythm and ring of the genuine ballad. Whittier's importance as a writer of ballads lies in his ability to tell a story, to throw over some simple incident the glamor of fancy or a touch of pathos, to see the picturesque and human side of his material, and to give it all in the fashion of the old ballad-makers.

In portraying the rustic life and manners of New England, Whittier did his best work. Such lyrics of his boyhood as "Memories," "The Barefoot Boy," "My Playmate," and "In School Days" reveal not only the home life of New England but disclose also the heart of Boyhood perfectly. Some of them, like "Telling the Bees," "First-Day Thoughts" and "The Meeting" relate pre-eminently to spiritual experience; others, like "The Huskers," "The Lumbermen," and "The Shoemakers" glorify the toil with which his people gained their livelihood. Whittier could write of this life vividly because he alone of our New England poets had lived outdoors with nature in all seasons of the year.

It is but natural that "Snowbound" (1866) should be Whittier's masterpiece. The theme was perfectly adapted to his mood and powers. He was nearly sixty, alone, and the family homestead, occupied for generations by his ancestors, and rich in personal associations, had gone into the hands of others. With unerring rightness of feeling he recreated in his "Flemish pictures" not only his own lost youth, but he pictured for all time the home life of rural New England as it once existed. Here are depicted with faithfulness and skill, the coming of the storm, the peaceful hearthside diversions while the snow is piled high without, the characteristics of individual members of the home, and of such others as the schoolmaster, with his introduction of local and foreign legend. As a charming picture of democratic life in the country this idyll does not suffer by comparison with "The Cotter's Saturday Night" or "The Deserted Village." In it Whittier was as impersonal and direct as he ever came to be, and the consequence is a well-nigh flawless work of art.

In one other respect Whittier deserves attention as a poet—he was a most intimate interpreter of the religious life. His religion was indeed the soul of his genius. As a writer of hymns he contributed in the poem "Our Master" such well-known selections as those beginning "We may not climb the heavenly steeps" and "Our Lord and Master of us all!" These are free from the dogmatism of a particular faith and have the passion of true devotion. They are humble, trustful, sincere. Such a spirit pervades also "The Eternal Goodness," and many another poem of simple aspiration.

Whittier's beautiful lines in "the Proem" ingenuously set forth the aims of his art, and what he believed were his shortcomings. From this view it is likely that few will dissent. "The harshness of an untaught ear" accounts for many of his bad rhymes. Sensuous charm had little appeal for him. His work suffered, also, from diffuseness. Besides much of it is too obviously didactic. Yet there are times, as in "Massachusetts to Virginia," when the very indignation of his appeal has poetry within it. There is little variety in form, yet in his simple meters there is often a fullness of life that is wanting in abler craftsmen—his better poems have character.

Most of the fiery stanzas which Whittier penned when the spirit of nationalism was more intense than it has been since are forgotten now with the issues that produced them. But when he turned from these to catch beauty in native hill and flower and stream he became our chief bucolic poet. He was provincial, but in the best sense:

like Crabbe he made vivid the life he knew, and the soil from whence he sprang. His sense of integrity and his insistence on the dignity of the individual carry their message still. In his unshakable faith in the spiritual order of the world he was a "very Galahad among poets"; he had "the holy heart of a George Herbert." He was not a first-rate poet, but his countrymen could ill afford to be without his best work.

Apart from the work of Whittier and of Mrs. Stowe, already noted, the conflict between North and South left its impress upon literature chiefly in the form of martial lyrics, the orations of Wendell Phillips, Charles Sumner, Daniel Webster, Henry Clay, John C. Calhoun, and the addresses of Abraham Lincoln. Songs and ballads like "The Battle-Hymn of the Republic," "Maryland! My Maryland," "Dixie," "Tenting on the Old Camp Ground," "Just Before the Battle, Mother," "Sheridan's Ride," "Marching Through Georgia," "John Brown's Body" and "Tramp, Tramp, Tramp, the Boys are Marching,"—these and many others served to keep up the courage of those involved in the conflict. The songs were easily parodied and were constructed too hastily to be seriously considered as art. Of the orations, Webster's "Reply to Hayne," because of its stress on nationality was perhaps the most forward-looking, though there was some-

thing of the platitudinous in Webster that begins
to tarnish. On the other hand, the addresses and
letters of Abraham Lincoln, because of their
simple sincerity, rank among the masterpieces of
rhetorical art. "The Gettysburg Address," the
"Second Inaugural Address," the "Farewell Address at Springfield" and the letter to Mrs. Bix-
by endure as literature because of their freedom
from artifice and their heartfelt genuineness. In
them a great spirit moved among the eternal
verities.

8. The Lyrics of Timrod, Hayne, and Lanier

Romanticism, the characterizing trait of the
Knickerbocker Group, the Transcendentalists,
and the Cambridge poets, was by no means confined to the writers of New York and New England. It found particular favor in the South.
Here the very organization of society was such
as to stress individualism, and love for the past.
Class distinctions, widely separating the aristocratic planter from the "poor white" and the
negro, kept up in the imagination of the South
a close connection with the feudal tradition of
Scott. At the same time, among the young men
of the manor, there was not a little of the Byronic.
On the other hand, there was also a sturdy middle
class, which maintained a tenaciously democratic
spirit. In this region, moreover, physical nature
is so florid and insistent that the cry for a "return to nature" could easily be heeded. It was

natural, then, that such literature as flourished in the South should deal with the luxuriance of nature, with personal feelings, or should revert to the glories of an earlier day.

Literature was regarded by the socially elect as light entertainment. Serious thinking concerned itself with political issues, and followed the traditions of the spoken word as practiced by Clay, Calhoun, and others. There were few centers, few publishing houses and magazines, few libraries. Nevertheless there was a reading public in the South that devoted its generous leisure to the romances of Scott, the oriental tales of Byron, and the essays of Addison which lined the walls of the manorial library. In time it supported the *Southern Literary Messenger* at Richmond and *Russell's Magazine* at Charleston and contributed to them its own sketches and romance, and its beautiful lyrics.

Out of the anguish and destitution of the Civil War there arose in the South three poets with as pathetic a story as our literature records. Henry Timrod (1830–1867), Paul Hamilton Hayne (1830–1886) and Sidney Lanier (1842–1881)—all rarely endowed with poetic gifts—found the pursuit of their careers interfered with by the call to arms. Each had his ancestral property swept away, each suffered from the exposures of life in the army, and after the ordeal each fought penury with broken health, yet kept his song cheerful and sweet even with death at the door.

Timrod and Hayne belonged to the small coterie at Charleston of which Simms, the novelist and poet, was the presiding genius, and *Russell's Magazine,* the literary organ. Hayne, the editor of that periodical during its brief career, 1857–1860, belonged to a family of social prominence, being a nephew of the opponent of Webster. As a writer of occasional verse, he was in constant demand and wrote entirely too much. His work bulks larger than that of Timrod and Lanier combined. Of sonnets alone he wrote perhaps as many as any American poet. Naturally a considerable portion of his work was imitative; to the romantic poets of England he was deeply indebted. But when, as in his poems on the pine-tree and the mocking-bird, he wrote of the sights and sounds of native wood and field, he rose occasionally above the merely graceful and melodious, and wrought with sincerity, conviction, and pathos.

Timrod, a truer poet, also wrote nature poems which in form and attitude owed a good deal to Wordsworth, Keats, and Tennyson but of which the atmosphere was that of the dreamy lower South. His most characteristic poem was "The Cotton Boll," prophetic of future prosperity. It may be compared with poems on similar themes, like Lanier's "Corn" and Bryant's "The Sower." "Carolina" and "Charleston" contain Timrod's impassioned stanzas in behalf of the South. In "Ethnogenesis" he hailed the birth of the Confederacy and in the "Ode at Magnolia Cemetery" and "The Unknown Dead" he paid tribute to the gallant sons who had fallen in the Lost Cause. In a lighter vein he wrote his charming "Katie," and his felicity of phrase and sincerity of thought found further happy expression in a series of sonnets. When Timrod was singing the beauty of his beloved Southland he was at his best.

The ablest of Southern writers, after Poe, was Sidney Lanier. Endowed with the gift of the twin arts, poetry and music, he gave a life-time of devotion in the endeavor to co-ordinate the two. His training, though limited, was in the cultivated traditions of the South. In childhood he read the older poets. From early youth he could play on almost every kind of instrument, but loved especially the flute. He came by his taste naturally, for several Laniers had been directors of music at the English court between the periods of Elizabeth and Charles II.

For one of Lanier's refined spirit the ordeal of the war proved especially severe, and he came out of his brief prison experience with health shattered; the rest of his life was a struggle, like Stevenson's, with consumption. The war gave him at the same time the contact with the actual world which he so much needed, and it served to give him a national outlook while that of his literary compeers was sectional.

After various attempts to gain a livelihood as clerk, teacher, lawyer, during the blundering period of Reconstruction, Lanier became at length first flutist for the Peabody Orchestra of Baltimore. He now also set about enriching his mind with that wide reading for which he had not had opportunity previously. He devoted himself to a mastery of the early periods of English literature, and during the last two years of his life was a lecturer on the subject in Johns Hopkins University. Out of this experience in lecturing grew his critical works, *The Science of English Verse* (1880) and *The Development of the English Novel* (1883).

Lanier first attracted public attention in 1875 by the publication of his poem "Corn." Soon his orchestrated protest in "The Symphony" against the crass materialism following the war won him the attention of Bayard Taylor, through whose mediation he was invited to write the Cantata for the opening of the Centennial Exposition at Philadelphia. In the few years that remained to him, Lanier was able to put forth only a slender volume of verse, but that volume contains the symphonies already referred to and his melodious poems and songs. "The Marshes of Glynn," with its sensuous opulence and moral suggestiveness, is his best poem. The "Song of the Chattahoochee" and the wistful lyric, "Evening Song," contain his most haunting melody. In the ballad form he contributed the simple compassionate "Trees and the Master" and the vigorous, Scott-like "Revenge of Hamish." His sonnet on "The

Mocking Bird" is well known, as is the nobly patriotic "Psalm of the West." The poem "Sunrise" was his buoyant death-bed song.

Poetry, as Lanier conceived it, was a variety of music. To him, rhythm and melody were more important than meaning. By his interest in metrical and stanzaic experimentation he belonged with Swinburne and Francis Thompson, whom he resembled also in his concern for movement, alliteration, and tone color, to the subordination of thought. In his devotion to beauty he was like Poe, though he leavened his conception with spiritual truth. His favorite subjects were nature and love and he dealt with both in a romantic manner. In the seven or eight years of his poetic composition he was becoming less vague than he had been at first, freer from over-luxuriant figures, and more spontaneous. Though he was not spared to attain to the fullness of his powers, Lanier contributed some of the sweetest strains to American song.

9. LATE ROMANTICS: THE METROPOLITAN POETS

After the Romantic Impulse in American literature had largely spent itself in the work of the major writers already discussed, there appeared, contemporaneously with Lanier, a group of lesser romantics who kept up the tradition throughout a transition period. This group of writers in New York City was known as the "Metropolitan

Poets.'' Most of them were not born in the
metropolis, nor did they have much to say about
it, but they were drawn together by mutual interests somewhat as the more intimate Knickerbocker Group had been drawn together a quarter
of a century before them.

The leading spirit of the ''Metropolitan Poets''
was a Pennsylvanian by birth, Bayard Taylor
(1825–1878). He had traveled extensively abroad,
had published his *Views Afoot* (1846), and then,
captivated by the Orient, introduced to his con-
freres the cult of the East in the ''Bedouin Song''
and other sensuous *Poems of the Orient* (1854).
His enormous energy also found expression in
novels, including *Hannah Thurston* (1863), a
satire on the *isms* of the mid-century, *The Story
of Kennett* (1866), a Pennsylvania idyll, and other
works of fiction. But his main ambition was to
be a poet after the manner of Shelley and Goethe.
Unfortunately, his verse was haunted too much
by the style of others and he paid the penalty of
shallowness for his versatility. The ''National
Ode'' lacked creative power; the pastorals of
Pennsylvania life were written with better understanding. Yet it seems likely that Taylor will be
remembered not for his verse but for his excellent translation, in the original meters, of *Faust*
(1871), and because of his having widely befriended aspiring writers.

Among those forming with Taylor a nucleus of
metropolitan writers was Richard Henry Stod-

dard (1825–1903), another devotee of beauty who poetized the Orient, and George Henry Boker (1823–1890), playwright and sonneteer, who was under the spell, also, of the Elizabethans. Boker's exotic verse is no longer read, but his sonnets are at last receiving due recognition. Stoddard was a lover of poetry rather than an inspired creator of it. Edmund Clarence Stedman (1833–1908) likewise did more through his anthologies and criticism to make the work of other poets known than he did by creating a few poems of the quality of "Pan in Wall Street." For him, a Wall Street banker, the Muse served as surcease from the cares and anxieties of business.

Others drawn into the coterie were the landscape painter, Thomas Buchanan Read (1822–1872), remembered only for the spirited "Sheridan's Ride" and "Drifting"; Charles Godfrey Leland (1824–1903), author of the amusing *Hans Breitmann's Ballads;* Richard Watson Gilder (1844–1909), editor of the *Century Magazine* during the first twenty-five years of its existence; and Thomas Bailey Aldrich (1836–1907), who fraternized with this Group during the early years of his career, and was perhaps the most finished of the creators of "art for art's sake." Gilder was a public-spirited man given to brooding on matters of art. His few intense and melodious lyrics are not so consequential as was his wide influence in improving public taste. Aldrich also reached a wide public during the 'seventies as editor of

Every Saturday, and during the 'eighties, as editor of the *Atlantic Monthly,* in his native New England. Besides his delightful boys' book, *The Story of a Bad Boy* (1869), and the clever hoax, "Marjorie Daw," Aldrich wrote sonnets and quatrains and lyrics almost as fastidiously worded as those of Herrick. His vivacity and wit further found expression in rather pleasing society verse. From the economic developments and social changes of the Reconstruction period he was as aloof as the rest of the "library poets." The chief service rendered by these late upholders of the romantic tradition was to discipline the more vigorous poets then in their formative years and to enable these younger poets with true creative urge to accomplish something.

IV

THE AMERICAN SCENE (Since 1860)

FOLLOWING the Civil War a spirit of intense nationalism spread over the country, a conscious awareness of the immensity of the new domain and a deepening appreciation for whatever was indigenous. There was a distinct break with the older tradition that had looked to Europe for inspiration. "The eight years in America from 1860 to 1868," said Mark Twain,[1] one of the leaders in national self-discovery, "uprooted institutions that were centuries old, changed the politics of a people, transformed the social life of half the country, and wrought so profoundly upon the entire national character that the influence cannot be measured short of two or three generations." The relatively unknown West, in the election of Lincoln, wrested political leadership from the Atlantic seaboard. As the imagination turned to the vast new frontier, the country as a whole became animated by the democratic spirit of that area. At the same time the romantic impulse was leavened by disillusionment with mid-

[1] In *The Gilded Age* (1873), p. 200.

dle-class economics and by a scientific temper that came to demand reality and yet more reality. Parlor poetry was too thin, and books of European travel and translations of old world classics with which the literary traditionalists tried to console themselves were of little moment to an age which wished to do its own thinking and for which nothing but genuineness would serve.

The break with European tradition had been heralded by Emerson in "The American Scholar" in 1837, but few had listened to him then. Longfellow and Lowell each voiced the same sentiment, but could not free themselves from British and German romanticism. It remained for Whitman, disciple of Emerson, but obedient to both the romantic and the realistic impulses, to give the impetus which made the new literature possible. His romantic individualism and mysticism, together with his keen sense of perception, welcoming the aid of science, and revolting against conventional modes of versification, fitted him to be the spokesman of a new movement; and these traits, united with an ardent faith in the future of "these States," made him the true prophet of Democracy.

1. WALT WHITMAN: PROPHET OF AMERICAN DEMOCRACY

From the first, Walt Whitman (1819–1892) has been the subject of controversy. His own generation was puzzled by the form of his verse and shocked by the frankness of his expression. The conservative New England group, excepting only Emerson and Thoreau, and Emerson not always, regarded him an upstart. There were others who, as the years passed, made of him a cult. In order, therefore, to distinguish whether he is an isolated and towering peak or a mere foothill it is necessary to let the good gray poet emerge from the myth that has settled upon him.

Whitman's youth was spent on Long Island, where he enjoyed a healthy outdoor life, declaiming the classics on the seashore or ardently hugging the ocean wave. Soon he was occupied at a printer's desk in Brooklyn, and thrilled crossing on the ferryboat to his beloved Manhattan, or eagerly conversing with cab-drivers and street-car conductors, or dropping in for a chat with the bohemians at Pfaff's. The first turning-point of his life came with a trip to New Orleans, where an erotic romance awakened the indolent drifter to an awareness of beauty and the meaning of sex. The creative spirit in him was no longer satisfied with writing journalistic rubbish and he turned to building houses in expanding Brooklyn, and more important still, to composing "Leaves of Grass." The next turn came when Emerson gave him almost the sole endorsement in a cold literary world. And last, there was the sublimation of his ego in the evil days that forced brother against brother, when his ministrations

as an army nurse deepened his art and spiritual-
ized it. The rest of his life was that of a broken
man, writing more verse, purging it in course of
time of redundancy, writing his own "puffs," los-
ing a government job because of the objection to
his verse by someone in authority, gaining at
length the favor of the British critics, spending
the years of decrepitude selling his books from a
basket in commonplace Camden, and, when paral-
ysis struck him down and money seemed sorely
needed, paying thousands of dollars for what
should be an appropriate tomb. In all the annals
of literature was there ever one like unto him?

For an intelligent approach to Whitman, it is
necessary to understand his use of the capital
"I." "I celebrate myself, and sing myself," he
says, but adds, "And what I assume, you shall
assume, For every atom belonging to me as good
belongs to you." He is not flaunting his ego,
therefore, but seeking to glorify the "divine average." True, there is a bit of the theatrical about
him: "I wear my hat as I please, indoors and
out." To some it seems Whitman suffered his
life long from a sense of inferiority and affected
a swagger to assert a masculinity he felt lacking.
To make sure none would feel unworthy of his
friendship, he avowed the evil within him as well
as the good. "I am not the poet of goodness
only, I do not decline to be the poet of wicked-
ness also." He wished to express the entire man.
"I am the poet of the Body," he chanted in an

age when athletics had not reached our colleges
and women were under the thrall of hoop-skirts,
"and," he added, "I am the poet of the Soul."
He insisted on glorifying the body in order to
give it a better soul.

Carnal though Whitman seemed, still he had
the ardor of the true mystic. There was in him
early a blending of religion and patriotism that
ultimately gave direction to his life. The gospel of Emerson's "Each and All" is writ large
across the pages of Whitman. "Not objecting
to special revelations, considering a curl of
smoke or a hair on the back of my hand just as
curious as any revelation," [2] expresses his attitude. A devoted patriot, he asserted that government only muddles when it tries to make a
people happy; they must do that for themselves.
"Democratic Vision" shows a genuine concern
for Americans to live up to their opportunities,
to have each citizen develop his personality in
order that a true democracy may be achieved.

America must, as Whitman says, "cease to
recognize a theory of character grown of feudal
aristocracies . . . and must promulgate her own
new standard, yet . . . accepting . . . the perennial elements, and combining them into groups,
unities, appropriate to the modern, the democratic, the West, and to the practical occasions
and needs of our own cities, and of the agricultural regions." As an expression of her true

[2] "Song of Myself," Stanza 41.

spirit, "America demands," he continues, "a poetry that is bold, modern, and all-surrounding and kosmical, as she is herself. It must in no respect ignore science or the modern. It must bend its vision toward the future, more than the past. Like America, it must extricate itself from even the greatest models of the past, and, while courteous to them, must have entire faith in itself, and the products of its own democratic spirit only. Like her, it must place in the van, and hold up at all hazards, the banner of the divine pride of man in himself. . . . Long enough have the People been listening to poems in which common humanity, deferential, bends low, humiliated, acknowledging superiors." Such a declaration marked a new era in our literature, and throughout his work Whitman's zeal showed no abatement in the endeavor to bring about the new order.

An obstacle to the appreciation of Whitman's verse, to some, is its apparent formlessness. Barrett Wendell spoke of the stanzas of "Brooklyn Ferry" as "confused, inarticulate, and surging in a mad kind of rhythm which sounds as if hexameters were trying to bubble through sewage." [3] Whitman adopted a lawless rhythmic movement, not because he had had no success with the established measures but because he could not sing of the great out-of-doors and the large faiths in life and death and affection in the sing-song of parlor

[3] Barrett Wendell: *A Literary History of America,* p. 473.

verse; for these he needed the diversified regularity in nature; her variegated arrangement of trees, the uneven rhythm of the sea-gull's wing, the unequal beat of wind and wave, the irregular curve of hills against the horizon. He felt that the idea to be expressed should govern the form, and in this later poets have been glad to follow him. He reverted to the principle of parallelism that underlies the poems of the Old Testament, Oriental epics, the poetry of *Ossian*. His rhythmical chants are keyed for the ear rather than the eye, as anyone may learn by reading aloud "When Lilacs Last in the Dooryard Bloomed" or "Out of the Cradle Endlessly Rocking."

Few poets have chosen so euphonious titles for their poems as he. To glance over the index to his lines is like reading a poem in free verse. For Whitman, the very names of objects have poetic connotation, as when he lists geographical names in trying to incarnate his country's spirit. Frequently he borrows words from foreign tongues—*allons, camerado, vivas, ambulanza*—or coins some of his own, like "tubercled," "experient"; not infrequently he seeks attention with a barbarism like "philosoph" or "promulge." Not all of these terms are chosen with equal felicity nor is there always rhythm or reason in his "cataloguing" of detail. In his endeavor to bring into focus immediately all the multifariousness of life, as might be done with a space-art like painting but not with a time-art like poetry, he lapses all too frequently into prosaic enumerations with only here and there a flash of inspiration.

Whitman may not be comprehended by reading a few of his poems selected here and there; from the first he regarded his poems as parts of a whole, "the deliberate and progressive unfolding of the conscious life of a man who is at once individual and typical"; and again he says, "The words of my book nothing, the drift of it everything." A good introduction to Whitman may be gained by reading "Democratic Vistas" and two other prose pieces too commonly neglected: the *Preface* to the 1885 edition of "Leaves of Grass" and "A Backward Glance O'er Travel'd Roads" (1888). These essays combined constitute perhaps the most important literary document since Wordsworth's Preface to the *Lyrical Ballads,* to which they form a striking supplement.

After reading the prefaces, ignoring for the time being the prose pieces the themes of which he stated more effectively elsewhere, one may go directly to the verse, preferably beginning with some of the later poems where he is freer from the belligerent mannerisms he felt necessary at first. "Sea Drift," "The Song of Joys," "When Lilacs Last in the Dooryard Bloomed" are beautiful and explicit and serve admirably toward giving one a liking for Whitman. Then may be read the prophetic "Pioneers! O Pioneers!" the poignant "Come Up From the Fields Father," the buoyant "Song of the Open Road," and that poetic response to nature's rhythms, "Crossing Brooklyn Ferry." One will of course not miss the tender threnody in more conventional verse form, "O Captain! My Captain!" When these have been enjoyed, it is time to chant the "Song of Myself," that amorphous glorification of the "divine average" in which Whitman struck the gamut of nearly everything he had to say. While it is undoubtedly true that "By Blue Ontario's Shore" and "A Song for Occupations" have the most compact statement of his central idea of universal sympathy, yet, as stated before, "Leaves of Grass" is a work to be comprehended in its totality and not judged from a few selections, however good.

The value in the content of "Leaves of Grass" is due, as the late Stuart P. Sherman has said,[4] "to its expression of what is proper and peculiar to American sentiment and civilization." What Whitman meant to him he explained further:

I love him for "By Blue Ontario's Shore" and "Sands at Seventy"; for expressing the American feeling about our own manners and customs; for responding to the splendor of American history and its magnificent and natural background; for chanting of the broad axe and the open road; for celebrating our own times and for seeing eternity focus in each present hour; for adoring the humane and reconciling God of Lincoln; for painting multitudes of common American men and women; for refusing to look down on any human soul; for accepting science and facing honestly the facts about his body and his mind; for diffusing fraternity;

4 In *Books*, June 13, 1926.

for understanding so much more about "equality" than his English critics; for making inventories of thousands of our own "objects curious"—states, cities, occupations, trades, tools,—inventories which now that he has touched them with his own immitigable adoration" stir me as the old Greeks were stirred by the Homeric catalogue of ships.

Others have felt that in reality Whitman's stock of cardinal ideas was small, that he owed most of them to Emerson, and that he repeated them excessively; that he was incoherent and diffuse, being unable to "select material susceptible to artistic treatment and to reject the rest";[5] that he stressed unduly the flesh and the appetites, treating love only in a fragmentary sense as a jealous emotion instead of "as a link in the evolution of the race, moral as well as biological"; that he was a poseur lacking a sense of humor and a knowledge of the past; that he ranted about America's manifest destiny "with the expansionist activities of political bandits"; that, after all, his knowledge of society was very limited, and that as the "poet of democracy" he has never reached the common people. Perhaps the most important indictment is that of George Santayana who characterizes his verse as "the poetry of barbarism." Its strength, he declares,[6] is "a blind and miscellaneous vehemence" which, "seeks to reveal and express the elemental

---

[5] The views here summarized are from Emory Holloway: *Whitman, an Interpretation in Narrative* (1926).

[6] In *Poetry and Religion*, p. 177 ff.

as opposed to the conventional" but which reduces experience to "moods and particular images." These whims are the product of a lazy, unsophisticated, and superficial fancy. He would, concludes Santayana, develop a nation of individualists "vigorous, comfortable, sentimental, and irresponsible."

The reader of Whitman is likely to take one or the other of the foregoing positions, so challenging, at least, is his work. To represent Whitman as a kind of "placid animal wallowing unreflectively in the stream of his own sensations"[7] is to ignore the new birth of his spirit in the baptism of the Civil War. Whitman's taste was not impeccable, but its greatest aberration was the poet's diffuseness. To assert that the poet of freedom has not been accepted by the common people is no charge against Whitman, for the "average man" is afraid of freedom.

Whitman was a prophet—that is his virtue when he is compared with some of his backward-looking contemporaries—and he can wait, as he declared, till "his country absorbs him as affectionately as he has absorbed it." By justifying faith in a democratic society he has a permanent hold not only upon his countrymen but prepares other people for the trend that the world is taking. If Whitman has derived much from Emerson, he has fulfilled that writer by creating a new pattern

[7] Stuart P. Sherman thus epitomizes Santayana's position. See Introduction to "Leaves of Grass" (1922), xviii.

of experience and character, a pattern which the younger poets have been glad to accept. His influence in bringing about the recent renaissance in poetry—some of it directly, and some of it by way of his French imitators—gives him historical significance apart from intrinsic merits. At the same time, this age is freeing itself from the excesses of the Whitman cult. In a less individualistic period it is possible that this process will go further in reducing the importance of the individual by setting over against him objectives of a superior order outside himself. It is in this direction rather than in some of the others that the ultimate weakness of Whitman lies.

2. The Frontier in Harte, Miller, Sill; Western Humor

The discovery of gold in California, with the mad rush of the ''Argonauts of '49'' across the trackless plains and through the mountain passes, the subsequent scramble for wealth in the mining towns, the lawlessness and excitement attendant upon the sudden acquisition or loss of fortune, opened one of the most picturesque periods in American annals. The zest for the frontier that had characterized Cooper's day was revived, and with a lavish hand and a rough jocosity literature strove to sublimate the spirit of the new frontier. Bayard Taylor's ''Eldorado'' and ''Rhymes of Travel'' first gave expression to the new-found

bonanza of the West; and Bret Harte supplied
the national curiosity with vivid stories of men
separated by almost the breadth of a continent
from civilization.

Bret Harte (1836–1902), the leader of the literary coterie at San Francisco after the war, was
not a native of California but of Albany, New
York. Only five years after the famous gold rush
of 1849, at the age of fifteen, he followed his
widowed mother to San Francisco, and engaged
successively in teaching, mining, and printing.
The rough life was not to his taste, but he had a
professional eye for it as literary material. After
having sharpened his pen on Irvingesque sketches
of the old Spanish missions in California, and
steeped himself in other men's styles by his
clever parodies, *Condensed Novels* (1867), he
made his "lucky strike" in 1868 with "The Luck
of Roaring Camp." This skillfully constructed
short story appeared in *The Overland Monthly,*
of which he had recently become editor. He followed it up with "The Outcasts of Poker Flat,"
"Tennessee's Partner," "Mliss," and other narrative sketches, which were hailed with public ac-
claim and were read for their humor as much as
for their strange material. The British press
praised the long-awaited "American" author,
and the *Atlantic Monthly* offered him ten thousand dollars if for a year he would write California stories exclusively for it. He left for
the East, never to return. His subsequent life,

after several years in and about New York, devoted to writing, was spent in Europe. There he held consular posts, and continued exploiting his Western material. He died in 1902 in England, a disappointed, expatriated man.

Bret Harte's reputation rests upon a few of his short stories. Early in his career he also wrote verse. "Plain Language from Truthful James," better known as "The Heathen Chinee," even won international fame, and his humorous dialect pieces and dramatic monologues once appealed widely. When he essayed longer works of prose fiction, as in *Gabriel Conroy* (1876), he failed lamentably in sustained suspense. But as a writer of short stories he is always sure of consideration, for he was a pioneer in adapting realism to the short story. It was he who gave impetus to the "local color" movement which was dominant in the last quarter of the century. He supplied the short story not only with a novel atmosphere but gave it picturesque characters and piquant dialect. He also simplified the theme by omitting details and reducing the number of characters.

Much in his manner he owed to Dickens. From him he had his fondness for contrasts: contrasts between individuals with but a single "humor," and incongruities of situation and character. He juxtaposed characters from low life with others from higher strata or an older civilization. To the influence of Dickens he owed, further, his fondness for humor and pathos, and his worst trait, theatrical sentimentality. Harte eschewed didacticism so far as direct expression of it was concerned; but every one of his stories was shot through with moral idealism. Among the outcasts of Poker Flat or in Lone Dog Camp he was bound to find his good-heart. He felt about his villains as Joaquin Miller has sung in his introductory lines on Byron:

> In men whom men condemn as ill
> I find so much of goodness still,
> In men whom men pronounce divine
> I find so much of sin and blot,
> I do not dare to draw a line
> Between the two, where God has not.

This search for the paradoxical amounted with Bret Harte to a mannerism that greatly impaired his work. There was indeed too much of the theatric in him for his work to last. Ostensibly a realist, and somewhat of an ironist in dwelling on life's inexplicable perplexities, he was too fond of melodrama for his realism to be trustworthy. Revengeful characters are not ordinarily flowers of devotion. Harte combined isolated extreme cases and made them appear to be the ordinary run of events. Compared with Mark Twain's, his attitude was rather that of an outsider who had felt the lure of the frontier but had not become indigenous to it. And therefore, "lacking sincerity and sympathy and moral background," as Professor Pattee has pointed out,[8] he has become in the history of American literature "a picturesque incident rather than a permanent force."

A more sincere presentation of the frontier appeared in the poetry of Joaquin Miller (1841–1913), the "Oregon Byron," though with him "local color" was painted thin over rather declamatory verse. Cincinnatus Hiner Miller, to give him his full name, was a picturesque figure in a migratory age. Born in a covered wagon bound for Oregon, living among miners and Indians at the foot of Mount Shasta, knocking at the door of the San Francisco coterie for recognition but gaining entrée into literature through the Pre-Raphaelites in London; planning to live in Italy, but returning to the Eastern states as bizarre publicity man for the "Western school"; settling at length as pacifist and prophet on San Francisco Bay, after having sowed poetic legends over the West from the Yukon to the Amazon— surely here was the man to express the frontier spirit.

There can be no question that the author of *Songs of the Sierras* (1871) knew his materials; but this rover was much too hasty and prolix to write with sustained beauty. His work is elemental yet somehow artificial because he lacked a "close mental grip"; occasionally he has the authentic strain, but there are many empty

[8] *Cambridge History of American Literature, II*, p. 381.

stretches in his verse, and passages that are
merely grandiose. His art is pictorial rather
than narrative, as might be expected. It put before the reader the rivers and canyons, the un-
tamed horses and buffalo, and restless adventures
of our Western scene. Poems like "Exodus for
Oregon," "Westward Ho!" depicting the westward movement, and others like "Columbus,"
with an analogous theme, or "The Last Taschas-
tas," describing the last stand of the red man, are
vivid pictures of our receding frontier. There is
a vigor in much of Miller's work that is attributable in part at least to his fondness for mono-
syllabic words. When his imagery is not over-
wrought, and his description is free from riotous
moralizing, he brings splendor and beauty to the
new provinces of song that he has annexed to our
literature.

Through Harte and Miller the country learned
to know the life of the Far West as it appealed
to men of action and large, blunt emotion. How
the Western scene affected an aesthetic soul, torn
in the struggle between doubt and faith, may be
seen in the poems of Edward Rowland Sill (1841–
1887). "The Fool's Prayer" is the best known
poem of this frail New England wanderer, but he
has many others equally imaginative, reflecting in
their pictorial riches the beauties of the "purer
world" of his adoption.

One of the first products to grow out of the
incongruities of the frontier was what Professor

Pattee has felicitously called [9] "the laughter of the West." It was quite different from the delicate wit of Lowell and Holmes, the pleasant urbanity of Irving, the gentle humor of Hawthorne, or even from the lampoons of the Jackson administration by Seba Smith. It was more intimate, being a by-product of the tremendous spread of newspapers among a new semi-literate reading public after the war. In form and expression it surmounted differences of station and temperament, assuming that everybody addressed would entirely understand whatever was said. George H. Derby (1823–1861) had in *Phoenixiana* (1855) anticipated most of the devices of the newer humorists, in his grotesque exaggeration, irreverence, euphemism, and whimsical *non sequiturs*. "The wind blew," he declared, "like well-watered roses." An undesirable citizen emigrated from his community in such haste that "he took nothing with him of his large property but a single shirt, which he happened to have about him at the time he formed his resolution." Josh Billings, as Henry Wheeler Shaw (1818–1885), author of *The Farmer's Allminax* (1860–1870), is better known, resorted to garbled spelling and dialect in his utterance of "hoss sense": "Young man, when yu hav tew sarch Webster's Dickshinnary tew find words big enuff tew convey youre meaning yu kan make up yure mind that you don't mean mutch."

[9] F. L. Pattee. *American Literature Since 1870* (1915), Chapt. 2.

Deliberate misspelling was employed also by the most famous of the earlier humorists, Artemus Ward, as the itinerant showman, Charles Farrar Browne (1834–1867) signed himself. He delighted in pure drollery and the sober utterance of nonsense. His travels acquainted him with the queer types of the period—Shakers, Mormons, Octoroons, Free Lovers, Spiritualists, Champions of Women's Rights, "Seseshers," Office Seekers, and what not. Something of his eccentricity of expression may be learned from the following narration of an experience with a Committee from the Woman's Rights Association:

I pitched my tent in a small town in Injianny one day last season, & while I was standin at the dore takin money, a deppytashun of ladies came up & sed they wos members of the Bunkumville Female Reformin & Wimin's Rite's Association, and they axed me if they cood go in without payin.

"Not exactly," sez I, "but you can pay without goin in."

"Dew you know who we air?" said one of the wimin —a tall and feroshus lookin critter, with a blew kotton umbreller under her arm—"do you know who we air, Sir?"

"My impreshun is," sed I, "from a kersery view, that you air females. . . . "

"Oh, whot,—whot!" screamed the female, swingin her umbrella in the air. "Oh, whot is the price that woman pays for her experience!"

"I don't know," sez I; "the price of my show is 15 cents pur individooal."

"& can't our Society go in free?" asked the female.

"Not if I know it," sed I.

"Crooil, crooil man!" she cried, & bust into teers.

"Won't you let my darter in?" sed anuther of the exsentric wimin, taken me afeckshunitely by the hand. "O please let my darter in,—shee's a sweet gushin' child of natur."

"Let her gush!" roared I, as mad as I cood stick at their tarnal nonsense; "let her gush!" Whereupon they all sprung back with the simultanious observashun that I was a Beest.

As a "column-writer" on various, papers, in particular the Cleveland *Plain Dealer,* Artemus Ward had a wide following, and as a lecturer he won the friendship of others besides, including even the prominent English writers of the day. His humor was collected and published in 1862 as *Artemus Ward: His Book,* to which was added *Artemus Ward in London* (1867).

Americans have proverbially loved a joke. Without a doubt fondness for frontier humor helped elect Abraham Lincoln President. His "yarns" and anecdotes endeared him to the masses. During the Civil War period, David Ross Locke (1833–1888), over the pompous signature of Petroleum V. Nasby, strengthened Union sentiment by his political satire published in the Toledo *Blade,* even as Thomas Nast (1840–1902), the father of American caricature, satirized corrupt government during the Reconstruction period. Of the other humorists of the period it suffices to mention Edgar Wilson Nye (1850–1896), known as "Bill Nye," and John Hay (1838–1905), co-discoverer with Bret Harte of Pike County material. More recently, "Mr. Dooley"

(Finley P. Dunne, 1867–   ), with his Irish-American humor, George Ade (1867–   ), with his fables in slang, Wallace Irwin (1876–   ), with his "Japanese schoolboy, Hashimura Togo," Carolyn Wells, with her nonsense parodies, and Irvin Cobb, and Ring Lardner have all contributed to the gayety of the American public. But at no other period has there been so significant an outburst of humor as that of the 'sixties and 'seventies. That laughter helped to disperse the sentimentalism in the national letters, and it helped bring about an era of realism.

3. Mark Twain (1835–1910)

The man who did most to lead the way to an indigenous literature was Mark Twain, as Samuel L. Clemens is known universally. In this thorough American the spirit of expansion that followed the war was incarnate. He understood the "divine average." He had had the good fortune to know many parts of his country at first hand; he had engaged in various occupations that kept him close to the ordinary idiom and the average point of view; and he profited by his experiences to the extent of maintaining his loyalty to democratic institutions throughout his vigorous career.

Born in 1835 of Virginia stock, and reared on the Missouri side of the Mississippi during the most picturesque period of its river life, the youth had up to the age of eighteen made contacts with small

town "pikes," negro slaves, and rivermen. He
had taken his "schooling" in the printer's trade,
had wandered as journeyman printer east to New
York and back again, had developed skill and
knowledge as a river-pilot during four years before the war, and had joined a self-recruited band
of Confederates that soon fell to pieces. Then
Wanderlust took him through six years of
crowded activity in the West, chiefly as reporter
and "funny-column" conductor during the boom
times of Nevada and California. Under the
tutelage of Artemus Ward and Bret Harte, he developed his gifts as a raconteur. He went still
farther west, to Hawaii, and lectured on that
island upon his return. His sense of humor, aided
by his irresistible drawl, made him a popular lecturer up to the end of his life.

In 1865 Mark Twain attained fame with the
publication in New York of his hoax, "The Cel-
ebrated Jumping Frog of Calaveras County."
The story was keyed to the jubilant, reckless
West. Liking the author's style, a newspaper
next sent him to Europe and the Holy Land to
report what he saw "with his own eyes." This
he did in *Innocents Abroad* (1869), to the utter
merriment of his countrymen who had been sus-
picious of such romantic accounts as *Outre-Mer*
and *Pencillings by the Way*, and now found their
suspicions confirmed. The irreverence of *Innocents Abroad* was not directed so much at old
world institutions, however, as at the romantic

tourist with his sentimental conception of art and travel.

More important books followed. First came *Roughing It* (1872), a social study of the days of the gold seekers with whom in the early 'sixties he had journeyed by stage-coach across the plains and mountains to Nevada. Then followed *Life on the Mississippi* (1883), with its intimate account of another phase of American civilization, now also vanished forever. *The Adventures of Tom Sawyer* (1876) and *The Adventures of Huckleberry Finn* (1884), picaresque romances both, marked the height of their author's powers, and *Pudd'nhead Wilson* (1894) concluded what has been well called "our American *Odyssey.*" The author collaborated with Charles Dudley Warner on *The Gilded Age* (1873), a somewhat poorly constructed novel of Reconstruction days, but interesting in its materials and noteworthy for Colonel Sellers. He also made several excursions into history: *The Prince and the Pauper* (1881), an anti-monarchical romance; *A Connecticut Yankee in King Arthur's Court* (1889), a delightful travesty on Malory's *Morte d'Arthur;* and the more serious historical novel, *Personal Recollections of Joan of Arc* (1896).

Mark Twain married an estimable woman of New England stock to whose censorship of his work he readily deferred; she, with the aid of Howells and others, turned him from hoaxes and burlesque autobiographies to the fields where his true talents lay. The Playboy had much of the gambler in him. He invested large sums of "easy" money in an unsuccessful publishing house and in a type-setting machine that proved a failure; but he retrieved his losses on the lecture platform. Oxford and Yale each bestowed the honorary degree of Litt.D. upon him, and he doubtless enjoyed the theatrical rôle of being a public character. In time, however, adulation bored him, and when, toward the end of his life domestic sorrow came to him, he developed into a philosophical pessimist. *What is Man?* (1906) and *The Mysterious Stranger* (1916), both written in 1898, and *The Man that Corrupted Hadleyburg* (1899) were the most noteworthy expression of his nihilism.

It was as a humorist that Mark Twain gained his reputation. The San Francisco Group that had prepared the way for him taught him an essentially oral method. If he did not quite acquire Artemus Ward's whimsical finesse or Josh Billings's seasoned wisdom, he found, on the other hand, that he could attain his ends by less obvious means than tricks like misspelling. Irreverence and exaggeration were the essence of his humor; both rested on incongruity, and depended for their effect on an assumption of innocent seriousness.

Of the camels in *Innocents Abroad* he writes: "They are not particular about their diet. They would eat a tombstone if they could

bite it." In *Huckleberry Finn,* "Aunt Sally . . .
was a-standing on top of the bed raising Cain,
and the rats was doing what they could to keep
off the dull times for her." Sometimes, he uses
the surprise of anti-climax, as when Tom Sawyer
in preparation for Sunday School "looked ex-
ceedingly improved and uncomfortable." At
other times his figures are exquisitely inappropri-
ate; as "Here comes the old man . . . looking
as absent-minded as year before last." Imperti-
nences add a dash of humor to his narrative every
now and then.

But it is needless to point out such devices.
One surrenders easily to the author's "yarn-
ing" and to that sober utterance of nonsense
which is the outstanding characteristic of
American humor. Not that Mark Twain was a
mere entertainer! He was an iconoclast who used
humor to attain his ends. Unfortunately, much
of his humor grew out of individual situations
and was not, as in Tom Sawyer and Huckleberry
Finn, centered in character and thereby insured
immortality. Because the humor in some of his
work was not organic, and because of its frequent
over-emphasis, it is yielding ground to his romance.

Mark Twain's ability at romance, his power to
recreate landscape and atmosphere, first appeared in *Roughing It.* Travel over the plains by
stage-coach, and life in the crude mining villages,
he had viewed through the eyes of a realist, and

now, under the glamor of imagination, his glowing narrative evoked the romantic atmosphere of those irresponsible days. The pony express, the Mormons, jackrabbits and coyotes, miners and desperadoes, Lake Tahoe and the sierras, Kilauea and the Sandwich-Islanders, all have their part in this epic of the golden West. The author recalls vividly the gambling spirit of the frontier, when a few successes caused an unreasoning optimism that shortly gave place to blackest despair. Like most of his books, *Roughing It* is very uneven in quality; but in none of them are there passages of more poetic beauty, grimmer irony, or more ebullient fun.

In *Life on the Mississippi* the Father of Waters became the epic symbol of the American Spirit. On its broad bosom a multifarious life came and went without regard to what might take place overseas. The author recaptured the active era that preceded the extensive use of railroads with the sympathy of one for whom the pilot's life had the strongest appeal. Graphic pictures of life in the river town, due appreciation of the hardships connected with steamboating, and poetic portrayal of the marvelous spell of the great river were united in this authentic romance. This work, except for somewhat desultory reminiscences in the second part of the book, shows Mark Twain's style at its best.

Tom Sawyer and *Huckleberry Finn,* his most popular books, depict boy life in the small Missouri town in which Mark Twain was reared, and, in a large sense, boy life anywhere. The former pictures the romantic attitude toward discipline and duty, the large element of superstition in boys reared with negroes, and the perennial spirit of adventure, centering, in this case, around a midnight murder and a treasure hunt in a cave. With the advent of *Tom Sawyer* the "Rollo" books lost their potency and the dime-novel that had enjoyed a clandestine popularity since the 'fifties came into literary respectability. In the narrative the mischievous lad's cleverness was set over against whatever was insincere in the institutional life of the small town; but of the simple virtues Tom was a champion. The episode of whitewashing the fence will not readily be forgotten by any reader of this vivid anecdotal story.

Huckleberry Finn, the pendent, is episodic also, but is somewhat more unified by its underlying philosophy. Through Huck's naïve but shrewd observations, the reader sees many kinds of society in the river towns and is brought face to face quite incidentally with profound social facts. The son of the town drunkard, left to shift for himself and to gain what ethics he may from nature, drifts down the river on a raft with a runaway negro, runs into the Grangerford-Shepherdson vendetta, meets with impostors like the "king" and the "duke," and handles the problem of stealing a negro out of slavery. It is an old plot—telling how men in hard straits have succeeded—and the spell lies in the richness and vividness of the detail. Not a little of the interest is owing to the realistic portrayal of the negro, Jim, who contrasts effectively with the didactic Uncle Tom of Mrs. Stowe. Most impressive of all is the relation established between the human scene and the broad, changing river, the author's "sense of the half-barbaric charm and the romantic possibilities in that grey wilderness of moving water and the rough men who trafficked on it." [10] The story is as simple as Gulliver's and it is as profound a study as Swift's famous book. It has the spirit of eternal youth and is a very gem of romance and humor.

For all his spontaneous humor, Mark Twain was at heart a serious man. His daughter reports that at home he talked largely on serious things with only an occasional humorous remark thrown in. A number of factors conspired to make him serious: his marriage, his financial losses, travel, honors, domestic sorrow, a philistine rationalism. All his life he was an ardent democrat, devoutly hating all sham and pretense, and throwing his protection around the weak. In *The Prince and the Pauper* he wrote a parable of democracy. In the *Connecticut Yankee* he tried, as he said, "to pry up the English nation to a little higher level of manhood." This quixotic satire on feudal institutions and their spurious chivalry reaches farther, however, until it

[10] *Cambridge History of American Literature, III*, p. 16.

touches all superstition. In *The Man that Corrupted Hadleyburg* the author laid bare human mendacity and avarice as has seldom been done, while in "Captain Stormfield's Visit to Heaven" he played havoc with the sentimentalist's hereafter. On the other hand, in his "Defense of Harriet Shelley" he wrote in passionate protest against Dowden's glorifying memoir of the poet, and he expressed his reverence for Joan of Arc with the loyalty and ardor of a medievalist in the cult of the Virgin.

Living at a period when many came under the influence of the brilliant orator, Robert G. Ingersoll, Mark Twain became an ethical and material determinist. To the question raised in *What is Man?* he replied, "a mere automaton." *The Mysterious Stranger* he conceived out of the depths of despair. The difference between it and the earlier books is so prodigious as to convince one there were two Mark Twains, a conviction confirmed by reading the *Autobiography*. But Mark Twain's pessimism, ironical as it may seem, is, at bottom, sentimental. Living in a utilitarian age, he staked his faith not on beauty, but on comfort. This explains his early contempt for Europe, and his later contempt for mankind. Yet a society that frustrates its imaginative life, he vaguely perceived, is futile; for man to be a mere cog in a comfort-grinding machine, he felt, takes the zest out of human issues. That a man need not accept the values that surround him, but may find his salvation in ever creating new values, he apparently failed to see.

Mark Twain's reputation, however, does not rest on his philosophy but on his portrayal of life in mid-nineteenth century America. He gave the bracing air of the prairie, the rising thrill of Western adventure and its hazard for new fortunes, the haunting beauty and picturesque romance of the stately Mississippi; and synchronized them with the new national aspirations. Out of it he evolved a humor, an infectious and hilarious nonsense, as rugged and free as the conditions that gave it birth. He is the incarnation of democratic America, best fulfilling Whitman's conception of the promise of American life. He has come nearer to giving the shirt-sleeve life of the average American than any other writer that this country has produced. He spoke the national idiom. And in world literature he belongs, as Howells has well said,[11] "with the great humorists of all time, with Cervantes, with Swift, or with any others worthy his company; none of them was his equal in humanity."

4. The Local Colorists

Following the completion of the first railroad to the Pacific coast in 1868, there came the extension of a network of transportation to all parts of the country. Newspapers sprang up every-

[11] W. D. Howells: *My Mark Twain* (1910).

where, recording local transactions. As the country became imaginatively aware of its enormous territory, its bleak and tropical extremes, its richness of sea-coast, mountain, lake, and river scenery, different sections grew eager to read about one another. Not only were they interested in the physical background of other regions, but they found appeal in the different racial stocks, with their peculiar history and resultant traditions. As a consequence, when Bret Harte rescued the short story from expressing the mystic and the grotesque and applied it to the picturesque life in a California mining town, he took the reading public by storm; he started a movement the ramifications of which went to every corner of the country. Harte himself was, properly speaking, a forerunner of the regionalistic movement, for in him local color was a means rather than an end. Yet through the interest aroused by him other writers bethought them of the riches of local custom and the best literary use to which they might be put. So pervasive was this sentiment that for a generation stories of local color held sway.

In the development of the "local color" movement several stages are perceptible. During the 'seventies, which marked the transition period from the older romance, regionalism arose in what were then frontier sections. The stories dealt in romantic fashion with picturesque types. Harte's "forty-niners," Eggleston's circuit-rid-ers, and Constance Fenimore Woolson's Mackinac traders belong here. Toward the close of the decade stories flourished in the older sections where a rich historical background made it possible to give the local color of social tradition. Cable's New Orleans Creoles, Miss Jewett's and Miss Wilkins's New Englanders, Joel Chandler Harris's Georgia negroes, Miss Murfree's Tennessee mountaineers, Page's old Virginians, and Helen Hunt Jackson's Spanish missionaries of California belong to the decade of the 'eighties when local color was in its heyday. With the 'nineties, the physical background rose to the importance at times of chief character in the story. Naturally such stories were located in regions where nature is particularly attractive or dangerous, as for example, the bayous of Louisiana, the Northern woods, the Western deserts, the Southern swamps, or the Alaskan ice-fields. The last phase of the movement was that in which the spirit of a community was the real essence of the tale, as in stories by Ellen Glasgow, William Allen White, Frank Norris, Margaret Deland, Zona Gale and others.

Some of the outstanding writers of the movement deserve further discussion. In the Middle West, at the very moment when Bret Harte was in the first flush of his success, Edward Eggleston (1837–1902) was describing the frontier life of Southern Indiana. Eggleston knew the frontier at first hand, having been born in the region he described and having traveled over much of the territory as a Methodist circuit rider. He had learned from the novels of Dickens and from Taine's *Art in the Netherlands* how the rough characters about him might be depicted, and the success of Lowell in *The Biglow Papers* had encouraged him to take pains with the handling of dialect. In 1871 he published *The Hoosier Schoolmaster*, a realistic portraiture of the home life of "poor whites," a book lacking somewhat the polish of Harte's stories, but perhaps even more memorable in character and in scene. Other novels followed, notably *The Circuit Rider* (1874), dealing with Indiana life before the war of 1812, and *The Graysons* (1888), in which Abraham Lincoln was shown during his youth in Indiana. Eggleston's stories, together with the domestic tales of J. G. Holland and the innocuous, even less distinguished romances of E. P. Roe, did much toward removing from the middle-class the objection to novel-reading. His later life was devoted to journalism and to history, but his real importance lay in the influence which his transcripts of Hoosier life lent to the rise of realism.

In New England, the later books of Mrs. Stowe, *The Pearl of Orr's Island* (1862) and particularly *Oldtown Folks* (1869), containing such a folk-type as Sam Lawson, prepared the way for the local colorists of that region. In this work she was aided by Rose Terry Cooke, with her sympathetic sketches of commonplace lives. But in this region

it remained for Sara Orne Jewett (1849–1909) to
usher in the movement with her *Deephaven*
(1877), a picture of the life of a decaying seaport. In such short stories as "The Dulham
Ladies" and "A Native of Winby," romantic
studies of individualists, the exodus from New
England to the West left its traces in a well delineated air of passivity. Mary Wilkins Freeman
(1862–   ), wrote sufficiently later to profit by
the realism that had come into vogue with the
influence of writers like Flaubert, Hardy, and our
own Howells. In collections of short stories like
A Humble Romance (1887) and *A New England
Nun* (1891), and in *Pembroke, a Novel* (1894) she
depicts with grim remorselessness her old maids,
daughters of cranks in villages or on forsaken
farms. Mrs. Freeman's realism is austere but not
cynical. With the utmost economy she shows her
eccentrics in revolt against the repressions
forced upon them by a decadent society. The
sentences are short, there is little comment, yet
her characters stand out, original and unforget-
table. Another writer of New England, Alice
Brown (1857–   ), has written dialect stories of
her native New Hampshire, skillfully constructed,
poetic in style, and warm in sympathy. The best
of her rural stories are found in *Meadow Grass*
(1895) and *Tiverton Tales* (1899), but, as Miss
Brown has been interested chiefly in other things,
Mrs. Freeman has remained the outstanding
regionalist of this section.

In the South, George Washington Cable (1844–1925) was the pioneer local colorist. This New Orleans accountant and reporter spent evenings investigating the Spanish and French archives of the city, and, having duly brooded over his materials, proceeded to reconstruct that rich and colorful life which seems so remote from anything American. Only Lafcadio Hearn has offered anything suggestive of it. *Old Creole Days* (1879), *Madame Delphine* (1881), and the novel, *The Grandissimes* (1880), represent a quaint Old South, with old world architecture and old world customs, a dreamy atmosphere of jasmine flowers and orange blossoms, in which move high-spirited men and beautiful women. The style is Gallic in lightness and subtlety. Little of a startling nature happens. But through innuendo and ellipses, a glimpse into character here, some conversation there, and a minor climax revealing another phase of character, the author brings the exotic atmosphere of Old New Orleans before the reader. Perhaps as characteristic a story as any is "Posson Jone," though some will prefer the moving little drama, *Madame Delphine*. The work of Cable, like that of the other writers of local color in the South, is romantic, but in the essentials it is true to human nature. The exquisite art of *Old Creole Days* has made it a classic.

Charles Egbert Craddock—as Mary Noailles Murfree (1850–1922) signed her work—deals with the "poor whites" of the Great Smoky Mountains, setting the cramped, barren lives of these people against the somber grandeur of the ranges. Her collection of short stories, *In the Tennessee Mountains* (1884), gives, with the insight of a careful observer, the feuds, the revivals, the raids on "moonshiners," the superstitions, the lovemaking of these simple, isolated folk. The local color of these stories partakes somewhat of the "exhibitional," because the grotesqueness of manners is dwelt upon to the relative exclusion of certain mental qualities. The use of dialect in Miss Murfree's stories is evidence of an attempt to make the presentation as realistic as possible.

An indication that the dialect type of story was coming into favor was *Marse Chan* (1884), by Thomas Nelson Page (1853–1922). In this volume, dialect was employed throughout the entire story. Page was not realistic, but highly romantic as a writer. His reconstruction of the aristocratic plantation days "befo' de wah," entitled *In Ole Virginia* (1887), was a group of artistic tales, told by a negro slave, to show how loyal such persons had been, and to indicate how much they suffered during the Reconstruction period. A more realistic transcript from the folk life of the Southern negro in the old regime was that of Joel Chandler Harris (1848–1908). His books *Uncle Remus, His Songs and Sayings* (1880) and *Nights With Uncle Remus* (1883), introduced to a host of delighted readers, Brer Rabbit and Brer Fox, and other creations of Afro-

American folk-lore. Harris told these stories for amusement; he was not concerned with the problem of connecting darky superstitions and the myths of the East; yet the tales are sound ethnologically and have documentary value. Brer Rabbit's helplessness typifies the negro, who, circumvented by the stronger forces about him, resorts to shifty tricks. His sense of humor is his saving grace. So well did Harris succeed in giving the workings of the negro imagination, the picturesque sensitiveness of mind and temperament, that Uncle Remus has become one of the few figures that Americans have added to the gallery of world fiction.

Other writers of provincial fiction in the South belong to the later stages of the movement. Will Harben, in *White Marie* (1889) and other works, told of the degenerate "cracker" type of humanity living in sections of Georgia and elsewhere. Alice French ("Octave Thanet") in *Knitters in the Sun* (1887) described the people of the Ozarks. F. Hopkinson Smith drew an affectionate picture of the Southland during plantation days in *Colonel Carter of Cartersville* (1891). James Lane Allen, and later, John Fox, Jr., described with considerable sentiment, the bluegrass region of Kentucky. Allen's collection of short stories, *Flute and Violin* (1891), and his romance, *A Kentucky Cardinal* (1894), belonged to that literature of locality which emphasized nature and environment, rather than dialect. In Louisiana, Grace King gave, in *Monsieur Motte* (1888), and in other stories, more realistic accounts of Creole life than Cable's; and Ruth McEnery Stuart, in *A Golden Wedding* (1893) and other tales, became the "laureate of the lowly."

The "local color" movement brought supremacy to the short story as a type of fiction. Few novels appeared during the 'seventies and 'eighties. The movement had its effect also upon verse, notably on that of John J. Piatt, John Hay, and James Whitcomb Riley, all born in Indiana, and on Irwin Russell of Mississippi, and Will Carleton of Michigan. In the course of its progress it passed from a stage of romantic dreaming at the first to an increasingly realistic presentation of materials, which culminated in the rise of "veritism" during the 'nineties, or degenerated into the commercially profitable, but artistically weak, historical fiction of that decade. Some of the writers adapted themselves to one vogue, and some to the other. Meanwhile, the cause of realism was being advanced by the outstanding novelists of the period, William Dean Howells and Henry James.

5. The Advance of Realism in Howells and James

Throughout his long career as "dean of American letters," William Dean Howells (1837-1920) made his influence felt as critic and novelist by decrying the mawkish sentimentalism that had appeared in much of the fiction after the 'fifties, and by substituting therefor a more honest transcript of manners, marked by far better artistry. His reticent realism maintained the favor of a large reading public and led the way to the thoroughgoing realism of today.

Like Mark Twain, Howells was a son of the virile Middle-West who worked his way up through rough-and-tumble journalism; but unlike him, he was contemplative by temperament, he loved the classics, and, instead of recording the rugged life about him, identified himself completely with the East. Born in 1837 at Martin's Ferry, Ohio, the son of a country printer with Swedenborgian leanings, the boy early showed a bookish inclination, and read not only all the great English authors, but the foreign as well, doting on Heine. With John J. Piatt he published *Poems of Two Friends* (1859), and he contributed other poems to the *Atlantic Monthly*. For writing a campaign life of Lincoln he was made consul at Venice. The appointment enabled him to study Italian, and to write his sketches of *Venetian Life* (1866), and *Italian Journeys* (1867).

On his return, the cosmopolite took up editorial duties, first with *The Nation*, then for fifteen years with the *Atlantic Monthly*, and last with *Harper's Magazine*. Naturally such connections gave him an immense influence. He encouraged unknown writers as dissimilar as Mark Twain and

Henry James, and gave recognition to many another. He became more and more interested in the writing of novels. In *Their Wedding Journey* (1871), *A Chance Acquaintance* (1873), and *A Foregone Conclusion* (1874) he exhibited the wholesome charm and felicity of expression for which he was to become famous, and a growing sense of realism as well. In turning from the waning transcendentalisms of New England to the delineation of actual life, he chose to present the conflict arising between different grades of sophistication.

When in 1882, Howells published *A Modern Instance,* his position as the leading American realist in fiction was assured. The book is a study of one of the author's pet antipathies, the "fresh" young man, and his degeneration. Besides the egotist, there is a jealous young wife, one of Howells's most vital heroines, and her father, Squire Gaylord, a shrewd, quiet, old lawyer and Yankee of Yankees. There are realistic scenes of New England winter and of newspaper life in Boston, and there is a trial scene in Indiana, vibrant with suppressed emotion. The author sought to rid his novel of the cheap theatricalities of the problem novel, and succeeded so explicitly that his characters seem to the unaccustomed reader to be undermotived. In some of the details, as for example, the logging-camp incident, the serial form in which the story first appeared is responsible for the lack of artistic proportion.

The book shows the keenest observation, however, and is thoroughly informed as to life.

The Rise of Silas Lapham (1884) reveals the development of character, as *A Modern Instance* had shown its deterioration. In this, the author's masterpiece, the self-made American who has always been dear to the imagination, but in his philistinism peculiarly representative of the Gilded Age, having made his fortune, experiences difficulty in attaining to a more cultivated social level; he retrieves his soul in the end, however, when his innate honesty triumphs over material adversity. The plot concerns not only a bankruptcy but a love affair in which, to everyone's surprise, the scion of culture marries the "other" girl. The author's rich knowledge of human nature, its foibles and secret aspirations, appears on every page, illuminating the relation of the lovers and shedding even a brighter light on the contrasted elderly pairs. From the interview of the opening scene, through the ordeal of the dinner episode, to the final triumph of his personal integrity, the bourgeois American is presented with a sympathy that might easily have lapsed into satire under a less skillful hand. Events follow one another with the delays and indirections attending such matters in actual life. Altogether, *Silas Lapham* is an interesting historical document of great value.

Almost as perfect in method and manner is *Indian Summer* (1885), which deals lightly with the loves of a man of forty. The Florentine background in this novel invites comparison with the work of Henry James that has a European setting. In this novel, as in the two preceding, the author revealed his increasing interest in character over plot. In his handling of the fine shades of conversation he proved himself the first American master of the art of dialogue.

And now, when Howells was past fifty, he experienced the most important change in his life. Under the influence of Tolstoy he, the conservative, became socialistically inclined. He did not become a militant radical, however, but continued his cheerful, lovable stories of commonplace lives, adding only a keener feeling for social injustice and a vision of life which, as he said, looked "toward the happiness of the whole human family." In *A Hazard of New Fortunes* (1889) the new social consciousness appears in the Marches, who relinquish their comfortable circumstances and learn how the other half lives. By 1894, in the symposium, *A Traveler from Altruria,* he ventured to criticize American life from the standpoint of an altruistic or ideal commonwealth. At a summer resort the visitor from another land sees all the social cleavages of American life; learns that every man must look out for himself; and finds that there are no individual rights save as they apply to the holder of property. The author's other studies in social ethics, *A World of Chance* and *The Quality of Mercy,* are negligible; it seems the conversion—if a mere deepening of tendencies already marked deserves the name—came so late that the gentle iconoclast had not the opportunity to know fully the complex structure of human society. When he returned, in *The Kentons* (1902), to making realistic transcripts from individual lives, he wrote one of his best books.

Howells's career as a critic began in 1886 when he moved from Boston to New York, to occupy an editorial position on *Harper's Magazine*. All manner of books now came under his scrutiny. In his armchair editorials he gave voice to his views on public affairs, in particular his opinions on questions of literary criticism. His best ideas, embracing his advocacy of realism, were republished under the title, *Criticism and Fiction* (1891). In *My Literary Passions* (1895) he offered further illuminating comment on many writers, concluding with an expression of his admiration for Tolstoy. *Literary Friends and Acquaintance* (1900) gave flesh and blood to the Cambridge group that had taken him in—Emerson, Lowell, Longfellow, Holmes; and it contained reminiscences concerning others, not of the Cambridge circle, Bayard Taylor, Mrs. Stowe, and many another whom he was privileged to know intimately during the course of a long career. *Heroines of Fiction* (1901), *Literature and Life* (1902), and the fine interpretation, *My Mark Twain* (1910), conclude what is significant in his critical writing. Howells's criticism of the work of others was catholic and humane, though naturally modified somewhat by his own leanings. His passion for the good sometimes stood in the way of his understanding the truth. But his tirelessness in denouncing romanticism and in advocating realism was helpful. It did much to implant better critical standards and improved therewith the quality of American fiction.

In addition to his criticism, Howells wrote acceptable farces, like *The Sleeping Car* and *The Mousetrap,* as well as short stories. His reputation, however, rests on his novels. As a novelist he has given the most considerable transcript of American life as yet made by one man. By virtue of his independence he was able to take large strides toward a more truthful presentation of life; yet today his realism seems modified and timid. The lighter ironies of existence he describes as well as his beloved Jane Austen; but heart-rending decisions such as people are obliged to make in real life, he seldom gives. His characters are conventional rather than heroic. Artistically his work is flawless, for Howells was a fastidious workman. His style is subtly informal, touched with humor and charm. In his decorum, however, he holds to a momentary period in human history. Only because of his reticence, Howells missed the greatness of those who draw the grand passions.

In the work of Henry James (1843–1916), the

crusading American who had conquered the frontier, turned back to the central settlement, the old world, in his quest for that beauty which was eluding him in the somewhat flat culture of the new world. During the Gilded Age this American had gone with Silas Lapham into business, or to perdition. Earlier, the innocent had ventured abroad and looked upon Europe with the eyes of an honest boor. But now he had arrived at a point where with Henry Adams he felt that the old culture had gone, and that for the development of a new one there was a lack of traditions. That there might be hope in the direction pointed out by Whitman in "Democratic Vistas" did not occur to him. So when he, now that he had attained leisure, turned his frank and honest face toward the European background, he servilely felt his lack of antecedents. Such is the "gesture" which may be studied in the earlier novels of Henry James.

For delineating this new venture of the leisured American, Henry James was admirably equipped. With his philosopher brother, William James, he had in youth been transplanted by his Swedenborgian father from one place to another, and had taken root in no city, system, or habit. He was an American mainly in the sense that he had been born in America, and had spent part of his youth there. Yet he never entirely divested himself of the American point of view. By the time he began writing, this passionate pilgrim had oscil-

lated so much between the new world and the old
that he had become a "fastidious connoisseur of
experience." After a brief Parisian contact, and
residence at various places on the continent, he
became rooted at length in the environs of London, where, on the eve of his death, he became a
citizen of Great Britain. Beginning as a writer
of international romances—international not as
concerned with conflicting loyalties, but with contrasting backgrounds—he came in time to cease
blushing for his countryman whom he had im-
paled before the citadels of culture, and denation-
alized his characters, became fussy over minutiæ,
and acquired an esoteric dialect that made his
work obscure to the uninitiated.

The work of Henry James falls into three
periods, representing an early, a transitional, and
a late manner. In the first period, between 1875
and 1885, he wrote novels that deal predominantly
with inexperienced Americans in a more cultured
European environment. *Roderick Hudson* (1875),
the story of a young sculptor abroad, was his first
success. It appeared in *The Atlantic Monthly*.
Then came *The American* (1877), the story of a
business man who was spurned by the old French
family into which he sought to marry. In *The
Europeans* (1878), the foreigners were introduced
in America to some of our less worthy traits. In
Daisy Miller (1879), his charming study of the
earliest American "flapper," he set that young
girl's independence skillfully against the old

world's sense of decorum, introducing at the same
time such interesting types as Daisy's mother and
brother, and young Winterbourne with his aunt.
Washington Square (1880) added further to the
author's reputation as a careful student of American manners; but the finest of his earlier works,
and perhaps his best novel, was *The Portrait of
a Lady* (1881). In the deft portraiture of this
generous-souled American girl in Florence, James
proved convincingly his ability to draw feminine
character amid contrasting civilizations.

During the second period, approximately from
1885 to 1901, James sought to penetrate to the
heart of English culture. But his attempt to give
in short stories and in plays the nuances of English life proved disastrous. To please himself and
to express the more intricate things he wished to
say, he wrote increasingly complex and abstract
novels. The chief works of this period were *The
Tragic Muse* (1890), in which the possibilities of an
artistic career were set over against family influence and political prospects; and *The Awkward Age* (1898), in which a young girl struggled
with her corrupt social environment. The reputation for unintelligibility, which the author helped
to foster by an involved style, was unfortunate,
for during his last period, from 1902 to the end,
he produced such genuine achievements as *The
Wings of the Dove* (1902), *The Ambassadors*
(1905), and *The Golden Bowl* (1906). In these he
returned to his study of Americans in Europe,

but his attitude toward his countrymen was no longer apologetic. Their integrity was contrasted effectively with the ethics of a lax society. *The Ambassadors* he regarded as his best constructed novel; it summed up, with rich deliberation, that large problem of the clash of civilizations which he had made peculiarly his own.

For an introduction to characteristic qualities of James's work, one of the earlier novels, *The American,* will serve. In this study the self-made American is one step beyond Silas Lapham. Through the sale of washtubs, and later of leather, he has rapidly amassed wealth and is now sojourning in Paris. Having plenty of leisure, he looks about and admires the treasures of art; but his real purpose is to find a perfect wife. He falls in love with the widowed daughter of the proud old French house of Bellegarde, feeling that she is "a kind of historical formation" whereas he is without antecedents. Though the daughter reciprocates his love, the family snubs him and drives her into a convent. Then he discovers that the mother and brother had earlier brought about the father's death, but with characteristic integrity he refuses to expose them. Here is the contrast between a man of unlimited self-reliance and a group of persons who are hedged in by the restraints of polite society. It is the Lapham-Corey relation transferred to a non-American background. Little happens; it is a situation rather than a plot, but flawless in out-

line. From a multitude of possible details the
author has selected just those that give the impression he wants. As his culture is unlimited,
the interest lies not so much in what goes on in
the heart as in what takes place in the mind. He
analyzes the characters as if he were conducting
a psychological clinic, but in the end the effect
is dramatic.

The truth is that James was by temperament a
critic, one who turned his critical intelligence into
the field of fiction. In his natural rôle he produced early, for the English Men of Letters series, his study of *Hawthorne*, an excellent piece
of work, though mistaken in regarding Hawthorne's environment as a handicap rather than
an opportunity. During his formative years
James was influenced also by Flaubert and by
Turgenev. When his reviews, contributed to the
better magazines, were collected, they were given
the title, *French Poets and Novelists* (1878).
They, together with *Partial Portraits* (1888) and
Essays in London (1893), contain as sound literary criticism as America has produced.

In view of the technical perfection of his novels,
James's theories on the art of fiction constitute his
most valuable contribution to criticism. They furnish the key to his work. It is his aim, he says, to
give imaginatively an appreciation of spiritual
values even amid temporal defeat. Delicacy he
dislikes seeing sacrificed to grossness. Action is
to be subordinated to the meanings and motives

of the story which center in a dominant impression suggesting something larger behind it. The art of fiction, he declares in his essay by that title, "is one of the *fine* arts"; . . . "a novel is in its broadest definition a personal, a direct impression of life"; its author must "possess the sense of reality." He adds, "Catching the very note and trick, the strange irregular rhythm of life, that is the attempt whose strenuous force keeps Fiction upon her feet." In the spirit of the scientist and artist, observing like a painter and analyzing like a psychologist, James sought to give the "air of reality."

The work of James presents, on a grand scale, aesthetic criticism of the leisure class in modern society. James was the first to have seen that the visiting of Europe by Americans constituted a social drama worth embodying in art. He introduced the method of comparative literature into fiction, and created a new *genre*. His field was, of course, a limited one. He knew enough about cosmopolitan life, but for supreme art his passionless detachment leaves something wanting. His work does not enlist the reader's sympathies so much as it engages his sense of perspective. It does not portray the primary passions, though it has some of the less easily assimilated ones. Perhaps, also, the author lacks narrative art; his later work certainly requires a second reading for the thought. On the other hand, James is the novelist of the few who appreciate beautiful technique. Authors like Edith Wharton and Joseph Conrad have profited by what he could teach them of technical skill. To American fiction he has bequeathed a fine artistic conscience.

It is time now to examine the work of the writers of minor importance who flourished during this period, novelists, dramatists, essayists, short story writers, and poets, who marked the transition from the old to the new, reflecting sometimes more intimately than their better known contemporaries "the voice of the democracy."

6. Convention and Revolt (1890–1928)

Convention and revolt, romance and realism, these are the ebb and flow of literary expression as they are of social life and manners. Because life is plastic, conventions form new attachments and acquire fresh content. When conventions harden they produce results.[12] The rebel against the old order usually goes to extremes, but those who follow change what has been explored into something enduring. If later the permanent and the universal lend sanction to that which was novel, the frontiers of art are to that extent advanced.

Such a transformation may now be traced in

[12] This thesis has been well established by John Livingston Lowes in *Convention and Revolt in Poetry* (1919).

various literary forms. During the 'nineties occurred the rebellion of the naturalistic novel
against the romantic type that had preceded it.
The revolt in poetry, though it had been gather-
ing force ever since Whitman's day, did not come
until the second decade of the new century.
About the same time the fight against convention
became acute in drama and in criticism. Before
considering in each instance the nature of the
revolt, it is desirable to know what was conventional at the time a change took place.

a. PROSE FICTION

When the vogue in local color was noted it was
observed that the short story had come to be the
most acceptable vehicle for the expression of regionalism. There was at the same time a school
of unlocalized art in short fiction, the most able
representatives of which were Thomas Bailey
Aldrich, Frank R. Stockton, H. C. Bunner, and
Ambrose Bierce. Aldrich's "Marjorie Daw"
depended for its popularity not on the region it
made known but on the sensation disclosed to its
reader at the very end. The story itself was a
mere anecdote, but it was told with whimsical
humor and a "patrician elegance" of style.
Stockton's "The Lady or the Tiger?" though
lacking the grace of "Marjorie Daw," went beyond it in making the impossible seem plausible,
and prepared the way for the legerdemain of O.

Henry. Bunner in "Short Sixes" was a fastidious craftsman who, in contrast to the more flamboyant local colorists, contributed to the short story a Gallic lightness of touch. Bierce recalled the manner of Poe in the collection which he finally entitled "In the Midst of Life," stories of a weird world, related with superb technique.

The humor of Stockton, the surprise of Aldrich, the reportorial skill of Bunner, something of the harlequinism of Artemus Ward, and of the theatricality of Bret Harte were united in William Sydney Porter (1862–1910), known everywhere as O. Henry. Beginning as a drug clerk in North Carolina, he had drifted to Texas, from whence he fled to Honduras because of financial irregularities for which he later went to prison. He had begun writing in Texas; and during his imprisonment and after his release, contributed to the Sunday supplements of New York newspapers. He wrote stories with Southern and Western, and even Latin-American setting, but his best work was done as prose laureate of the metropolis.

O. Henry was enormously prolific. It is not necessary, however, to read all of his two hundred and fifty stories to understand the peculiar technique which he employed. He is perhaps at his best in such stories as "The Furnished Room," "The Gift of the Magi," "A Municipal Report," "Mammon and the Archer," "A Lickpenny Lover," "An Unfinished Story," and "The Last Leaf." His is a deft craftsmanship in which directness of expression, slang, indirect quotation, confidential asides, striking similes, all have their part, but in which the unexpected turn at the end is the unique feature. It is calculated artifice. But so cleverly does this apparently careless raconteur conceal his point that one is always startled by the outcome; besides, the same trick is never quite repeated.

Here is the tragedy and comedy of everyday existence related by one who loves to smile on the pranks of fortune. Hypocrisy and cant receive short shrift. There are exaggeration, irreverence, and everywhere there is "punch." Here are the thrill and picturesque action of the "movie." Many have since tried to imitate O. Henry's skill in construction and his brilliant style, but their journalization of the short story has generally weakened the form. More significant than his contribution to technique, however, was O. Henry's drift, with others, toward the humanized short story with new social content.

In the meantime, how were matters faring with the longer prose fiction? By the middle of the 'nineties the novel vied once more with the short story for public favor and won supremacy in the following decade through the vogue of historical romance. This popular literary form, which had dominated in the fiction that was produced before the Civil War, had appeared only sporadically

after it, in some of the work of John Esten Cooke
and of Edward Eggleston, and in the sensation-
ally popular *Ben-Hur* (1880) of Lew Wallace.
But with the revival of romance in England, by
Stevenson and Kipling, and, aided most of all
by the ardor of patriotism stirred up by the war
with Spain in 1898, a host of "best-sellers" appeared, recalling the glories of the nation's past,
and pointing to its manifest destiny. Mary Johnston went to the traditions of the Old Dominion
and embellished them somewhat in *To Have and
to Hold* (1899); S. Weir Mitchell in *Hugh Wynne*
(1897) told with reposeful style of the Revolution
when it raged near the Quaker City; Paul
Leicester Ford, the historian, drew on his fund
of information for *Janice Meredith* (1899), another story of the Revolution; and Winston
Churchill made his reputation by placing before
the public his conception of various historical
figures: Paul Jones in *Richard Carvel* (1899);
Abraham Lincoln in *The Crisis* (1901); and
George Rogers Clark in *The Crossing* (1904).
There were, of course, many other historical
novelists. Some, like Charles Major, even went
back to the days *When Knighthood was in Flower*
(1898). F. Marion Crawford (1854–1909), with a
cosmopolitan training like James's, had sent his
Zoroaster (1885) from Italy, and now turned his
talent at story telling to the period of the
Crusades in *Via Crucis* (1898), and to the times
of John of Austria in the entertaining romance,

In the Palace of the King (1900). Crawford was not primarily a historical novelist—he wrote novels of manner like *Mr. Isaacs* (1882) and *Saracinesca* (1887), laid in various countries—yet so strong was the vogue of costume romance that he, like others, was drawn into it. As time went on, the spirit of realism forced writers to become more accurate in their use of history and thereby to jeopardize the romantic quality of their work. Rather than do this, most writers turned to other methods and materials, and after 1905, when the public had become satiated, the type rapidly declined.

A more important trend in fiction, during the 'nineties, was the rise of naturalism. According to this doctrine, originally announced by Zola, human conduct is based upon physical desire in a world that is a welter of confusion. This conception, which was materially advanced by the progress of science, is in direct conflict with conventional standards of decorum. A leader in opposing the tradition of reticence and optimism, though hardly a naturalist, was Hamlin Garland (1860‒   ), historian of the Middle Border. Garland was born on a Wisconsin farm, and moved with his parents, as he relates in *A Son of the Middle Border* (1917), to Iowa and later to the Dakotas. His knowledge of farm conditions, came, therefore, from actual contact with its back-breaking toil and privations; and his conception, following Eggleston's *Schoolmaster* and

Kirkland's *Zury,* displaced that found in the idyllic pastorals that had preceded. *Main-Travelled Roads* (1891–1898) was a collection of iconoclastic short stories in which he applied the method of the French and Russian realists to the country of corn and wheat-raising and to the rural customs he so well knew. Life on the farm, as he understood it, was an unrelieved round of hard work, especially severe for the women, for many of whom it meant tragedy. In the short story, Garland could best give vent to his indignation. "Under the Lion's Paw" rebels with the fervor of a "single-taxer" against the injustice of rural economics to the renter, and "Among the Corn-Rows" has like intenseness. *Prairie Folks* (1892–1898) also quivers with reality, but he did not hit his stride again until he produced that graphic "document" of rural life, *A Son of the Middle Border.* The literary theory on which Garland created his work he set forth in *Crumbling Idols* (1893). These essays ably presented the doctrines of the new "veritism" and were widely influential.

With the publication of *Maggie, a Girl of the Streets* (1893) and *The Red Badge of Courage* (1895) by Stephen Crane (1871–1900), naturalism became more definitely established. In the latter novel, instead of that sentimental reveling in a glorious past which had been the mode of rococo romance, there appears the realism of the mud and stench of battle. With amazing convincingness the

author takes a raw recruit through the actualities
of the Civil War and records his reactions to that
grim enterprise. It is a pungent, intense recital
that rivals Conrad's *Lord Jim* as a study of the
psychology of fear. Indeed, Conrad, as well as
Howells and others, came to regard Crane the
outstanding genius among the younger realists.
His verse, too, stands in remarkable contrast to
that of his age.

Crane unfortunately died young, as did Frank
Norris (1870–1902), who was in many respects
like him. Norris, too, had been a war correspond-
ent, and he had conceived a hearty dislike for the
loose manner of provincial romance. In protest,
he had written the vigorous *McTeague* (1899),
and later, *The Responsibilities of the Novelist*
(1903), a companion volume to Garland's *Crumbling Idols*. He planned a trilogy of stories, com-
prising "the Epic of Wheat," which was to deal
on a national scale with the staff of life. *The
Octopus* (1901) treated the struggle between the
California wheat-growers and the railroad, the
conflict between agriculture and commerce for a
fair price. *The Pit* (1903) dealt with the un-
scrupulous manipulation of the wheat-market on
the Chicago board of trade. The third story was
to have been called *The Wolf,* and was to deal
with the exportation of grain to relieve a European famine, but the work was left unfinished by
the author's untimely death. *The Octopus* vividly
actualized life in rural California, and is Norris's

masterpiece. Norris sought in all his writing, whether it dealt with farming, or shark-fishing, or the bohemian life delineated in his less-known books, to portray with undeviating honesty the elemental facts concerning human nature.

Jack London (1876–1916) was the most widely popular of the naturalistic school, rising and disappearing like a comet. This street urchin of San Francisco, full of the zest of life, early went with the gold-seekers to the Klondike, shipped as a common sailor to the South Seas, was for a time an oyster-pirate, and then a coal-heaver, wandered in the slums of London, and rounded off his adventurous career on a ranch in California. Out of this heterogeneous experience came a quantity of stories that amazed and thrilled his readers. From his contact with the basic elements of human nature, moreover, came his philosophy of life as a struggle for the survival of the fittest. It also made him a socialist. Huxley and Nietzsche were his favorite reading. Men at bottom, he believed, were brutes, as he indicated in *The Call of the Wild* (1903), in *The Sea-Wolf* (1904), or in the Marxian *Martin Eden* (1909).

In *The Call of the Wild* London applied human psychology to the conduct of a dog taken from civilization and impressed into drawing a sledge in Alaska; the dog makes his escape and returns to the wild, becoming the head of a pack of wolves. The narrative is full of adventure, moves

rapidly, and has much of the poetry of the North-
land in it. His reputation once established, London poured forth with journalistic abandon tale
after tale dealing with "red blooded" supermen,
indulging in fights and rejoicing in storms. But
his pen was too headlong, and what should have
been virile became melodramatic. Nevertheless,
he most truly represents the prevailing taste of
the decade before the World War, opposing with
Kipling the aestheticism of the 'nineties.

Of the naturalistic novelists now living, Theodore Dreiser (1871–   ) is the Nestor. As early
as 1900 he published *Sister Carrie,* in which life
is portrayed on the level of instinct. This thesis
he has courageously maintained through the
years. What we call civilization, he asserts, ex-
ists only on paper. So-called society is in reality
a jungle in which the struggle for existence is
won by the physically strong and mentally ruthless. Consequently, his characters are irresponsible followers of their desires. In their efforts
at self-realization they evade penalties, and so
challenge every law and custom. The author is
bewildered by all this chaos, but he feels, with
pity, that people exist thus and it is for him to
portray them candidly.

After an interval of a decade, appeared *Jennie
Gerhardt* (1911), another study of the disintegra-
tion of a girl's character under the pressure of
her environment. It was followed by *The Finan-
cier* (1912) and *The Titan* (1914), depicting the

shocking methods of "big business." *The Genius*
(1915), which was suppressed for its alleged in-
decencies, made Dreiser known to a wider public.
In 1925, after another ten years, appeared *The
American Tragedy,* marking the author's advance
to artistic detachment. It shows dramatically
and convincingly how ideas of crime take posses-
sion of a young man's mind, disintegrating his
personality.

All of Dreiser's works are "as full of details
as a day's shopping." Not only are they prolix;
the style is heavy and uncertain, for Dreiser is
a slow, confused thinker. His plots are amorphous and the details frequently blur the outline
of the story. He is not at home with well-bred
characters like those of Henry James, but he has
a tender understanding of elemental, vulgar
humanity. Because he evades no circumstances
in the delineation of his characters' lives, and so
opens to other writers the way to the use of all
sources of material, he is perhaps the most powerful of our present-day writers of fiction.

Another type of novel in which distinguished
work is being done is the novel of social manners.
In this type French and English models have
been followed largely and women have, on the
whole, been most successful. Edith Wharton
(1862–   ) has written accomplished novels of
New York society life with its social compulsions
and the tragedies that grow out of it. Mrs.
Wharton began her writing with short stories in

the manner of Henry James. She adheres in her
work to something like the Greek conception of
fate, and maintains an impartial irony toward
both her social climber and the smart set on whose
wheel of decorum the non-conforming individual
is broken. *The House of Mirth* (1905) is a well-
conceived satire of flash-culture and of some of
the futilities of fashionable life in the big city,
and so is *The Age of Innocence* (1920), which
goes back to the conservative 'seventies. In her
masterpiece, *Ethan Frome* (1911), the setting is
not the metropolis but New England; yet even
here are felt the social compulsions, and, in addition there is the compulsion of poverty. A man
whom fate has thwarted in every way, falls in
love with the cousin of his invalid wife, and so
forgets his lot for a time. But poverty allows
him no hope of escape from his thralldom, and,
in a rebellious moment he seeks oblivion by coast-
ing with his loved one into a tree. The charming
cousin is maimed for life and the crippled Ethan
spends his days in remorse. Slight and episodic
as the story appears, Mrs. Wharton, through the
power of her art, lifts it above a mere rural tragedy into the realms of the universal. On the
whole, Mrs. Wharton favors for her themes characters that are well-bred, straightforward, and
purposeful. She brings to her work an excellent
craftsmanship, a fine understanding of human
psychology, and brilliant diction. Her quiet irony
is the delight of sophisticated minds.

Robert Herrick (1868–   ), in his treatment
of the changing status of women, set a scholar's
conscience against the exuberant complacence of
the opening years of the century. In such novels
as *The Common Lot* (1904), *Together* (1908) and
One Woman's Life (1913), he dealt austerely with
a civilization that makes its women parasites. He
satirized the extravagances of such culture as
would have the individual cut a false figure in the
world rather than maintain her personal integrity. *Together,* a study of the problem of
modern marriage, has perhaps been the author's
most important book.

Ellen Glasgow (1874–   ) has written novels
which have both historical and provincial background but in which the treatment is from a
national point of view. Her use of realism as
early as 1900 in *The Voice of the People* is the
more remarkable inasmuch as writers of Virginia
have ordinarily romanticized the Old Dominion
as a land full of colonels, old mansions, and
ravishing beauties. In such works as *Virginia*
(1913), and *Barren Ground* (1924) appears an
affectionate derision of the old South. The common theme in Miss Glasgow's novels is the fleet-
ing and illusory nature of love. Her fondness for
depicting a community through its most symbolic
individuals is well illustrated in *The Miller of Old
Church* (1911), with its upward push of the
"lower classes." The pervasive elements in Miss
Glasgow's world are her sense of the profound

interdependence of man and nature, her ready humor and exceptional wit, her unmistakably ethical consciousness, her breadth and vision, and her lucidly beautiful style. The most recent successes of this gifted social analyst are *The Romantic Comedians* (1926) and *They Stooped to Folly* (1929).

Willa Cather (1875–   ) is at the same time a realist and a poet. Her work is fresh and autochthonous, revealing life on the rolling landscapes of the Middle West or the arid regions of the Southwest. She herself came out of a small Nebraska town where she made contacts with German, Swedish, and Bohemian pioneers. After receiving a "Puritan" upbringing, she passed through the state university into the field of journalism, and then into fiction. She believes in living out one's potentialities. The best in her characters is called forth in *O Pioneers!* (1913) and *My Ántonia* (1918), vivid memoirs, depicting the primitive battle with soil and elements. Alexandra, the heroine of *O Pioneers!* finds romance in acquiring forsaken farms; a husband is to her only incidental. The story of the pioneers as Miss Cather tells it has a wistful, sad beauty. In *One of Ours* (1922) the elect individual is frustrated for a time by the benumbing circumstances of the Nebraska farm, but he outgrows his restrictions when he enlists in the army and gives his life in the fight against Germany. In *A Lost Lady* (1924) the artist-heroine, stifled for a love worthy of her, descends to lower planes.

The story of this artist's deterioration links with an earlier one of Miss Cather's, *The Song of the Lark* (1915), in which another artist, a singer, subordinates everything to her one talent, yet expands her life by preserving it. *A Lost Lady* is the book that Miss Cather has enriched most with the poetry and wisdom of her imagination. Her latest book, *Death Comes for the Archbishop* (1927), attests again to the fact that Willa Cather is an important artist.

Another novelist of social life whose art is as important as his ideas is Booth Tarkington (1869–   ). This popular novelist of the lighter side of urban society, in particular of the minor foibles of youth, first achieved fame in *The Gentleman from Indiana* (1899). His humorous studies of boyhood and adolescence, *Penrod* (1914), and *Seventeen* (1916), are delightfully reminiscent of the hilarities of youth, without much realization of the serious side which usually lies underneath much of the fun. *The Magnificent Ambersons* (1918), a domestic satire with laughable details, is in some respects the author's most notable work, though *Alice Adams* (1921), a study in social deterioration, shows no falling off in his ability to manage dramatic situations, or to handle clever dialogue and gentle satire. Tarkington delineates the lives of complacent folk who, whatever their ambitions, settle down in the end to a life of routine. In his cozy Indiana there is no sophisticated sickness of life but, instead, there are probity, humor, and the comforts of conformity.

Joseph Hergesheimer (1880–   ) is a romantic realist who has a decided preference for bric-à-brac and aristocratic manners. His dramatic presentation of polite society he suffuses with an atmosphere of rich beauty. Lonely dreamers appear in it, and exotic heroines from the tropics or the opulent Orient. Their creator loves to exercise the historical imagination. *The Three Black Pennys* (1917) goes back to the period of Washington and Jefferson, and delineates the lives of several generations thereafter in the iron regions of Pennsylvania. *Java Head* (1919), with its decorative Manchu heroine, is laid in Salem a century ago, at the close of its seafaring days. In *Linda Condon* (1919) there is a simple exotic beauty who realizes that her position in life will disappear with her beauty, but is glad to have given her sculptor lover his vision. *The Bright Shawl* (1922) is laid in Cuba during the 'eighties; *Balisand* (1924), in eighteenth-century Virginia. Hergesheimer's sensuous imagery is suggestive of Conrad and his genteel atmospheres are reminiscent of Galsworthy; but he is a notable artist in his own right—a gifted stylist and a dramatic story-teller.

Sinclair Lewis (1885–   ) has been the leader in the revolt against the complacency of village life in America. In the enormously popular *Main*

Street (1920) he reproduced with fine realistic detail the drab and gossipy life of the small town of the Middle West. His heroine rebels against the dullness of the place, and through her aspiration for something better has caused many readers of the book to resent the tendency of modern democratic civilization to standardize everything. In *Babbitt* (1922) Lewis went still further in his analysis of complacency, directing his satiric thrusts at the bustling, self-sufficient, commonplace business man of our cities. With all the products of civilization at his disposal, Babbitt is restless and unsatisfied. In his boredom he gropes in unfruitful directions for the happiness and beauty he has missed through glib conformity; he is pleased when his children obey their genuine impulses, since that seems to be the way to true happiness. In *Arrowsmith* (1925), a satire on the medical profession, the author's thesis is that the search for scientific truth is well-nigh impossible in a world which judges only by results. In *Elmer Gantry* (1927) the "muck-raking" is extended to the clergy. Mr. Lewis has too strong a satiric vein to give an entirely truthful picture of contemporary life yet there are in his novels many vividly reported passages that accurately depict our usages.

Sherwood Anderson (1876–   ) likewise rebels against the standardized lives of his countrymen, though with more poetry and less wit than Lewis. He has brooded over man's rebelliousness

but is frankly mystified by the complex problems
of human existence. He, like Lewis, favors being one's genuine self rather than accepting the
advantages of material prosperity. *Winesburg,
Ohio* (1919), a collection of naturalistic tales, has
been Anderson's most noteworthy contribution to
contemporary fiction. It portrays revolt against
all those things which deny the spirit of man—
things like industrial prosperity and stern custom, which make the common life seem banal, and
in opposition to which human desire is the ever-
present witness. *A Story Teller's Story* (1924)
looks forward to intellectual and spiritual triumphs.

James Branch Cabell (1879–   ) devised an
escape from what to him is an ugly world when
he invented Poictesme, an imaginary medieval
country, the characters of which are the ancestors
of his Virginians. Conceiving that life is a vast
comedy in which birth, aspiration or failure, and
death are perpetually re-enacted, he has peopled
his chimerical world with rogues and heroes from
old world romance, has set over them Count
Manuel, and given them magnificent adventures.
The hero of *Jurgen* (1919) has a Faustian day
of amours but finds he has not the strength to
enjoy himself forever. *Domnei* (1913) is the
author's version of some such idealistic romance
as *Aucassin and Nicolette,* together with an adaptation of the Virgin cult. In *The Cream of the
Jest* (1917), a comedy of evasions, Kennaston, the

poet, becomes Horvendile in his imaginary world, between which and the real world he shifts back and forth nightly. In the allegory, *Figures of Earth* (1921), the hero is Count Manuel himself, experiencing love that ends in disappointment. *The Silver Stallion* (1926) brings the Poictesme series to an end, with *Something About Eve* (1927), furnishing an epilogue of disenchantment. In *Beyond Life* (1919) and *Straws and Prayerbooks* (1924) Cabell has given his theories, but these are less important than his imaginative work. In point of style he is without an equal among American writers today, but his work, being somewhat precious, has not reached so many readers as it deserves.

There are many other voices, notably John Dos Passos, Ernest Hemingway, and Louis Bromfield, that seek to interpret through creditable fiction our changing life, but the main trend has been indicated by the more critical of the novelists already mentioned.

b. POETRY

During the years when the short story was in the ascendancy, the poetic field was comparatively barren. One "last pale Indian-summer flower of Puritanism" was blossoming in its retired shade, unnoticed until late but giving forth a fragrance that was to inspire the poets who were to follow. The reference is, of course, to Emily Dickinson

(1830–1886), a sensitive soul, whose concentrated bits of verse marked her during the 'nineties, a precursor of the "imagists." Miss Dickinson, save for one tragic attachment, in which the lovers "scrupled to take their bliss at another's cost," lived a cloistered existence. Driven in upon herself, she found relief in verse of rare insight and pungency. She recorded, with a mind at once daring and naïvely responsive to the simplest things, the whims and fancies of that inner life, its child-like aphorisms, its startling excursions into another world, its lyric cry of the heart. To her, the verses were too sacred to give to the public, but with their publication since her death they have found secure popular favor.

While Miss Dickinson was producing her laconic poems of introspection, the public that had enjoyed John Hay's ballads of homely life on the frontier and recited Will Carleton's ballads of farm life in Michigan, were reading that "laureate of the People," James Whitcomb Riley (1849–1916). The Hoosier poet, who had lived in a small town and who had been successively itinerant sign-painter, vaudeville actor, and drummer in a medicine-show, knew the small-town view of things, the humdrum routine of its life and the respite to be obtained from reflections on the old swimming-hole, the old hay-mow, the old trundle-bed, the old glee club, and recollections of old Aunt Mary, old sweethearts and old-fashioned roses. He knew, too, its love for children and the sentiment with which it liked to recall its own childhood on the farm. He could strike off a gesture or a character inimitably, and his lines abounded in folk-wisdom. The optimism with which he always managed to look upon things ingratiated him with his readers—or hearers—for Riley was a platform-artist, whose sense for vocal expression was one of his unique gifts. The artless sing-song of his meters helped endear him to his public.

Sharing with Riley in the humor and sentiment of newspaper balladry was Eugene Field (1850–1895). He, too, was a poet of childhood, as is well attested by "Little Boy Blue" and other child lyrics; he was, in addition, a clever parodist whose high spirits doted on anything that would fill a column, even such clever variations upon Horace as went into his *Echoes from the Sabine Farm* (1893).

During the 'nineties more than twice as much poetry was published in the United States as had appeared in the two preceding decades. In England this period was characterized by the art for art's sake reaction against Tennyson and the Mid-Victorians and by imitations of the French *fin de siècle* symbolists. The American poet most susceptible to the cult was Richard Hovey (1864–1900). But though Hovey affected the picturesqueness of these writers, and was at one time closely associated with Maeterlinck, he was too robust to live the life of a poseur; their heavily perfumed atmosphere was too close for him, and with Bliss Carman he took to the open road, they two singing the song of comradeship. Three volumes of *Songs From Vagabondia* (1894–1900), they published together, and Hovey composed some rollicking Dartmouth songs of good fellowship.

Mere fraternity was not enough for Hovey, however, as may be seen in "Spring," which passes from the conviviality of the well-known Stein Song to the idea of "the greater tomorrow [that] is on its way." During the Spanish war Hovey wrote a regrettable number of jingoistic poems, even as Kipling was sounding his notes of imperialism from across the sea. Hovey's reorientation in "Unmanifest Destiny" disclosed a larger view, but his life was cut off before he had time to develop a true international outlook. His early death put an end also to what appeared to be a most promising cycle of Arthurian poetic drama. "Launcelot and Guenevere" (1907) did appear, but most readers prefer his vigorous lyrics, in which without doubt his genuine talent lay.

Another poet born in the Middle West, who was educated in the East, and who died young, was William Vaughn Moody (1869–1910). Moody's outlook differed from Hovey's in its larger view of the nation's destiny. He had an acquaintance with ancient and modern literature and did not shut the past from vital experience. He possessed a passionate zest for life, and in his gift of expression was one of the most richly endowed of American poets. His best poems deal with social justice and with patriotism. In "Gloucester Moors" he sounded the questioning spirit that was to mark the new century. He conceived of the earth as a ship careening through space to some unknown port, its voyage disturbed by the noise of injustice towards the passengers in the hold. In "The Brute" he looked upon the factory system as an example of social maladjustment. Moody was not a pessimist but viewed a problem in the light of all its implications. In "The Quarry" he had his country remonstrate against the partitioning of China; and in one of the noblest American odes, "An Ode in Time of Hesitation," he warned his countrymen against imposing imperialism upon the Philippine people who had no issue at stake in the war with Spain. Such independent criticism of national affairs had been unknown among the placid poets of an earlier era. Moody attempted, further, a fresh synthesis out of spiritual values and materialistic determinism. The sardonic poem, "The Menagerie," was his comment on the evolutionary struggle. All of his work was characterized by a deft mastery of technique, even to the extent of elusive metaphors and recondite diction. He has not reached the masses, but he has been beloved by the poets, who in one way and another have carried on his tradition.

Another scholar and mystic who has written

poetry of a high order is George Santayana (1863–   ). This son of Spain who was educated in the United States, and later taught philosophy at Harvard University, began his creative career by writing mystical love lyrics and reflective verse of an austere sort. *Sonnets and Other Verses* (1894), is the dramatic record of his growth of spirit in his passage from orthodoxy to a wider sense of knowledge and beauty; in spirit, it suggests Moody's union of Platonism and naturalism. So flawless and sincere are these pieces that they would lend distinction to any nation's literature.

The spirit of unrest prevailing in the industrial world, of which note was taken in some of the poems of Moody, found its most forceful expression in "The Man With the Hoe" (1899), by Edwin Markham. This protest in behalf of the oppressed toilers of the world was inspired by Millet's well-known painting with the same title, and has been quoted widely. In "Lincoln, the Man of the People," Markham voiced also the ideal of a democracy.

Another form of protest appeared in the verse of Stephen Crane, who has already been discussed for his fiction. Crane set himself in opposition not only to the "genteel" views of the older poets, but to the regularity of their form of expression as well. *The Black Rider and Other Lines* (1895) and *War is Kind* (1899) anticipated the "free verse" of later poets; and the bitter irony of his naturalistic vision of life has enjoyed popularity during the post-war decade.

The first years of the new century were unproductive in poetry. But by 1915 the renaissance was in full swing. The movement that had been begun by Whitman, and had gathered force in Hovey and Carman's *Songs of Vagabondia,* found direction in the naturalism of Stephen Crane, the imagism of Emily Dickinson, and the humanitarianism of Markham. It embodied itself in a new "school" of poets, who had a definite program. They launched a magazine with a catholic attitude toward contributions, and all but made poetry a "best seller."

The "new" poetry was not without romantic elements—the old individualism, humanitarianism, and love of nature were retained—but the sense of observation was more acute and the outlook on life more rational. The movement, in the first instance, was directed against Victorian smugness and sentimentalism which had been entrenched in American literature from the days of Irving and Longfellow to those of Riley. It furthered, instead, a scientific and critical attitude toward life. It objected to the *clichés* of the older poets, and substituted therefor the language of everyday speech. Old standards of versification were cast to the winds, and "free verse" and "imagism" became the order of the day. There was abundant zest for experience. Nothing, if rightly viewed, was regarded as too trivial or

ugly to serve for poetic material. By the time
the *Spoon River Anthology* of Masters appeared
in 1915 the new movement was definitely on its
way.

When the furore over this book had subsided
somewhat, critics pointed out that Edwin Arling-
ton Robinson (1869–   ), had since 1897 been
employing the technique which now made the
Spoon River Anthology famous. In a series of
sonnets characterized by directness of utterance
and sharpness of epithet he had studied crucial
moments in the lives of ordinary people. He had
in fact flown into the face of a decade that wor-
shipped "efficiency" and had made a study of
apparent failures like Richard Cory, Miniver
Cheevy, and Captain Craig. His disillusionment
concerning life was set down with ironic detachment; his doomed creatures were etched in reticence rather than sung with florid melody. Yet
the delineation of their struggle against an un-
kind fate is heartening too. Something of the
poet's austerity he no doubt owes to his New
England ancestry. In any case, Robinson is a
painstaking artist; his poetry has profundity and
precision. He, like Hovey and Moody, has been
interested in the Arthurian legends, giving in
"Merlin," "Launcelot," and the more recent,
"Tristram," an unheroic but distinguished version of life at a medieval court.

What seemed an important aspect of the new
movement was the program of the Imagists. Led

by Ezra Pound and then by Amy Lowell, this group, which included Hilda Doolittle and John Gould Fletcher, sought to liberate verse from the bondage of convention by returning to the use of common speech. Their program reads much like Wordsworth's, upon whom they made war. They insisted on employing only the exact word rather than such generalities as Wordsworth had used, or as had been indulged in even by Whitman; they sought new rhythms for the expression of new moods; they insisted on absolute freedom in the choice of subject; and they tried to make a sharp, because clearly concentrated image, the vehicle of poetic expression. Like Wordsworth, they frequently violated their own precepts, but undoubtedly their experimentation helped to make poetry more flexible.

Amy Lowell (1874–1925), in *Men, Women and Ghosts* (1917), did most to illustrate what the Imagists sought to do. Her poem, "Patterns," uses a lady, her prim dress, the formal garden paths, and the war to bring out the prevailing image. It is a poem of striking beauty and pathos. It is written in cadenced verse with rhymes irregularly placed. Miss Lowell also experimented with "polyphonic" prose, as may be observed in the use of meter, assonance, alliteration, "return," and rhyme, in "Spring Day." But Miss Lowell's importance to the new movement lay less in these things than in her militant leadership.

Robert Frost (1875–   ), like most of the newer poets, does not write "free verse," but employs largely colloquial blank verse. He, like Robinson, interprets decadent New England life, but his work is in much truer sense native to that region; it is as indigenous as its granitic countryside, its woodpiles and dusty blueberries, as apple picking and mending wall. He has as little concern as Robinson for institutional life, or reform, but he loves neighborliness and family ties. Where Robinson is direct, he is leisurely and soft-spoken. Somehow, he manages to put the tones of actual speech into his verse, the reticences of Yankee idiom and its vernacular sounds. He has spoken of himself as a mystic who states always a part for the whole. Certainly there is more in *North of Boston* (1914) than the naturalism of its rock-ribbed austerity. The haze of Indian summer lies on its hard hills and the repressed lives that eke out a living among them.

In America the poetry of the people has been found in adaptations of English ballads that lingered in the pioneer fastnesses, particularly of Kentucky and the Carolinas, though in the course of time a more truly native spirit has appeared in the folk-poetry of various regions. There have been ballads of miners and steamboat pilots, mostly in the Pike County dialect; and the Hoosier ballads of Riley were close to the soil. Besides the ante-bellum songs of the negro reported by Harris and Irwin Russell, there have

been the racy rhymes of Paul Laurence Dunbar
and the negro spirituals.[13]   The spirit of Indian
originals has in recent years been most success-
fully conveyed in verse by Lew Sarett, and
the songs of the cowboy have been collected and
recited and sung by John A. Lomax.[14]

But the poet of the people today is Vachel
Lindsay (1879–   ).   His verse has expressed
the jazz rhythms of the negro, the boisterous
evangelism of the Salvation Army, the dream of
romance of our Chinese laundrymen, as well as
the beauty and sociability of the hearth and the
neighborhood.   He is a provincialist, but he relates his themes to the world at large.   His
whimsy sometimes leads directly to the gods.   In
method he continues the oral tradition that has
so constantly affected American style.   He began
his career as a traveling minstrel, singing and
preaching the "gospel of beauty"; and he has
adapted in his later method the lyric recitation
of the ancient Greeks to what he calls "the higher
vaudeville."   "General Booth Enters Heaven"
tells of a mid-Western heaven as conceived by a
Salvation Army mind, yet the appeal of the poem
is general.   "The Congo" looks into the deeper
racial experience of the negro and relates his uncertain lot to modern civilization.   "The Chinese

13 Collected in *A Book of Negro Spirituals* (1926) by J. W.
Johnson.
14 *Cowboy Songs* (1914) and *Songs of the Cow Camp and the
Cattle Trail* (1919).   See also Louise Pound's *American Ballads
and Songs* (1922).

Nightingale," pure fantasy, yet as impressive as anything he has written, depicts an Asiatic's yearning for beauty in the world of Oriental romance. In his strident idiom, Lindsay sometimes mistakes enthusiasm for inspiration, but it is pleasant to read the vigorous lines of this provincial idealist.

Of quite different temper is Lindsay's fellow Illinoisan, Edgar Lee Masters (1868–). With satiric realism he laid bare four or five years before *Main Street* and *Winesburg, Ohio,* the frustrated impulses towards a more humane life in a mid-Western village. *The Spoon River Anthology* (1915), with its confessions of vice, in ironic contrast to the glowing epitaphs of representative citizens of the community, stirred the country as no book of poems had ever done before. Some readers were interested because of the scandal it revealed; others delighted in its challenge to minor conventionalities; and still others saw beneath the grocery-store gossip, America in microcosm. The immediate model for the epitaphs was the *Greek Anthology,* but the characters were types the author had known personally in his practice as a criminal lawyer. Their drab life he set forth without reticence, though it may be added, with perhaps too great rebelliousness against conformity for the highest achievement in art.

In the poetry of Carl Sandburg (1878–), the "laureate of industrial America," there appears the glorification of muscular power, and the beauty of elemental things. This son of a Swedish immigrant has been buffeted about by the industrial system till he speaks with raw, indignant realism of the things that he has known. The factory, the railroad, smoke and steel, the slum, the prairie, cornhuskers, construction gangs; he has known them all, and he sounds his barbaric yawp against brutality and sham. Yet he reserves a heart of pity for things as they are. He sees beauty in the varying moods of nature, in childhood, and in homely ways and places. He has eschewed rhyme and metrics, and has borrowed the language of the street in order to grip close the thought he has wanted to express. Undoubtedly there is much in his work that is underdone, but there is no question that he has widened the rhythmic patterns of verse or that in his best work he has the true fire.

Of the more conventional lyricists mention must be made of Adelaide Crapsey, with her "cinquains" of fragile loveliness; Sara Teasdale, with her haunting lyrics of love; Joyce Kilmer, for the simple charm of his "Trees"; and Alan Seeger for his inspiring, "I Have a Rendezvous with Death." Contemporary experimenters are named in the Appendix. This account of American poetry may come to a close with a brief observation on the work of Edna St. Vincent Millay (1892–   ). This young poet, whose "rough-and-tumble" is so characteristic of the verve and audacity and willfulness of modern youth, has written lyrics and ballads and sonnets that are fresh and direct and full of zest for experience. Forward or high-hearted, she has written of freedom and joy and gallantry with sincerity and incisiveness, and with penetrating wit. Her volume, *Renascence and Other Poems* (1917), reveals the sweep of her imagination, and her sonnets on what has been called a "Winged Love," and on Euclid, have melody, color, and strong emotion. Because she loves life so ardently, knowing that it is haunted by mortality, such pieces as "Departure" and "Lament" have the utmost poignancy. So brilliant and graceful a writer promises well for the new era of poetry.

C. THE ESSAY AND CRITICISM

When the bewildering chorus of new poets—Amy Lowell, Robert Frost, Vachel Lindsay, Edgar Lee Masters, Carl Sandburg, and others—had enjoyed their nine days' wonder, and their enthusiasm had infected such novelists as Theodore Dreiser, Sinclair Lewis, and Sherwood Anderson, who carried on their program of realism, there arose a number of critics who gave the new movement their aid and support. They took up the cudgels, in the first instance, against tradition, and soon had arrayed against them some stalwart defenders of the conventions. The quar-

rel early took the nature of the old inquiry
whether there is an American culture, and if so,
what are its bases? But before going into their
problem it is desirable to trace the advance of
the literary essay from the older period to the
new.

The essay written before 1860, by men like
Washington Irving, Donald G. Mitchell, and
George William Curtis, had flourished in an atmosphere of established traditions. But, with the
dissolution of the old culture and the dawn of an
exuberant Americanism after the Civil War, the
essay of the classical tradition no longer found
favor, and its place was taken by a more factual,
incisive type of essay. The nature essay, combining scientific accuracy and power of expression,
became, in the hands of John Burroughs and John
Muir, an important literary type during the last
quarter of the century.

An essayist who was at once a formative influence on out-of-door writing and the natural successor of Curtis and the contemplative essayists
was Charles Dudley Warner (1829–1900). Warner was a man of wide culture and sympathy, editor of the *Library of the World's Best Literature*
and the American Men of Letters series, and for
many years one of the editors of *Harper's Magazine*. *My Summer in a Garden* (1870) looked
forward to the nature essayists, while his *Backlog
Studies* (1872) had more of the personal charm
and pleasing humor of Donald G. Mitchell.

Much more significant nature-writing was that of Warner's contemporary, John Burroughs (1837–1921). Burroughs grew up on a farm in New York, with little formal education. He became a government clerk at Washington, where from 1864–1873 he associated intimately with the obscure Whitman. All this while he kept up an interest in out-door life, retiring at length to a retreat on the Hudson where he could write with his eye on his bird and animal neighbors, and where, as he said, he hoped to entice some of the shy thoughts that would not come down to the village. He wrote many books, of which *Wake Robin* (1871), *Winter Sunshine* (1875), *Locusts and Wild Honey* (1879), and *Walt Whitman, a Study* (1896), are the most valuable.

In *Wake Robin,* perhaps his most representative book, Burroughs writes intimately of bees, the speckled trout, strawberries, the blue-bird, and the birds of the hemlock forests. Others have written on these subjects but none with such contagious joy. He wrote of nature with an artistic interest. He was a poet, not only by virtue of his widely quoted "Waiting," but by reason of the rhythmic quality of much of his prose. Some of it might have been written as free verse.

Many of the views of Burroughs on religion, philosophy, and literature he derived or deduced from Emerson, Thoreau, and Whitman. In his scorn for the representatives of the "genteel tradition" he was at one with the later rebels.

In fact, he welcomed the modern movement in literature as early as 1860, in an essay on "Expression," in which he repudiated a bloodless academicism. In 1903, his essay in the *Atlantic* entitled "Real and Sham Nature History," effectively pilloried the "nature-fakers," to use the term coined by his friend, Theodore Roosevelt. In his later work Burroughs became more speculative, pushing beyond scientific materialism to spiritual values. To see and think clearly, to live simply and look into the universe humbly—this was for him the way of truth.

John Muir (1838–1914) was a more penetrating interpreter of nature than Burroughs, more systematic in his study, and he made more important additions to human knowledge. This man of the mountains was born, as he tells in his absorbing autobiography, *The Story of My Boyhood and Youth* (1913), in Scotland, was educated in Wisconsin, and was thereafter at home in the Sierra Nevadas. His first love had been botany; later, his passion was for glaciers, and for the giant sequoias of his beloved Yosemite. By sixty, when he published his first book, he had had a thorough schooling in facts. *The Mountains of California* (1894), *Our National Parks* (1901) and *My First Summer in the Sierras* (1911) eloquently testify to his love of rocks and storms and moving waters. "The world needs the woods!" was his cry. And he saw to it that the forests were conserved. There was something of the poet in him.

"Come with me, along the glaciers," he ex-
claimed, "and see God making landscapes."
There is a theory that the responsiveness of
Americans to the out-of-doors is a race memory
of contact with the wilderness.[15] If this be so,
these nature writers disclose the most genuinely
American traits of our literature.

Not so indigenous are the writers of the informal essay. Among these, Samuel McChord
Crothers (1857-1927) fell heir to the mantle of
Holmes. The play of humor and the graceful
manner that characterize his work are found at
their best in such collections of essays as *The
Gentle Reader* (1903), and in such individual essays as "The Ignominy of Being Grown-up,"
"The Merry Devil of Education," and "The
School of Polite Unlearning." Most of these,
contributed originally to the *Atlantic Monthly*.
display a "mind richly stored in literary treasure." Agnes Repplier (1858-   ), has been
more critical of conventional views of things,
particularly of makeshift opinions. From *Books
and Men* (1888) to her latest magazine article her
essays have exhibited the Gallic sparkle of her
wit and the lambent play of such satire as is the
delight of cultivated readers. The most pleasing
of contemporary writers of the informal essay is
Christopher Morley (1890-   ), who, as a "columnist" as well as poet and novelist, has made

[15] See H. S. Canby: "Back to Nature," *Yale Review*, July,
1917.

the post-war decade considerably merrier than it might have been.

The most enduring work that has been done in the essay is that by critics of American civilization like Henry Adams, George Santayana, William James, and Woodrow Wilson. Henry Adams (1838–1918) marked the culmination of the intellectual movement associated with the earlier New England. In *The Education of Henry Adams* (1906–1918) a book which is much more than an intimate autobiography of a disillusioned man, this younger son of an eminent American family may be observed during the last half of the century seeking some way through the multiple contradictions of life in an age of science and democracy. So far as he could see, all was futility; such balm as his spirit found, lay in the mystical enthusiasms of the cathedral-building Middle Ages. His excellent *Mont Saint Michel and Chartres* (1904), is the expression of his "escape" from the rising culture of the West, even as a European setting furnished an anodyne for Henry James. George Santayana (1863–   ), in his excursion through the past, *The Life of Reason* (1905), found that apparently blind industrialism may re-create the world through idealism. But the teachings of this classic have not even yet been absorbed to any appreciable extent. William James (1842–1910), not ordinarily regarded a man of letters, though he has such a claim by virtue of his imaginative power, his liberating spirit, and his style, has been an important force in dealing with the problems of contemporary civilization. The philosophy of pragmatism has had strong appeal for Americans interested in practical results. It did much toward giving sanction to the revolt against outworn institutions. The addresses of Woodrow Wilson (1856–1923), particularly those redefining the meaning of Democracy and those pertaining to the entrance of the republic upon international affairs, also possess literary value as criticisms of our civilization.

In literary criticism the conflict between tradition and change has been most pronounced. On the side of the conservatives have stood Paul Elmer More, Irving Babbitt, George Edward Woodberry, John Jay Chapman, Henry Seidel Canby, and Stuart P. Sherman. Against these have been arrayed John Macy, Van Wyck Brooks, Ernest Boyd, and H. L. Mencken. The conservatives have maintained a "humanistic" attitude toward life, in contrast to a naturalistic one; that is, they oppose the analogy between the life of man and nature, saying that the true man is spiritual, rather than a creature of the senses merely, and they bid him study his humane traditions to make himself more completely man rather than place any hope upon what nature, whether the nature within him or external nature, may do for him. Accordingly, a critic like Mr. More (1864–   ) has found in the rich human experience recorded by the ancient Hindu sages, by Plato, and in the Bible, the basis for his humanism. Naturally, his interpretation of literary men has reference to their being the spiritual voices of their generation. With his scholarly method, judicial attitude, and literary finish he has been the nearest approach in America to the great French critic, Sainte-Beuve. Professor Babbitt has centered his criticism on the vagaries of romanticists. W. C. Brownell (1851–1928), by his careful analyses has helped to set standards of taste for the fruitful development of later literature. His *French Traits* (1889), *American Prose Masters* (1909), and *Victorian Prose Masters* (1910), and his essays on criticism, standards, and style have the insight and repose of distinguished criticism. George E. Woodberry, (1855–   ), who is a poet as well as a critic, has made an aesthetic evaluation of letters in his six volumes of *Collected Essays* (1921). His *Appreciation of Literature* (1909) has helped many a student into a more humane kind of life.

In 1913 John Macy offered the first assault upon the critics of tradition in his little book, *The Spirit of American Literature*. But the battle royal between the forces of Puritanism and those of naturalism was waged from 1918 to 1925 between Stuart Sherman and H. L. Mencken. Sherman, in articles later collected in such books as *On Contemporary Literature* (1917), *Americans* (1922), and *The Genius of America* (1923), sought to defend the traditions of the founders of American institutions against what seemed to him the flippant attacks of the younger generation as exemplified, among others, by Randolph Bourne in *Youth and Life* (1913); and Mencken, with Nietzschean wrath, in various articles collected subsequently as *Prejudices,* condemned all Puritans and academic "conformists." The outcome of the argument was that Sherman took a more liberal attitude toward matters and Mencken began to read better books. As a critic, Sherman was a disciple of Matthew Arnold in identifying literary criticism with criticism of civilization. He had a beautifully finished style, together with more perspective than his opponent, and was achieving national authority in letters when his untimely death occurred, in 1926. Mencken possesses a wide and curious learning in many arts, and has a brilliant, if raucous style, but he lacks calm and is obsessed by a journalist's passion for contemporaneousness. He has, however, through his various writings, including those as editor of *The American Mercury,* established a definite place for himself in contemporary thought. For the conservatives, Henry Seidel Canby's *Saturday Review of Literature* is maintaining a high standard in literary reviews. The fight with tradition continues, and criticism in America is at present in a state of chaos.

d. DRAMA

The conflict with convention appeared in the drama chiefly as opposition to the standardizing influence of conditions in the theatre, and issued in much greater freedom in experimentation than had ever been enjoyed before. In the period after the Civil War, American drama was as weak as it had been in the period prior to it. But foundations were laid for later activity. Managers like Augustin Daly were adapting plays, from whatever source, for use by their companies. Players like Edwin Booth, Charlotte Cushman, Lawrence Barrett, and Richard Mansfield were favorites on the stage, in many instances having parts written for them. Dion Boucicault cast his lot with American playwrights, adapted numberless foreign plays, and developed the traveling stock company. Bronson Howard established playwriting as a profession, and won popular applause with his farce comedy *Saratoga* (1870), and his stirring war play *Shenandoah* (1889). While David Belasco collaborated on melodramas, William Gillette and James A. Herne, both actors, introduced into the theatre the realistic method that was coming into fiction. Western life was dramatized, but the plays were spectacular rather than literary. Steele MacKaye and Augustus Thomas, through their experiments, and William Winter, through his criticism of stagecraft, however, were preparing the theatre for a better day. By 1890, the movement for more artistic plays, which had started shortly before in England and on the Continent, reached this country.

Clyde Fitch (1865–1909) was for twenty years the most popular and prolific craftsman of the new era in drama. Some of his earlier plays, *Nathan Hale* (1899) and *Barbara Frietchie* (1900), had historical themes, but he was most successful with the comedy of manners. In *The Climbers* (1901), he satirized the ambitions for wealth and social standing of a mother and two daughters who deteriorate under the ordeal. In *The Girl With the Green Eyes* (1902), and *Her Great Match* (1905), he displayed further his exceptional knowledge of women, the former being an entertaining study of jealousy, and the latter, a play pertaining to a love affair between a girl with democratic instincts and a foreign prince. *The Truth* (1907) presented a wife given to flirting and lying until she was enmeshed to such an extent that the author's final reconciliation proved rather unconvincing. All these plays have clever dialogue and move briskly, but, being the work of the superficial craftsman, they are not profound.

A more serious purpose underlies the plays of Augustus Thomas (1859–   ). *The Witching Hour* (1907) is a study of the influence of telepathy and heredity on the destinies of a group. *As a Man Thinks* (1911) has to do with the reconciliation—through a cultivated Jewish physician

—of an estranged couple, alienated through the double standard of morality. These plays show acute observation of "things about town," and have excellent sequence of events, leading to strong climaxes.

Most thoroughly American in its material was *The Great Divide* (1906), of William Vaughn Moody (1869–1910), poet and scholar. The theme of this play was the clash between the culture of New England represented by the morally scrupulous Ruth Jordan and the temperament of the Far West in the person of the rough but genuine Stephen Ghent. Ruth, having in an emergency accepted her abductor, cannot bear the idea of being a primitive prize and escapes to her Eastern home; but when Stephen follows her and gives evidence of genuine love and understanding, she becomes reconciled to him. Though indifferently successful on the stage, this play has literary merit, and is an excellent presentation of important elements in the American scene. Moody's interest in the rebirth of an individual through devotion to another or to an ideal is illustrated also in *The Faith Healer* (1909), in which a man with healing power feels that his love for a woman will jeopardize his ability to work miracles, but learns that the union will simply increase his powers. The play has a mystical atmosphere, and lacks the general interest of *The Great Divide;* moreover, there is a weakness in that the healer's gifts are not powerfully impressed. Moody had previously projected a trilogy of poetic dramas, but lived to complete only *The Masque of Judgment* (1900) and *The Firebringer* (1904). The central conception is the inseparableness of God and man, and it is executed with fine imaginative mingling of classical and Biblical imagery.

A number of dramatists developed contemporaneously with Moody. Richard Hovey (1864–1900) and Josephine Preston Peabody (1874–1922) wrote poetic plays. Hovey lived to finish only *Launcelot and Guenevere* (1907), of his projected romantic trilogy, but Miss Peabody attained recognition with *The Piper* (1909), and *The Wolf of Gubbio* (1913). Langdon Mitchell (1862–   ), son of the novelist S. Weir Mitchell, satirized divorce in *The New York Idea* (1906). *The College Widow* (1906) by George Ade (1866–   ) was once a popular type comedy, as Booth Tarkington's (1869–   ) *The Country Cousin* (1917), and *Clarence* (1919), were later. Charles Rann Kennedy (1871–   ), in *The Servant in the House* (1907), illustrated the brotherhood of man when really practiced rather than merely proclaimed. Percy Mackaye (1875–   ) wrote excellent masques and community pageants, poetic dramas, and a play, *The Scarecrow* (1908), satirizing social pretensions. Rachel Crothers (1878–   ) cleverly satirized social life from the feminine viewpoint in *A Man's World* (1909), *He and She* (1916), and *Expressing Willie* (1924).

About 1915, considerable experimentation appeared in the native theatre; stage devices were imported and adapted, and technique was loosened. The popularity of the motion picture made changes on the legitimate stage imperative. At the same time, opposition to the commercial syndicate, which had controlled bookings of important theatres throughout the country, reached a crisis. Because of this situation, but even more because of a nation-wide enthusiasm for dramatic expression, the little theatre movement came into being. Following the experimentations of the Neighborhood Players, the Washington Square Players, and the Provincetown Players, the smaller towns, which had been objecting to the poor road shows that had been sent to them, began fostering community plays. Drama groups, giving amateur playwrights a chance to develop, sprang up not only in the colleges but in virtually every county seat.

An important aspect of the movement was the encouragement it gave to the one-act play. Indeed, so prolific has been the production of one-act plays that America bids fair to excel in this type as it has excelled in the short story. Able exponents of the one-act play are George Middleton (1880–   ), author of *Embers* (1911), and Percival Wilde (1887–   ), critic and playwright.

More important is Susan Glaspell (1882–), one of the pioneer contributors to the success of the Wharf Theater at Provincetown. With her husband, George Cram Cook, she wrote a delightful parody on psychoanalysis, *Suppressed Desires* (1915), and brought her intelligent and passionate mind to bear on domestic relations in *Trifles* (1916). Stuart Walker, with his Portmanteau Plays and his small but adequate stage, carried the little theatre to widely scattered communities. The most important playwright discovered by the little theatre is Eugene O'Neill.

Eugene O'Neill (1888–) could not have been more fortunate than to come into the theatre at a time when experimentation was giving a hearing to young and daring artists. He brought to his work a varied experience. He had been suspended from college, had gone to Honduras to prospect for gold, had shipped to South America and engaged in commercial work there, had given that up in disgust and gone to South Africa, and, when a seaman's life had palled on him, he had settled down in New York as an actor and reporter. Meanwhile, he had read Conrad and Nietzsche; and now, because of his tropical exposure and reckless living he was obliged to spend half a year in a sanitarium for tuberculosis. During these months of enforced idleness he began writing plays based on the harsh life which he had encountered. Under Professor George Pierce Baker, then at Harvard, he was trained to think dramatically, and was ready to experiment with the Provincetown Players. After writing a number of one-act plays dealing with his favorite theme, the sea—plays that already exhibited his instinct for the potency of pure sound—he made his debut on the professional stage with *Beyond the Horizon* (1920).

In many respects, *Beyond the Horizon* is O'Neill's best play. It is the story of two brothers, one a dreamer who should have been a sea-rover, but remains a farmer, and the other, who was a born farmer but became a sea-rover, because the girl that belonged to him pledged herself to his brother. The practical brother amasses wealth on his voyage, while, on the farm, the dreamer's romance fails to prove the successful match the young people expected it to be. With relentless strokes the dramatist pictures the decay of this household where love has waned and poverty and disease have stalked in. The brother returns to find the husband, ever unable to live without illusions, dying on the hill at sunrise and with yearnings for the romantic lure "beyond the horizon." In its record of the unavoidable mistakes, resulting in consequences which the victims were unable to foresee, the play has something of the fatality of Greek drama.

The Emperor Jones (1921), *The Hairy Ape* (1922), and *Anna Christie* (1922), continued their author's success in dealing with thwarted individuals. In the first two, O'Neill became an "expres-

sionist," seeking to sublimate the changing mood
of successsive scenes by such accompanying maneuvers as the beating of tom-toms and the use of
automatons. In a later play, *The Great God Brown*
(1926), the dual personality of Brown is portrayed by the putting on and taking off of masks.
In *Strange Interlude* (1928), the dramatist has
carried his experimentation still further. By
an adroit use of the soliloquy and the aside he
has tried to convey, much as the novelist does,
what the characters think as well as what they
say to each other; and by means of nine acts, with
an intermission after the fifth, he has sought to
give the sense of the passage of time that here-
tofore has been considered the peculiar province
of the novel. O'Neill is above all an experimen-
talist, so avid of new forms as not always to master his material, but ever pressing on to untried
ways of envisaging the human scene.

The drama of revolt has since the World War
had successes besides those of O'Neill. *Miss Lulu
Bett* (1921), by Zona Gale (1874–   ), pictured
the protest of a village drudge against dullness.
George S. Kaufman (1889–   ) and Marc Con-
nelly (1890–   ) made dullness interesting by
contrasting it with cleverness in *Dulcy* (1921);
they continued the nimble play of their wit on the
theme of domestic relations in *To the Ladies*
(1922). This theme has also been dealt with suc-
cessfully by George Kelly (1887–   ), in *The
Show-Off* (1924), and in *Craig's Wife* (1926).

The most persistent impulse in American drama,
the comedy type, reappeared in *The Boomerang*
(1916), by Winchell Smith (1871–   ), and
was accorded a remarkable run in *Lightnin'*
(1918), as acted by Frank Bacon. Almost as popular was Frank Craven's *The First Year* (1920),
which dealt hilariously with the predicaments of
a young married couple. The most phenomenal
patronage was enjoyed by Anne Nichols's *Abie's
Irish Rose* (1922), in which love laughs at the
locksmiths of race prejudice. Some of these
plays, it must be admitted, owed their popularity
to their timeliness rather than to extraordinary
merits.

Another episode in recent dramatic history has
been the development of the provincial play.
Primitive types such as inhabit the mountain
regions of Kentucky and Carolina have appealed
powerfully to the imagination of the public. Paul
Green (1894–   ), developed by F. H. Koch, has
been the outstanding figure in bringing this picturesque folk-drama to the people. His best collections of one-act plays, *The Lord's Will* (1925)
and *Lonesome Road* (1926), have exploited the
primal poetry of the negro race and the tragedies
among the Southern tenant farmers. There have
been other plays of Carolina mountaineers, notably Harold Williamson's *Peggy* (1922), Lula Voll-
mer's *Sun-Up* (1923), and Hatcher Hughes's *Hell-
Bent fer Heaven* (1924), and it is likely that only

a beginning has been made in depicting regional peculiarities in the theatre.

Without question, the new movement in drama has had more far-reaching results than the corresponding one in poetry. The country as a whole is alive to a dramatic renaissance. With the renewed interest in play-making, as expressed in community players, in drama leagues, and in the dramatic workshops of all the larger universities, it may not be too much to hope that before long the many-colored complexity of the common life will have that serious rendering in drama which has long been overdue.

APPENDIX

A. AN ADDITIONAL LIST OF AMERICAN WRITERS WITH A FEW REPRESENTATIVE WORKS

1. EARLIER WRITERS

ALLSTON, WASHINGTON (1779–1843). Essayist and poet. *The Sylphs of the Seasons* (1813).

ARTHUR, T. S. (1809–1885). Novelist. *Ten Nights in a Bar Room* (1855).

AUDUBON, JOHN JAMES (1780–1851). Naturalist. *The Birds of America* (1827–1838).

AUSTIN, JANE G. (1831–1894). Novelist. *Standish of Standish* (1889); *Betty Alden* (1891).

BALDWIN, JOSEPH G. (1815–1864). Humorist. *Flush Times of Alabama and Mississippi* (1853).

BANCROFT, GEORGE (1800–1891). Historian. *History of the United States* (1834–1874).

BANGS, JOHN KENDRICK (1862–1922). Humorist. *A House-Boat on the Styx* (1895).

BARR, AMELIA E. (1831–1918). Novelist. *A Bow of Orange Ribbon* (1886).

BARTRAM, WILLIAM (1739–1823). Naturalist. *Travels* (1773–1778).

BEECHER, HENRY WARD (1813–1887). Clergyman and novelist. *Norwood* (1866).

BELLAMY, EDWARD (1850–1898). Novelist. *Looking Backward* (1888).

BROOKS, MARIA GOWEN ("Maria Del Occidente") (1795–1845). Poet. *Zophiel* (1833); *Idomen* (1843).

BROOKS, PHILLIPS (1835–1893). Theologian. *Sermons and Hymns* (1878).

BROWNELL, HENRY HOWARD (1820–1872). Poet. *War Lyrics and Other Poems* (1866).

BURDETTE, ROBERT J. (1844–1914). Humorist. *Hawk-eyetems* (1877); *Hawkeyes* (1879); *Chimes From a Jester's Bells* (1897).

BURNETT, FRANCES HODGSON (1849–1924). Novelist *Little Lord Fauntleroy* (1886).

BUTLER, WILLIAM A. (1825–1902). Poet and Novelist. *Nothing to Wear* (1857); *Domesticus* (1886).

CARLETON, WILL (1845–1912). Poet. *Farm Ballads* (1873); *City Ballads* (1885).

CARY, ALICE (1820–1871) and CARY, PHOEBE (1824–1871). Poets. *Poems* (1849).

CAWEIN, MADISON J. (1865–1914). Poet. *Bloom of the Berry* (1887); *Days and Dreams* (1891); *A Voice on the Wind* (1902).

CHILD, LYDIA MARIA (1802–1880). Novelist. *Hobomok* (1824); *The Rebels* (1825).

CHOPIN, KATE (1851–1902). Story-writer. *Bayou Folk* (1894).

COOKE, PHILIP PENDLETON (1816–1850). Poet. *Frois-sart Ballads* (1847).

CRANCH, CHRISTOPHER P. (1813–1892). Poet. *Poems.* (1844); *The Bird and the Bell* (1875); *Ariel and Caliban* (1886).

CUMMINS, MARIA S. (1827–1866). Novelist. *The Lamp-lighter* (1854).

CURTIS, GEORGE WILLIAM (1824–1892). Essayist and orator. *Nile Notes of a Howadji* (1851); *Prue and I* (1856); *From the Easy Chair* (1891, 1893, 1894).

DAVIS, RICHARD HARDING (1864–1916). Journalist and story-writer. *Gallegher* (1891); *Van Bibber* (1892); *Soldiers of Fortune* (1897).

DENNIE, JOSEPH (1768–1812). Essayist. *The Lay*

Preacher (1795); Editor, the *Port Folio* (1806–1817).

FESSENDEN, T. G. (1771–1837). Poet. *Terrible Tractoration* (1803).

FISKE, JOHN (1842–1901). Historian. *Beginnings of New England* (1889); *Old Virginia and Her Neighbors* (1897).

FOSTER, STEPHEN C. (1826–1864). Song-writer. *Old Folks at Home* (c. 1851); *My Old Kentucky Home* (c. 1853).

FREDERIC, HAROLD (1856–1898). Novelist. *In the Valley* (1890); *The Damnation of Theron Ware* (1896).

GARRISON, WILLIAM LLOYD (1805–1879). Journalist. *The Liberator* (1831–1865).

GRADY, HENRY W. (1851–1889). Orator. *The New South* (1886).

GREELEY, HORACE (1811–1872). Editor. *Recollections of a Busy Life* (1868).

HALE, EDWARD EVERETT (1822–1909). Story-writer. *My Double and How He Undid Me* (1859); *The Man Without a Country* (1863).

HARRIS, CORRA (1869–   ). Novelist. *A Circuit-Rider's Wife* (1910).

HEARN, LAFCADIO (1850–1904). Essayist. *Chita* (1889); *Out of the East* (1895); *Japanese Fairy Tales* (1903).

HEDGE, F. HENRY (1805–1890). Poet and essayist. *Parnassus* (1874); *Ways of the Spirit* (1877).

HERNE, JAMES A. (1839–1901). Dramatist. *Hearts of Oak* (1879); *Shore Acres* (1893).

HIGGINSON, THOMAS WENTWORTH (1823–1911). Essayist. *Cheerful Yesterdays* (1898); *Old Cambridge* (1899); *Contemporaries* (1899).

HOLLAND, JOSIAH GILBERT (1819–1881). Poet, editor

and novelist. *The Bay Path* (1857); *Bitter Sweet* (1858); *Arthur Bonnicastle* (1873).

HOLLEY, MARIETTA (1844–1926). Humorist. "Samantha" books by "Josiah Allen's Wife" (1873–1914).

HOOKER, THOMAS (1586–1647). Theologian. *The Soul's Vocation* (1638); *The Saint's Dignity and Duty* (1658).

HOWE, JULIA WARD (1819–1910). Poet. *Battle Hymn of the Republic* (1862).

INGRAHAM, J. H. (1809–1866). Novelist. *The Prince of the House of David* (1855).

JACKSON, HELEN HUNT (1831–1885). Novelist and poet. *Verses* (1870); *A Century of Dishonor* (1881); *Ramona* (1884).

JAMES, WILLIAM (1842–1910). Psychologist. *The Will to Believe* (1897); *The Varieties of Religious Experience* (1902); *Pragmatism* (1907).

JEFFERSON, THOMAS (1743–1826). Statesman. *Notes on Virginia* (1782).

JOHNSTON, RICHARD MALCOLM (1822–1898). Novelist and editor. *The Dukesborough Tales* (1871).

KEY, FRANCIS SCOTT (1780–1843). Poet. *The Star-Spangled Banner* (1814).

LARCOM, LUCY (1826–1893). Poet. *Ships in the Mist* (1859); *Wild Roses of Cape Ann* (1880); *A New England Girlhood* (1889).

LAZARUS, EMMA (1849–1887). Poet. *Admetus* (1871); *Songs of a Semite, the Dance of Death* (1882).

LONGSTREET, AUGUSTUS BALDWIN (1790–1870). Humorist. *Georgia Scenes* (1835).

MOTLEY, JOHN LOTHROP (1814–1877). Historian. *Rise of the Dutch Republic* (1856); *History of the United Netherlands* (1860–1868).

NEAL, JOHN (1793–1876). Novelist and editor. *Sev-*

enty-six (1823); *Brother Jonathan* (1825); *The Down-Easters* (1833).

NORTON, CHARLES ELIOT (1827–1908). Essayist and translator of Dante. Translation of *Divina Commedia* (1891); *Letters* (1893).

O'BRIEN, FITZ-JAMES (1828–1862). Journalist and story-writer. *The Diamond Lens* (1858); *What Was It?* (1859).

ODELL, JONATHAN (1737–1818). Tory satirist. *The American Times* (1780).

PARKER, THEODORE (1810–1860). Transcendental preacher. *Sermons for the Times* (1843).

PARKMAN, FRANCIS (1823–1893). Historian. *The Oregon Trail* (1849); *The Conspiracy of Pontiac* (1851); *Pioneers of France in the New World* (1865); *The Jesuits in North America* (1867); *Montcalm and Wolfe* (1884).

PARSONS, THOMAS WILLIAM (1819–1892). Poet and translator of Dante. *Chetto di Roma* (1854); *On a Bust of Dante* (1854).

PERCIVAL, JAMES GATES (1795–1856). Poet. "To Seneca Lake" (1843).

PHILLIPS, DAVID GRAHAM (1867–1911). Novelist. *The Great God Success* (1901); *Old Wives for New* (1908).

PIKE, ALBERT (1809–1891). Poet. *Dixie* (1861).

PINKNEY, EDWARD COATE (1802–1828). Poet. *Rodolph and Other Poems* (1823); *The Indian's Bride* (1824).

PRESCOTT, WILLIAM HICKLING (1796–1859). Historian. *Conquest of Mexico* (1843); *Conquest of Peru* (1847).

ROE, E. P. (1838–1888). Novelist. *Barriers Burned Away* (1872); *Opening a Chestnut Burr* (1874).

RYAN, ABRAM JOSEPH (1839–1886). Poet. *Poems* (1880).

SEDGWICK, CATHERINE M. (1789–1867). Novelist. *Redwood* (1824); *The Linwoods* (1835).

SHERMAN, FRANK DEMPSTER (1860–1916). Poet. *Madrigals and Catches* (1887); *Little Folk Lyrics* (1892).

SIGOURNEY, LYDIA HUNTLEY (1791–1865). Poet and essayist. *Letters to Young Ladies* (1833); *Pocahontas; Past Meridian* (1854).

SMITH, SAMUEL F. (1808–1895). Hymn-writer and clergyman. *America* (1832).

SMITH, SEBA (1792–1868). Humorist. *Life and Writings of Major Jack Downing* (1833).

SPOFFORD, HARRIET PRESCOTT (1835–1921). Story-writer. *The Amber Gods* (1863).

STOCKTON, FRANK R. (1834–1902). Novelist. *Rudder Grange* (1879).

TABB, JOHN BANNISTER (1845–1909). Poet. *Poems* (1894); *Lyrics* (1897); *Child Verse* (1899); *Later Poems* (1910).

THAXTER, CELIA L. (1836–1894). Poet. *Driftweed* (1878).

THOMPSON, MAURICE (1844–1901). Novelist. *Alice of Old Vincennes* (1900).

TORREY, BRADFORD (1843–1912). Naturalist. *Friends on the Shelf* (1906).

TOURGÉE, ALBION W. (1838–1905). Novelist. *A Fool's Errand* (1879); *Bricks Without Straw* (1880).

WARD, ELIZABETH STUART PHELPS (1844–1911). Novelist. *The Gates Ajar* (1868).

WARE, WILLIAM (1797–1852). Novelist. *Zenobia* (1838); *Aurelian* (1848).

WARNER, SUSAN (1819–1885). Novelist. *The Wide, Wide World* (1850); *Queechy* (1852).

WARREN, MERCY OTIS (1728–1814). Dramatic satirist and historian. *The Adulateur* (1773); *The Group* (1775).

WASHINGTON, BOOKER T. (1859–1915). Educator. *Up From Slavery* (1901).

WESTCOTT, EDWARD NOYES (1847–1898). Novelist. *David Harum* (1898).

WHIPPLE, EDWIN PERCY (1819–1886). Essayist. *Literature and Life* (1849); *American Literature and Other Papers* (1887).

WILSON, AUGUSTA EVANS (1835–1909). Novelist. *St. Elmo* (1866).

WINTER, WILLIAM (1836–1917). Essayist. *Shakespeare's England* (1888); *Shadows of the Stage* (1892–1893).

WINTHROP, THEODORE (1828–1861). Novelist. *Cecil Dreeme* (1861); *John Brent* (1862); *Edwin Brothertoft* (1862).

WIRT, WILLIAM (1772–1834). Essayist. *Letters of the British Spy* (1803); *Life of Patrick Henry* (1817).

WOODWORTH, SAMUEL (1785–1842). Poet and editor. *The Old Oaken Bucket* (1817).

WOOLSON, CONSTANCE FENIMORE (1848–1894). Novelist. *Castle Nowhere* (1875); *Anne* (1882); *East Angels* (1886); *Jupiter Lights* (1889).

2. RECENT AND CONTEMPORARY WRITERS

AIKEN, CONRAD (1889–   ). Poet, critic and novelist. *Earth Triumphant* (1914); *Blue Voyage* (1927).

ATHERTON, GERTRUDE (1859–   ). Novelist. *Senator North* (1900); *The Conqueror* (1902); *The Splendid Idle Forties* (1902).

AUSTIN, MARY (1868–   ). Playwright and novelist. *The Land of Little Rain* (1903); *The Arrow Maker* (1911).

BACON, JOSEPHINE DASKAM (1876–   ). Poet and novelist. *Smith College Stories* (1900).

BAKER, RAY STANNARD (1870–   ). Essayist. *Adventures in Contentment* (1907).

BATES, KATHARINE LEE (1859–   ). Critic and poet. *America, the Beautiful* (1911).

BEEBE, WILLIAM (1877–   ). Naturalist. *Jungle Peace* (1918).

BELASCO, DAVID (1859–   ). Dramatist. *Madame Butterfly* (1895); *The Girl of the Golden West* (1905); *The Return of Peter Grimm* (1911).

BENÉT, WILLIAM ROSE (1886–   ). Poet. *Merchants From Cathay* (1913). (Brother of Stephen Vincent Benét.)

BENÉT, STEPHEN VINCENT (1898–   ). Poet, novelist. *John Brown's Body* (1928).

BODENHEIM, MAXWELL (1892–   ). Poet. *Mimi and Myself* (1918).,

BOK, EDWARD (1863–   ). Essayist. *The Americanization of Edward Bok* (1920).

BRADFORD, GAMALIEL (1863–   ). Biographer. *American Portraits* (1922); *Damaged Souls* (1924).

BRANCH, ANNA HEMPSTEAD. Poet. *Rose of the Wind* (1910).

BROMFIELD, LOUIS (1898). Novelist. *The Green Bay Tree* (1924); *Early Autumn* (1926).

BROOKS, VAN WYCK (1886–   ). Critic. *America's Coming of Age* (1915); *Ordeal of Mark Twain* (1919); *Emerson and Others* (1927).

BROUN, HEYWOOD (1888–   ). Columnist and essayist. *Seeing Things at Night* (1921); *Anthony Comstock* (1927).

BYNNER, WITTER (1881–   ). Poet and playwright. *Young Harvard* (1907); *Tiger* (1913); *Grenstone Poems* (1917).

CHAMBERS, ROBERT W. (1865–   ). Novelist. *Cardigan* (1901); *The Fighting Chance* (1906).

CHAPMAN, JOHN JAY (1862–   ). Poet and critic.

Emerson, and other Essays (1898); *Songs and Poems* (1919).

CLEGHORN, SARAH N. (1876–   ). Poet, novelist. *A Turnpike Lady* (1907); *Portraits and Protests* (1917).

COBB, IRVIN S. (1876–   ). Story-writer and humorist. *Roughing It De Luxe* (1914); *Back Home* (1915); *Paths of Glory* (1915).

CORBIN, ALICE (MRS. WILLIAM P. HENDERSON). Poet. *Adam's Dream* (1907); *The Spinning Woman of the Sky* (1912).

CRAPSEY, ADELAIDE (1878–1914). Poet. *Verse* (1915).

CUMMINGS, E. E. (1894–   ). Poet. *Tulips and Chimneys* (1923).

DELAND, MARGARET (1857–   ). Novelist. *John Ward, Preacher* (1888); *Old Chester Tales* (1899); *The Iron Woman* (1911).

DELL, FLOYD (1887–   ). Novelist. *Moon-Calf* (1920).

DOOLITTLE, HILDA (MRS. RICHARD ALDINGTON) ("H. D.") (1886–   ). Poet. *Sea Garden* (1916).

DOS PASSOS, JOHN (1896–   ). Novelist. *Three Soldiers* (1921); *Manhattan Transfer* (1925).

DUBOIS, WILLIAM E. (1865–   ). Essayist. *The Souls of Black Folk* (1903); *Darkwater* (1920).

DUNBAR, PAUL LAURENCE (1872–   ). Poet. *Lyrics of Lowly Life* (1896).

ELIOT, T. S. (1888–   ). Poet. *Poems* (1920).

ERSKINE, JOHN (1879–   ). Novelist and essayist. *Private Life of Helen of Troy* (1925); *Galahad* (1926).

FERBER, EDNA (1887–   ). Story-writer. *So Big* (1924); *Showboat* (1926).

FICKE, ARTHUR DAVISON (1883–   ). Poet (*alias* "Anne Knish"). *Sonnets of a Portrait Painter* (1914).

FINGER, CHARLES J. (1871–   ). Story-writer and

essayist. *Tales from Silver Lands* (1924–25); *Romantic Rascals* (1927).

FISHER, DOROTHY CANFIELD (1879–   ). Novelist. *The Bent Twig* (1915); *The Brimming Cup* (1921); *Rough-Hewn* (1922).

FULLER, HENRY B. (1857–   ). Novelist. *The Cliff-Dwellers* (1893); *On the Stairs* (1918).

GALE, ZONA (1874–   ). Novelist, story-writer, dramatist. *Miss Lula Bett* (1920, dramatized 1921).

GEROULD, KATHERINE FULLERTON (1879–   ). Story-writer and Poet. *Vain Oblations* (1914); *The Great Tradition* (1915); *The Aristocratic West* (1925).

GLASS, MONTAGUE (1877–   ). Humorist. *Potash and Perlmutter* (1913); *Abe and Mawruss* (1915).

GUITERMAN, ARTHUR (1871–   ). Poet. *The Mirthful Lyre* (1918); *Ballads of Old New York* (1919).

HARRISON, HENRY SYDNOR (1880–   ). Novelist. *Queed* (1911); *V. V.'s Eyes* (1913).

HAWTHORNE, JULIAN (1846–   ). Biographer and novelist. *Nathaniel Hawthorne and His Wife* (1884); *Archibald Malmaison* (1899).

HECHT, BEN (1893–   ). Novelist. *Erik Dorn* (1921).

HEMINGWAY, ERNEST (1898–   ). Novelist and poet. *In Our Time* (1924); *The Sun Also Rises* (1926).

HEYWARD, DUBOSE (1885–   ). Poet, novelist, playwright. *Carolina Chansons* (1922); *Porgy* (1925).

HOWE, E. W. (1854–   ). Novelist. *The Story of a Country Town* (1883).

HUNEKER, JAMES G. (1860–1921). Essayist. *Iconoclasts* (1905); *Egoists* (1909).

HURST, FANNIE (1889–   ). Story-writer. *Lummox* (1923); *Humoresque* (1923); *Mannequin* (1926).

KENNEDY, CHARLES RANN (1871–   ). Dramatist. *The Servant in the House*.

KILMER, JOYCE (1886–1918). Poet. *Trees, and Other Poems* (1915).

KREYMBORG, ALFRED (1883–   ). Poet. *Love and Life* (1908); *Mushrooms* (1916); *Others, an Anthology of New Verse* (1916, 1917, 1919).

LARDNER, RING W. (1885–   ). Humorist. *You Know Me, Al* (1915); *Gullible's Travels* (1917); *The Big Town* (1921).

LEONARD, WILLIAM ELLERY (1876–   ). Poet and dramatist. *The Vaunt of Man* (1912); *Two Lives* (1925).

LEWISOHN, LUDWIG (1882–   ). Critic and novelist. *The Modern Drama* (1915); *Upstream* (1922).

LINCOLN, JOSEPH C. (1870–   ). Poet and novelist. *Cape Cod Ballads* (1902); *Cap'n Eri* (1904).

MACY, JOHN (1877–   ). Critic. *The Spirit of American Literature* (1913); *The Critical Game* (1922).

MARQUIS, DON (1878–   ). "Columnist" and playwright. *Hermione* (1916); *The Old Soak* (1921).

MATTHEWS, BRANDER (1852–   ). Essayist. *The Historical Novel* (1901); *A Study of the Drama* (1910); *A Study of Versification* (1911); *A Book About the Theatre* (1916); *These Many Years* (1917).

McCUTCHEON, GEORGE BARR (1866–1928). Novelist. *Graustark* (1901); *Brewster's Millions* (1903); *Beverly of Graustark* (1904).

McFEE, WILLIAM (1881–   ). Novelist. *Casuals of the Sea* (1916).

MERWIN, SAMUEL (1874–   ). Novelist. *Anthony the Absolute* (1914).

MONROE, HARRIET (1860–   ). Poet and editor of magazine. *Poetry* (1912–   ); *Poets and their Art* (1926).

MORLEY, CRISTOPHER (1890-   ). Essayist, poet, novelist. *Parnassus on Wheels* (1917); *Shandygaff* (1918); *The Haunted Book Shop* (1919); *Where the Blue Begins* (1922).

NATHAN, GEORGE JEAN (1882–   ). Dramatic critic. *The Popular Theatre* (1918); *The World in Falseface* (1923); *Land of the Pilgrim's Pride* (1927).

NEIHARDT, JOHN G. (1881–   ). Poet. *Song of Hugh Glass* (1915); *Song of Three Friends* (1919).

NEWTON, A. EDWARD (1863–   ). Essayist. *The Amenities of Book Collecting* (1918); *A Magnificent Farce* (1921).

NICHOLSON, MEREDITH (1866–   ). Essayist and novelist. *The House of a Thousand Candles* (1905); *A Hoosier Chronicle* (1912); *The Provincial American* (1913); *The Valley of Democracy* (1918).

NORRIS, KATHLEEN (1880–   ). Novelist. *Mother* (1911); *Certain People of Importance* (1922).

PERCY, WILLIAM ALEXANDER (1885–   ). Poet and critic. *Sappho in Levkas* (1915).

PERRY, BLISS (1860–   ). Essayist. *A Study of Prose Fiction* (1902); *The Amateur Spirit* (1904); *Park Street Papers* (1909).

PHELPS, WILLIAM LYON (1865–   ). Essayist. *Essays On Modern Novelists* (1910); *The Advance of English Poetry* (1918).

POOLE, ERNEST (1880–   ). Novelist. *The Harbor* (1915); *The Family* (1917).

POUND, EZRA (1885–   ). Poet. *Spirit of Romance* (1910); *Canzoni* (1911).

QUICK, HERBERT (1861–1926). Novelist. *Vandemark's Folly* (1922); *The Hawkeye* (1923).

RANSOM, JOHN CROWE (1888–   ). Poet. *Poems about God* (1919); *Grace After Meat* (1924).

REESE, LIZETTE WOODWORTH (1856–   ). *A Handful of Lavender* (1891); *A Wayside Lute* (1909).

RICE, ALICE HEGAN (1870–1921). Novelist. *Mrs. Wiggs of the Cabbage Patch* (1901); *Lovey Mary* (1903).

RICE, CALE YOUNG (1872–   ). Poet, dramatist. *Collected Plays and Poems* (1915).

RICHMOND, GRACE S. Story-writer. *The Second Violin.*

RIDGE, LOLA. Poet, critic. *Sun-up and Other Poems* (1920).

ROBERTS, ELIZABETH MADOX. Poet and novelist. *The Time of Man* (1926).

ROGERS, WILL (1879–). Humorist. *Rogerisms* (1919).

SARETT, LEW (1888–). Poet. *Many, Many Moons* (1920); *Slow Smoke* (1925).

SEEGER, ALAN (1888–1916). Poet. *Poems* (1916).

SETON, ERNEST THOMPSON (1860–). Naturalist. *Wild Animals I Have Known* (1898).

SHELDON, EDWARD (1886–). Dramatist. *Salvation Nell* (1908); *The Nigger* (1910); *The Boss* (1911); *Romance* (1914).

SINCLAIR, UPTON (1878–). Novelist and essayist. *The Jungle* (1906); *The Brass Check* (1919); *The Goose-Step* (1923).

SINGMASTER, ELSIE (1879–). Novelist. *John Baring's House* (1920).

SLOSSON, ANNIE TRUMBULL (1838–1926). Story-writer. *Seven Dreamers* (1891); *Aunt Abby's Neighbors* (1902).

STRUNSKY, SIMEON (1879–). Essayist. *Sinbad and His Friends* (1921).

TEASDALE, SARA (1884–). Poet. *Rivers to the Sea* (1915); *Love Songs* (1917); *Flame and Shadow* (1920).

THOMAS, EDITH M. (1854–1922). Poet. *In Sunshine Land* (1895); *The Dancers* (1903).

TIETJENS, EUNICE (1884–). Poet and novelist. *Body and Raiment* (1919).

UNTERMEYER, LOUIS (1885–). Essayist. *The New Era in American Poetry* (1919).

VAN DOREN, CARL (1885–). Critic. *The American Novel* (1921); *Many Minds* (1924).

VAN DYKE, HENRY (1852–   ). Essayist and poet. *The Poetry of Tennyson* (1889) ; *Fisherman's Luck* (1899) ; *The Blue Flower* (1902).

VAN LOON, HENDRIK WILLEM (1882–   ). Historian. *The Story of Mankind* (1921).

VAN VECHTEN, CARL (1880–   ). Critic. *Peter Whiffle* (1922) ; *Nigger Heaven* (1926).

VESTAL, STANLEY (W. S. CAMPBELL). Poet and biographer. *Kit Carson* (1927).

WATTS, MARY S. (1868–   ). Novelist. *Nathan Burke* (1910).

WHEELOCK, JOHN H. (1886–   ). Poet. *The Human Fantasy* (1911) ; *Black Panther* (1922).

WHITE, STEWART EDWARD (1873–   ). Novelist. *The Blazed Trail* (1902).

WHITE, HERVEY (1866–   ). Novelist. *Differences* (1899) ; *Quicksand* (1900).

WHITE, WILLIAM ALLEN (1868–   ). Novelist and journalist. *The Real Issue* (1896) ; *A Certain Rich Man* (1909) ; *In the Heart of a Fool* (1918).

WIDDEMER, MARGARET (1880–   ). Novelist and poet. *Factories* (1915).

WIGGIN, KATE DOUGLAS (1859–   ). Novelist. *Rebecca of Sunny-Brook Farm* (1903) ; *The Old Peabody Pew* (1907).

WILDER, THORNTON (1897–   ). Novelist. *The Bridge of San Luis Rey* (1927).

WILLIAMS, WILLIAM CARLOS (1883–   ). Poet. *Poems* (1909).

WILSON, WOODROW (1856–1924). Statesman. *Mere Literature* (1893) ; *A History of the American People* (1902) ; *The New Freedom* (1913).

WISTER, OWEN (1860–   ). Novelist. *The Virginian* (1902) ; *Lady Baltimore* (1906).

WYATT, EDITH F. (1873–   ). Poet. *The Wind in the Corn* (1917) ; *The Invisible Gods* (1923).

B. A SKETCH OF AMERICAN PERIODICAL LITERATURE

1. NEWSPAPERS; IMPORTANT EDITORS

In a democracy the chief habitual reading matter for multitudes is the penny newspaper. One does not look for much of literary value where there must be such haste as may bring to the breakfast table an account of the nation's doings within the past twenty-four hours. Yet so diversified is the province of modern newspapers and so readable is their style that the nation's thought is shaped largely by them. Nor is their influence confined to political matters; they reflect the changes in the national idiom. Literary men throughout the course of American journalism have conducted "columns," or have served as editors; and many a poem or sketch has first found its readers through the medium of the newspaper.

Journalism had considerable cultural significance in the early life of the country; for want of news the periodicals frequently contained essays, poems, and other literary matter.[1] As a whole, Colonial news sheets were poor and usually had short shrift. The Boston *News Letter*, however, a small four-page, double-column folder, established in 1704, was among the more successful. *The New England Courant*, established in 1721, is of interest despite its short life, because it was conducted by an older brother of Benjamin Franklin, and served the younger man for his Spectator-like prentice work in the Silence Dogood essays. The *Courant* was the organ of "The Hell-fire Club" and was unique in not being a reprint of current English journals. In the early years of the eighteenth century half of the colonies had each

[1] Consult Elizabeth C. Cook's *Literary Influences in Colonial Newspapers, 1704–50*. 1912.

a Gazette, appearing weekly; and by the time the colonists severed their relations with the mother country the number of newspapers had grown to thirty-seven. In them the poetry and satire of the Revolution appeared. The first daily newspaper, *The Pennsylvania Packet and Daily Advertiser,* was established at the close of the war.

Not, however, until the New York *Evening Post* began to flourish in 1801, under strong Federalist patronage, and more particularly when in 1828 it began its half century of notable editorship under William Cullen Bryant, did American journalism rise to a position of respect. The high, conservative ideals maintained by Bryant were continued under such later editors as Carl Schurz, E. L. Godkin, and others. Several rival papers soon came into the field. The New York *Sun,* established in 1833 as the first American penny newspaper, was for thirty years after the Civil War, under the editorship of Charles A. Dana, one of the nation's most influential newspapers. In 1835 the New York *Herald,* under the elder and the younger James Gordon Bennett, began its notable career of newsgathering. Perhaps the best known journalist of his day was Horace Greeley, founder in 1841 of the New York *Tribune.* With the aid of such writers as George Ripley, Charles A. Dana, and George William Curtis, the *Tribune* advanced materially the literary standards of journalism. The New York *Times,* founded in 1851 by Henry J. Raymond, and continued more recently by Adolph S. Ochs, has been in the main a political organ, though its weekly book reviews also command wide attention. The New York *World,* begun in 1860, became a force to be reckoned with in 1883 when Joseph Pulitzer introduced the sensational exposure of public abuse. In literature his name is inseparably associated with the encouragement he has given American writers by offering annual prizes for the best work in the various fields of literary endeavor.

Outside the metropolis, some of the best known newspapers of literary significance in recent years have been the Boston *Transcript*, the Springfield (Mass.) *Republican*, the Louisville *Courier-Journal*, the Philadelphia *Public Ledger*, the Atlanta *Constitution*, the *Christian Science Monitor*, the New Orleans *Picayune*, and the San Francisco *Examiner*.

2. Defunct Magazines of Literary Importance

Although there had been sporadic, flamboyantly patriotic attempts to establish magazines in the last half of the eighteenth century, no literary magazine worthy of the name appeared until Joseph Dennie at Philadelphia founded *The Port Folio*. Established in 1801 as the weekly newspaper of a Federalist coterie, the periodical became in 1806 a monthly magazine of "polite letters," with such contributors as John Quincy Adams, Charles Brockden Brown, and Dennie himself; it reviewed American and English books up to 1827. In Boston, *The Monthly Anthology*, begun in 1803, was prominent in making that city an intellectual center. It was edited "by a society of gentlemen," who also supported the Boston *Athenaeum*, and who in 1815 established the *North American Review*. From 1823 to 1845 the New York *Mirror* appeared weekly. It published, among other things, Willis's "Pencillings by the Way," and Poe's "The Raven." When the annuals rose to supremacy during the thirties, *Godey's Lady's Book* was established at Philadelphia and enjoyed a long period (1830–1876) of appeal to women readers. Among its best known contributors were Longfellow, Poe, Holmes, and Bayard Taylor. *The New England Magazine*, 1831–1835, published the early work of Longfellow,

Hawthorne, Whittier and Holmes. *The Dial*, 1840–1844, the quarterly of the New England Transcendentalists, published many of the writings of Margaret Fuller, of Bronson Alcott, of Emerson and Thoreau, and others.

A definite attempt to encourage American writers was made by *The Knickerbocker Magazine*, 1833–1859. Contributors to its pages were Bryant, Irving, Halleck, Longfellow, Whittier, Holmes, and many secondary writers. A similarly genteel tradition was maintained by *Knickerbocker's* contemporary at Richmond, *The Southern Literary Messenger*, 1834–1864. Edgar Allan Poe, of course, did most to enlarge the circulation of this magazine, but among prominent contributors were N. P. Willis, C. F. Hoffman, R. W. Griswold, and J. G. Holland from the North; Dickens, Thackeray, and G. P. R. James, of England; and P. P. Cooke, J. W. Legaré, J. P. Kennedy, P. H. Hayne, Henry Timrod, and Sidney Lanier from the South. *The Southern Quarterly Review*, 1842–1857, possessed a certain old-fashioned distinction through its connection with Charleston and Columbia. But more important for Charleston's literary life was *Russell's Magazine*, 1857–1860, because it was the mouthpiece of Simms and his literary coterie. At Baltimore, *The Saturday Visiter* published some work of Poe; and *The Southern Magazine*, in the period from 1871–1875, published some of the writings of Lanier, Hayne, Gildersleeve, and others. The spirit of the West found expression in the late thirties in *The Western Monthly Magazine*, 1833–1837, and in *The Western Messenger*, 1835–1841, both published in Cincinnati.

Meanwhile there appeared in Philadelphia *Graham's Magazine*, formerly the *Gentleman's Magazine*, which, because of the high pay it offered—twelve dollars a page—reckoned among its contributors almost every prominent American writer of the time, and enjoyed a circulation of 135,000 copies. In this city, *Lippincott's* furnished writers an active market from 1868–1916. But as early as 1850, with the establishment of *Harper's New Monthly Magazine,* New York attained to supremacy as a publishing center, a position which it virtually monopolizes today. In this city, *The Democratic Review,* founded in 1837, developed into an important political journal. For a little more than a decade, 1866–1878, *The Galaxy,* edited by Richard Grant White, supplied entertaining illustrated fiction. *Putnam's,* established in 1853, and having been merged successively with *Emerson's Magazine* and *Scribner's Monthly,* and, having absorbed *The Critic* and *The Reader,* before it, in turn, was taken over by the *Atlantic,* maintained a consistent market for the better writers of the period up to 1910. The metamorphosis through which *Putnam's Magazine* passed was representative of the lot of many other American journals.

In the far West *The Overland Monthly,* 1868–1875; 1883–, under the original editorship of Bret Harte, furnished an outlet for the humorists of that section, including Mark Twain. In Chicago, *The Dial,* 1881–1918, maintained a high standard as a fortnightly literary review. The aforementioned magazines are, of course, only the more prominent of those which once brought American authors before their public. As repositories of literary expression and media for the exchange of opinion, they well illustrate the importance of our periodical literature in stabilizing public taste and in furthering new ideals in American letters.

3. CURRENT MAGAZINES WITH LITERARY TRADITION

The reading of magazines is in America more general than the reading of books. Much that appears in magazines today may be reprinted tomorrow in books. Coincident with the rise of magazines, it will be recalled that

a favorite form of entertainment, the short story had its
beginnings. Later, the publication in serial form of
some of the best American novels was achieved through
the medium of such magazines as *The Atlantic Monthly,
Harper's Magazine, The Century Magazine,* and *Scribner's Magazine.* Important poetry and criticism have
likewise made their initial appearance in them.

Of the magazines that still survive the one that has
enjoyed the longest career is *The North American
Review.* Established in 1815 and modeled on the great
English qaurterlies, the *Review* maintained its scholarly,
non-partisan policy throughout the war between the
states; with its removal from Boston to New York, in
1878, it became a monthly and subsequently changed
its editorial policy to include short articles on popular,
timely subjects by leading writers of the day. Among
its editors have been Richard H. Dana, Edward Everett,
James Russell Lowell, Charles Eliot Norton, William
Dean Howells, Henry Adams, Henry Cabot Lodge, and
George Harvey. Other reviews that have survived are
The Forum, founded in 1886; *The American Review of
Reviews,* in 1890; *The Yale Review,* dating from 1892,
when it absorbed *The New Englander; The Bookman,*
established in 1895; *The Sewanee Review,* 1892, and
The South Atlantic Quarterly, 1901. These, together
with the more recently significant *Virginia Quarterly
Review,* and *The Saturday Review of Literature,* are
supplying serious and important discussion of American
literary, political, economic, and historical interests.

Of the popular literary magazines with diversified
reading matter, *Harper's Monthly Magazine* is the
oldest. Founded in 1850, it began a new departure. It
published serially the fiction of Dickens, Bulwer, and
other British novelists; reprinted significant British
reviews (though the eclecticism of *Littell's Living Age,*
Boston, 1844, had anticipated this); and supplied illus-

trations. Henry M. Alden, who for fifty years, 1869–1919, was its editor, established special departments like "The Editor's Easy Chair"—departments conducted with distinction by George William Curtis and William Dean Howells. In later years *Harper's* printed more and more the work of American writers, encouraging young authors like Richard Harding Davis, Mary Wilkins Freeman, and Stephen Crane.

The most distinctly literary magazine has been *The Atlantic Monthly*. It is a significant fact that the *Atlantic* has attained a wide popularity without sacrificing high standards. When it was founded in Boston in 1857, by Francis H. Underwood, Lowell was its editor and Holmes contributed serially *The Autocrat of the Breakfast Table*. Sooner or later every American writer of distinction has contributed to its pages. It has had such distinguished editors as James Russell Lowell, James T. Fields, William Dean Howells, Thomas Bailey Aldrich, Horace E. Scudder, Walter Hines Page, Bliss Perry, and Ellery Sedgwick.

Next in age is *The Century Magazine,* begun in 1870 and continued until 1881 under the name of *Scribner's Monthly*. The editor during this early period, J. G. Holland, an author of rather commonplace books in prose and verse, knew how to enlist the services of well-known writers. His successor, when the name was changed to the *Century,* was Richard Watson Gilder, a man of poetic taste and journalistic ability. He published serially Howells's *A Modern Instance,* Stedman's articles on American poets, and illustrated articles on history. From the first the *Century* encouraged Southern contributors. It has consistently included articles of timely import.

Scribner's Magazine, which should not be confused with *Scribner's Monthly,* just mentioned, did not appear until 1887. It has been interested in matters pertaining to art, music, nature, and travel, as well as in literature proper, and has included among its contributors H. C. Bunner, Sarah Orne Jewett, Joel Chandler Harris, R. H. Stoddard, T. B. Aldrich, T. W. Higginson, and, more recently, W. C. Brownell, Winston Churchill, Meredith Nicholson, and others. None of the foregoing magazines has been the voice of any one school; all have contributed to giving American authors their audience.

4. Other Magazines Expressing Contemporary Thought

In conclusion, it seems fitting to mention a few magazines that represent in a measure the great diversity of taste to which current periodicals minister. Every trade now has one or more periodicals devoted to its interests, but it is the intention here to name merely a few of those of more direct importance to the student of literature.[2] Unquestionably *The American Mercury,* under the editorship of H. L. Mencken, has done most to discount the sentimental attitude in American life and letters. At the same time it has given opportunity to young writers who have had something virile and trenchant to offer. *The Dial,* not to be confused with the critical fortnightly published in Chicago, 1881–1918, has advanced the frontiers of the seven arts by publishing articles, poems, drawings, and stories with a definitely modernistic trend. *Vanity Fair* likewise enjoys the patronage of intelligent, sophisticated readers. It has had articles of distinction on the theatre. American humor has found notable expression in *Puck,* during the editorship of H. C. Bunner, and more recently in *Life* and *Judge,* both popular comic weeklies. Journals appealing especially to women, like *The Ladies' Home*

[2] The reader desiring fuller information about periodical literature will find it in Algernon Tassin's *The Magazine in America* (1916).

Journal, The Delineator, The Woman's Home Companion, and others, bring many authors of repute before a wide reading public. There are weeklies, also, literary and political, like *The Nation, The New Republic, The Outlook, Collier's,* and *The Literary Digest* which keep the public informed on current issues. Most widely read of the weeklies is *The Saturday Evening Post,* founded long ago by Benjamin Franklin. It furnishes our material civilization timely articles about its markets, and literary pabulum as well, by some of the best known of contemporary writers.

C. A SELECTED BIBLIOGRAPHY

I. HISTORICAL

Cambridge History of American Literature. 1917–21. 4 vols. (Contains authoritative discussion and invaluable bibliographies.)

Manly, J. M. and Edith Rickert: Contemporary American Literature. Bibliographies. 1922.

Marble, A. R.: Heralds of American Literature (through Brown). 1907.

Moses, M. J.: The Literature of the South. 1910.

Parrington, V. L.: Main Currents in American Thought. 1927– . 3 vols.

Pattee, F. L.: A History of American Literature since 1870 [to 1900]. 1915.

Richardson, C. F.: American Literature (1607–1885), 1887, 1889.

Riley, Woodbridge: American Thought. 1915.

Rusk, R. L.: The Literature of the Middle Western Frontier. 1925. 2 vols.

Trent, W. P.: A History of American Literature. 1903.

Tyler, M. C.: A History of American Literature from 1607 to 1765. 1878.

Tyler, M. C.: A Literary History of the American
Revolution. 1897.

Wendell, Barrett: A Literary History of America. 1900.

Whitcomb, S. L.: Chronological Outlines of American
Literature. 1894.

Woodberry, G. E.: America in Literature. 1908.

II. Collections

1. *General*

Alderman, E. A. and others (ed.): Library of Southern
Literature. 1908–23. 17 vols.

Cairns, W. B.: Early American Writers. 1912.

Foerster, Norman: American Poetry and Prose. 1925.

Newcomer, Andrews, Hall: Three Centuries of American Poetry and Prose. 1917.

Pattee, F. L.: Century Readings in American Literature. 1919; 1926.

Payne, L. W.: American Literary Readings. 1917;
Later American Writers. 1927.

Prescott, F. C. and J. H. Nelson: Prose and Poetry of
the Revolution. 1925.

Shafer, Robert: American Literature. 1926.

Snyder, F. B. and E. D.: A Book of American Literature. 1927.

Stedman, E. C. and E. Hutchinson: A Library of
American Literature. 1887–1890. 11 vols. (The
last volume has brief biographies.)

Stedman, E. C.: An American Anthology. 1900.

Trent, W. P.: Southern Writers. 1905.

Trent, W. P. and B. W. Wells: Colonial Prose and
Poetry. 1901.

2. *Poetry*

Boynton, P. H.: American Poetry. 1918. (Appendix
has critical material.)

Braithwaite, W. B.: Annual Anthology of Magazine Verse (since 1914).

Bronson, W. C.: American Poems. 1912.

Eggleston, G. C.: American War Ballads and Lyrics. 1889.

Griswold, R. W.: Poets and Poetry of America. 1842; Female Poets of America. 1848.

Higginson, T. W. and E. H. Bigelow: American Sonnets. 1890.

Lomax, J. A.: Cowboy Songs. 1914; Songs of the Cow Camp and the Cattle Trail. 1919.

Matthews, Brander: American Familiar Verse. 1904.

Monroe, H. and A. C. Henderson: The New Poetry, an Anthology. 1917, 1923.

Page, C. H.: Chief American Poets. 1905.

Pound, Louise: American Ballads and Songs. 1922.

Rittenhouse, J.: A Little Book of Modern Verse. 1913. A Second and Third Book of Modern Verse also.

Stevenson, B. E.: Poems of American History. 1908, 1922.

Untermeyer, L.: Modern American Poetry. 1919, 1925.

Wilkinson, Marguerite: New Voices. 1919; 1928.

3. *Prose*

Babbitt, Irving, and others: Criticism in America. 1924.

Baldwin, C. S.: American Short Stories. 1904.

Bronson, W. C.: American Prose. 1916.

Carpenter, G. R.: American Prose. 1898.

Foerster, Norman: Chief American Prose Writers. 1916.

Griswold, R. W.: Prose Writers of America. 1847.

Hanscom, E. D.: The Heart of the Puritan. 1917.

Matthews, Brander: The Oxford Book of American Essays. 1914.

Pattee, F. L.: Century Readings in the American Short Story. 1927.

Payne, W. M.: American Literary Criticism. 1904.

4. *Drama*

Baker, G. P.: Modern American Plays. 1920.
Koch, F. H.: Carolina Folk-Plays. 1922.
Mantle, Burns: The Best Plays (annually since 1919).
Mayorga, M. J.: Representative One Act Plays by American Authors. 1919.
Moses, M. J.: Representative Plays by American Dramatists. 1918–25. 3 vols.
Quinn, A. H.: Contemporary American Plays. 1923.
Quinn, A. H.: Representative American Plays. 1917, 1925.

III. Biography

1. *General*

Adams, O. F.: A Dictionary of American Authors. 1897, 1905.
Appleton's Cyclopedia of American Biography. 1886–89. 6 vols.
Beers, H. A.: Connecticut Wits and other Essays. 1920.
Boynton, P. H.: Some Contemporary Americans. 1924.
Cooper, F. T.: Some American Story-tellers. 1911.
Dictionary of American Biography. 1928– .
Duyckinck, E. A. and G. L.: Cyclopedia of American Literature. 1856, 1865, 1885. 2 vols.
Fields, J. T.: Yesterdays with Authors. 1871.
Higginson, T. W.: Cheerful Yesterdays. 1899.
Sherman, S. P.: Americans. 1922.
Trent, W. P. and John Erskine: Great American Writers. 1912.
Tyler, M. C.: Three Men of Letters. 1895. (Dwight, Barlow, Berkeley.)
Who's Who in America. 1899– .

2. *Individual Authors* (including best edition of their Works).

Alcott, A. Bronson.
>Life by Honoré Willsie Morrow. 1927.
>Works, ed. by R. W. Emerson. 1912.

Aldrich, Thomas Bailey.
>Life by Ferris Greenslet. 1908.
>Works, Riverside ed., 9 vols. 1907.

Brown, Charles Brockden.
>Life in Erskine's Leading American Novelists. 1910.
>Works, pub. by McKay. 1887. 6 vols.

Bryant, William Cullen.
>Life by Parke Godwin, 1883; John Bigelow (AML) [3] 1890; W. A. Bradley (EML) [3] 1905; J. G. Wilson's Bryant and his Friends. 1886.
>Works, ed. by Parke Godwin. 1883–84. 6 vols.

Burroughs, John.
>Life by Clara Barrus. 1925; The Real John Burroughs by W. S. Kennedy, 1924.
>Works, Houghton. 23 vols. 1921; *The Heart of Burroughs's Journals* (1928).

Clemens, Samuel Langhorne (Mark Twain).
>Life by Albert B. Paine, 1912, 3 vols; see also Howells's "My Mark Twain" in *Literary Friends and Acquaintance,* 1900, and V. W. Brooks's *The Ordeal of Mark Twain,* 1920; the *Autobiography* (1924) is less valuable than *Mark Twain's Letters.* 1917. 2 vols.
>Works, 1910, 25 vols. does not include *The Mysterious Stranger,* 1916, and *What is Man?* 1917.

Cooper, James Fenimore.
>Life by T. R. Lounsbury (AML) 1883. *Correspondence of Cooper.* 1922.

[3] *AML* refers to the American Men of Letters Series; *EML* to the English Men of Letters Series.

Works, 33 vols. Mohawk ed.; The Houghton Mifflin
Co. ed. has introductions by Cooper's daughter.

Crane, Stephen.

Life by Thomas L. Beer. 1924.

Works, Follett ed. 1925. 12 vols.

Crèvecoeur, Hector St. John.

Life by Julia B. Mitchell. 1916.

Letters (Everyman ed.); and *Sketches of Eighteenth
Century America.* 1926.

Dickinson, Emily.

Life by Martha D. Bianchi. 1924.

Complete Poems. Houghton. 1925.

Edwards, Jonathan.

Life by A. V. G. Allen. 1889, 1896.

Works of President Edwards, 1881. 4 vols.

Emerson, Ralph Waldo.

Life by J. E. Cabot; G. E. Woodberry (EML);
O. W. Holmes (AML); O. W. Firkins. See also
Correspondence of Carlyle and Emerson; and the
essay by Matthew Arnold in *Discourses in
America.*

Works, Centenary ed. 1903. 12 vols. and the
Journals, 1909–14. 10 vols. *The Heart of Emerson's Journals,* ed. by Bliss Perry, 1926 is excellent.

Franklin, Benjamin.

Life by J. B. McMaster (AML), 1889. Phillips
Russell's *Benjamin Franklin, the First Civilized
American,* 1927, may be consulted.

Writings of, with Life and Introd. by A. H. Smyth.
1905. 10 vols.

Freneau, Philip.

Life by Mary S. Austin, 1901.

Poems of, ed. by F. L. Pattee. 1902–07. 3 vols.

Fuller (Ossoli), Margaret.

Life by T. W. Higginson (AML), 1884.

Gilder, Richard Watson.

Letters of, 1916.

Complete Poems of, 1910.

Harris, Joel Chandler.

Life by Julia C. Harris. 1918.

Works: *Uncle Remus, His Songs and Sayings* (1880) and *Nights with Uncle Remus* (1883).

Harte, Bret.

Life by H. C. Merwin, 1911; T. E. Pemberton, 1903; H. W. Boynton, 1903.

Works, 1896–1903, 20 vols. Letters of, ed. by Geoffrey Bret Harte, 1926.

Hawthorne, Nathaniel.

Life by G. E. Woodberry (AML) 1902; Henry James (EML) 1880; G. P. Lathrop, 1876; Julian Hawthorne, 1884; Recollections by Bridge, 1893; M. D. Conway, 1891; *Rebellious Puritan* by L. Morris, 1927; Herbert Gorman, 1927.

Works, Riverside ed., 12 vols. 1882–84. 15 vols. includes biography.

Hayne, Paul Hamilton.

Complete Poems, 1882.

No adequate biography.

Holmes, Oliver Wendell.

Life by J. T. Morse, 1896, 2 vols.

Works, Riverside ed., 1891, 14 vols. Cambridge ed of Poems in 1 vol.

Howells, William Dean.

Life by O. W. Firkins, 1924; by D. G. Cooke, 1922.

Life in Letters of W. D. Howells, 1928.

No collected ed. Harper and Houghton Mifflin publish his books.

Irving, Washington.

Life by P. M. Irving, 1862–63; C. D. Warner (AML), 1881; G. S. Hellman, 1926. See also

Journals of (ed. by W. P. Trent and G. S. Hellman), 1919, 3 vols.

Works, Knickerbocker ed., 40 vols., 1897.

James, Henry.

Life by Rebecca West, 1916; see also V. W. Brooks's *The Pilgrimage of Henry James,* 1925, and J. W. Beach's *Method of Henry James,* 1918.

Works, New York ed., 1907–17, 26 vols. incomplete, but has critical prefaces. Letters of, ed. by Percy Lubbock, 2 vols., 1920.

Lanier, Sidney.

Life by Edwin Mims (AML), 1905.

Poems by, 1884.

Lincoln, Abraham.

Life by Nicolay and Hay, 1890; see also D. K. Dodge's *Lincoln, Master of Words.* 1924.

Complete Works, Nicolay and Hay ed., 1894, 2 vols.

Longfellow, Henry Wadsworth.

Life by Samuel Longfellow (letters and diary), 1891, 3 vols.; T. W. Higginson (AML), 1902; Herbert Gorman's *Victorian American,* 1926.

Works, Riverside ed., 11 vols. 1886. Cambridge ed. of Poems and Plays in one volume.

Lowell, James Russell.

Life by H. E. Scudder, 1901, 2 vols.; Ferris Greenslet, 1905; see also Letters ed. by C. E. Norton, 1894, 2 vols., and E. E. Hale's *Lowell and his Friends,* 1899.

Works, Riverside ed., 11 vols. 1891. Cambridge ed. of Poems in 1 vol.

Mather, Cotton.

Life by Barrett Wendell, 1891, 1925; see also K. Murdock's *Increase Mather,* 1925, and his *Selections from Works of Cotton Mather,* 1926.

Melville, Herman.

Life by R. M. Weaver, 1921; John Freeman

(EML), 1926; Meade Minnigerode's *Some Personal Letters of Herman Melville*, 1922, has also a bibliography; *Life*, by Lewis Mulford, 1929.
Works, Standard ed., 1924, London, 16 vols.

Miller, Cincinnatus Hiner ("Joaquin").
No adequate biography. See F. L. Pattee's *American Literature since 1870*, and the Introduction to Stuart P. Sherman's edition of Poetical Works of Joaquin Miller, 1923.

Moody, William Vaughn.
Poems and Plays, 1912, 2 vols. contains Life by J. M. Manly.

Paine, Thomas.
Life by M. D. Conway, 1892, 2 vols.
Works of, ed. by M. D. Conway, 1894.

Poe, Edgar Allan.
Life by G. E. Woodberry, 1909, 2 vols.; Hervey Allen's *Israfel*, 1926, 2 vols.
Works, Virginia ed., 1902, 17 vols. now out of print; Stedman and Woodberry ed., 1895, 10 vols. Poems ed. by K. Campbell, 1917, and Short Stories ed. by K. Campbell, 1927, are good single volumes.

Porter, William Sidney ("O. Henry").
Life by C. A. Smith, 1916.
Works, 1911, 12 vols. C. A. Smith's *Selections*, 1922, is the best single volume of his work.

Riley, James Whitcomb.
Life by Marcus Dickey, 1922.
Works, Biographical ed., 1913, 6 vols.

Sewall, Samuel.
Samuel Sewall and the World he Lived in. N. H. Chamberlain. 1897.
Samuel Sewall's Diary. Abridged. 1927.

Simms, William Gilmore.

    Life by W. P. Trent (AML), 1892. See Erskine's *Leading American Novelists.* 1910.

    Novels, 18 vols., 1859; 1886. Poems, 1853, 2 vols.

Stedman, Edmund Clarence.

    Life and Letters, Laura Stedman and G. M. Gould, 1910, 2 vols.

    Poems, 1908, is the best one volume edition.

Stowe, Harriet Beecher.

    Life by C. E. Stowe, 1889; Life and Letters, by Annie Fields, 1897.

    The Novels and Stories of Harriet Beecher Stowe, 1910, 10 vols.

Taylor, Bayard.

    Life and Letters by Marie Taylor and Horace Scudder, 1884. 2 vols.

    Life by A. H. Smyth (AML), 1896.

    Works, Household ed., 1870, 14 vols.

Thoreau, Henry D.

    Life by F. B. Sanborn (AML), 1882. See also W. E. Channing's *Thoreau, the Poet-Naturalist,* 1873; L. Bazalgette's *Henry Thoreau, Bachelor of Nature,* 1924; J. B. Atkinson's *Henry Thoreau,* 1927.

    Works, Riverside ed., 11 vols. 1894, or Walden ed. 20 vols., which includes the *Journal. The Heart of Thoreau's Journals,* 1927.

Timrod, Henry.

    Life by G. A. Wauchope, 1915.

    Poems, Memorial ed., 1901.

Twain, Mark (See Clemens, Samuel L.).

Whitman, Walt.

    Life by Bliss Perry (AML), 1906; G. R. Carpenter (EML), 1909; John Bailey (New EML), 1926; John Burroughs, 1896; E. Holloway, 1926. See also G. Santayana's *Poetry and Religion,* 1900.

    Works, Camden ed., 10 vols., 1902; or, Leaves of

Grass, Inclusive Edition, 1924; Complete Prose
Works, 1898; and Uncollected Poetry and Prose
of Walt Whitman, 1921, 2 vols.

Whittier, John Greenleaf.

Life and Letters by Samuel Pickard, 1907; G. R.
Carpenter (AML), 1903; T. W. Higginson
(EML), 1902; Bliss Perry, 1907.

Works, Riverside ed., 7 vols. 1888. Cambridge ed.
poems in one vol.

Willis, Nathaniel P.

Life by H. A. Beers (AML), 1885. Contains a discussion of Annuals.

Woolman, John.

The Journals and Essays, Gummere ed., 1922. Also
in Everyman's Library.

IV. CRITICISM

1. *General*

Adams, Henry: The Education of. 1918, 1927.

Andrews, C. M.: Colonial Folk-ways. 1919.

Beard, Charles and Mary: The Rise of American Civilization. 1927.

Beer, Thomas: The Mauve Decade. 1926.

Boynton, P. H.: Some Contemporary Americans. 1924.

Brooks, J. G.: As Others See Us. 1908.

Brooks, Van Wyck: America's Coming of Age. 1915.

Brooks, Van Wyck: Emerson and Others. 1927.

Brownell, W. C.: Democratic Distinction in America.
1927.

Crawford, Mary C.: Social Life in Old New England.
1914.

Dondore, Dorothy: The Prairie in the Making of Middle
America. 1926.

Earle, Alice Morse: Customs and Fashions in Old New

England. 1893. (Other books by Miss Earle should also be consulted.)

Eggleston, E.: The Transit of Civilization from Europe to America. 1901.

Ellsworth, W. W.: A Golden Age of Authors. 1919.

Fisher, S. G.: Men, Women, and Manners in Colonial Times. 1897.

Foerster, Norman: Nature in American Literature. 1923.

Foerster, Norman and others: The Re-Interpretation of American Literature. 1928.

Frank, Waldo: Our America. 1919.

Frothingham, O. B.: Transcendentalism in New England. 1876.

Gaines, F. P.: The Southern Plantation. 1924.

Goddard, H. C.: Studies in New England Transcendentalism. 1908.

Hazard, Lucy: The Frontier in American Literature. 1927.

Jones, Howard M.: America and French Culture, 1750–1848. 1927.

Kittredge, G. L.: The Old Farmer and his Almanack. 1905.

Lawrence, D. H.: Studies in Classic American Literature. 1923.

Macy, John: The Spirit of American Literature. 1913.

Mencken, H. L.: The American Language. 1919, 1923.

Mesick, Jane L.: The English Traveler in America, 1785–1835. 1922.

Minnigerode, Meade: The Fabulous Forties. 1924.

Mitchell, D. G.: American Lands and Letters. 1897–99. 2 vols.

More, Paul Elmer: Shelburne Essays. 11 vols. 1904–

Mumford, Lewis: The Golden Day. 1926.

Nicholson, Meredith: The Hoosiers. 1900.

Pattee, F. L.: Sidelights on American Literature. 1922.

Perry, Bliss: The American Mind. 1912.

Perry, Bliss: Park Street Papers. 1908.

Perry, Bliss: The Praise of Folly and Other Papers. 1923.

Phelps, W. L.: Howells, James, Bryant and Other Essays. 1924.

Phelps, W. L.: Some Makers of American Literature. 1922.

Rusk, R. L.: Literature of the Middle Western Frontier. 1925. 2 vols.

Schlesinger, A. M.: New Viewpoints in American History. 1925.

Sherman, Stuart P.: The Genius of America. 1923.

Spiller, R. E.: The American in England. 1926.

Swift, Lindsay: Brook Farm. 1900.

Tandy, Jennette: Crackerbox Philosophers. 1925.

Venable, W. H.: Beginnings of Culture in the Ohio Valley. 1891.

Wright, T. G.: Aspect of Early Literary Culture in New England. 1917.

2. *Poetry*

Lowell, Amy: Tendencies in Modern American Poetry. 1917.

Lowes, J. L.: Convention and Revolt in Poetry. 1919.

Monroe, Harriet: Poets and their Art. 1926.

Onderdonk, J. L.: A History of American Verse. 1901.

Otis, W. B.: American Verse, 1625–1807. 1909.

Perry, Bliss: A Study of Poetry. 1920.

Stedman, E. C.: Poets of America. 1885.

Untermeyer, L.: The New Era in American Poetry. 1919.

Weirick, B.: From Whitman to Sandburg. 1924.

Wilkinson, Marguerite: Contemporary Poetry. 1923.

3. *Drama*

Dickinson, T. H.: The Case of American Drama. 1915.

Dunlap, William: History of the American Theatre. 1832.

Hornblow, A.: A History of the Theatre in America. 1919. 2 vols.

Krow, A. E.: Play Production in America. 1916.

Moses, M. J.: The American Dramatist. 1911, 1917, 1925.

Nathan, G. J.: The Critic and the Drama. 1922.

Quinn, A. H.: A History of American Drama. 1923–27. 3 vols.

Sayler, O. M.: Our American Theatre. 1923.

Seilhamer, G. O.: History of the American Theatre, 1749–1797. 1888–91. 3 vols.

4. *Essays and Criticism*

Brownell, W. C.: American Prose Masters. 1909.

Cairns, W. B.: Development of American Literature, especially Periodicals, 1815–33. 1898.

Foerster, Norman: American Criticism. 1928.

Howells, W. D.: Literary Friends and Acquaintance. 1900, 1910.

Lee, James Melvin: History of American Journalism. 1917.

Payne, W. M.: Leading American Essayists. 1910.

Tassin, Algernon: The Magazine in America. 1916.

5. *Prose Fiction*

Baker, E. A.: Guide to the Best Fiction, 1913; Guide to the Best Historical Fiction, 1914.

Erskine, John: Leading American Novelists. 1910.

Loshe, L. D.: The Early American Novel (to 1830). 1907.

Michaud, Regis. The American Novel Today. 1928.

Pattee, F. L.: The Development of the American Short
  Story. 1923.
Perry, Bliss: A Study of Prose Fiction. 1902.
Phelps, W. L.: Essays on Modern Novelists. 1910.
Van Doren, Carl: The American Novel. 1921.
Van Doren, Carl: Contemporary American Novelists.
  1922.

INDEX